How Do Astronauts Scratch an Itch?

Other Books by David Feldman

✄

Imponderables®

How to Win at Just About Everything

Why Do Clocks Run Clockwise?
and Other Imponderables®

Who Put the Butter in Butterfly?
and Other Fearless Investigations into
Our Illogical Language

When Do Fish Sleep?
and Other Imponderables®
of Everyday Life

Why Do Dogs Have Wet Noses?
and Other Imponderables®
of Everyday Life

Do Penguins Have Knees?
An Imponderables® Book

When Did Wild Poodles Roam the Earth?
An Imponderables® Book

How Does Aspirin Find a Headache?
An Imponderables® Book

What *Are* Hyenas Laughing At, Anyway?
An Imponderables® Book

HOW DO Astronauts Scratch an itch?

An
Imponderables®
Book

DAVID FELDMAN
illustrated by Kassie Schwan

BERKLEY BOOKS, NEW YORK

HOW DO ASTRONAUTS SCRATCH AN ITCH?
AN IMPONDERABLES BOOK®

A Berkley Book / published by arrangement with
the author

PRINTING HISTORY
G. P. Putnam's Sons edition / October 1996
Berkley trade paperback edition / October 1997

The Putnam Berkley World Wide Web site address is
http://www.berkley.com

ISBN: 0-425-15984-1

BERKLEY ®
Berkley Books are published by
The Berkley Publishing Group, a member of Penguin Putnam Inc.,
200 Madison Avenue, New York, New York 10016.
BERKLEY and the "B" design
are trademarks belonging to Berkley Publishing Corporation.

PRINTED IN THE UNITED STATES OF AMERICA
10   9   8   7   6   5   4   3   2   1

For
DENNIS
and
HEIDE WHELAN

Contents

Preface

If you picked up this book, snared by the catchy title, hoping that you'll find out how astronauts go to the bathroom in space, we're sorry to disappoint you. You see, anytime an astronaut gives a speech or goes to a cocktail party, that's the first question on everyone's lips. And astronaut bathroom habits have been written about more often than Cher has had plastic surgery.

Nope. Our job is to track down the mysteries of everyday life that you can't answer by consulting reference books, and we answer them by consulting experts in every conceivable field (this book sent us to skywriters, jigsaw puzzle makers, safety pin manufacturers, and karate teachers, among many others).

And we don't whip up these questions out of thin air, either. Almost all the Imponderables in this book come from readers who have lost sleep mulling over these knotty mysteries. Aware of the torment that Imponderability can cause, and as a reward for the suffering they've endured, we offer a free autographed copy to the first reader to send in an Imponderable that we publish, along with our grateful acknowledgment in the book.

Two other sections round out *Imponderables* books. In the "Frustables" section, we ask readers to help solve some of the mysteries that have eluded our grasp, and in the Letters section, we allow those readers who for some strange reason don't agree with us the opportunity to vent their spleen in prose.

This is our ninth in the series of *Imponderables* books, and you may not be stunned to know, the next one will be our tenth. We're planning to do a few things to make the tenth book special. One element is a contest. No, we're not talking Publishers Clearinghouse kind of bucks here, unfortunately, but we hope you'll have fun competing, especially longtime readers. And there are some prizes that we think you'll like. For details, see *"Imponderables X Contest"*

(Whoever thought there would be more *Imponderables* books than Rocky movies?) located just after the "Imponderables" section.

What else is happening at Imponderables Central? We're particularly excited about three developments. We are still planning to undertake the scary project of solving the mysteries of the opposite sex, and we continue expanding our involvement on the Internet, including an *Imponderables* web site. The back of the book will tell you how you can get involved with either.

And we're launching "David Feldman's Imponderables Game," a board game based on these books. In fact, these are among the prizes for our contest. Sure, $10 million is nice, but would you trade it for an Imponderables Game?

Enough of the preliminaries. We want to find out why lizards don't get sunburned after sitting out in the sun all day!

Why Do Many Mattresses Have Floral Graphics on Them?

*A*ll the bedding experts we spoke to concurred on the purpose of the flowers on mattresses: They are there to look pretty.

Not to be pedantic, but technically the flowers aren't on the actual mattress, but on its cover, which folks in the sleepbiz call the "ticking." We spoke to Curt Scarborough, of ticking manufacturer Culp Co., who told us that the floral graphics are part of their competitive marketing strategies. After all, rows of white mattresses all look alike; the bedding industry has become design oriented; many mattresses not only sport flowers but also solid colors besides white (blue seems to be the most popular variant).

We gently reminded our sources that pretty flowers don't do much good when they are covered up by sheets. They just as gently reminded us that our argument was beside the point. The purpose of the flowers is not to command our attention at home but to attract us in the store.

Why flowers, instead of, say, images of elephants or kiwifruit? Susan Swinney, of TieTex, told *Imponderables* that women are the dominant buyers of mattresses, and women respond to floral patterns. If men bought more mattresses than women, perhaps we'd see tickings with pictures of camshafts, stereo speakers, and leggy supermodels.

Submitted by Scott Fiore and Brian Miller of Lancaster, Pennsylvania. Thanks also to Ginelle Watkins, of parts unknown.

How Do They Keep More Than Two Pieces of a Jigsaw Puzzle from Fitting Together? Is Every Piece Unique?

Although you could argue that anyone who embarks upon fitting together a 1,000-piece jigsaw depiction of a beefsteak tomato already has masochistic tendencies, no puzzler wants to be further frustrated by encountering two pieces that fit into the same spot. So it behooves jigsaw puzzle companies to forestall this potential problem.

Milton Bradley's solution to the twin-piece possibility is decidedly low-tech: Its designers draw the puzzle freehand. A designer makes a line drawing of a potential puzzle pattern, and then blueprints are created. Inspectors then check to make sure that every piece is unique, is the right size, and that every piece interlocks, snugly fitting into its adjoining neighbors.

Mark Morris, public-relations director of jigsaw giant Milton Bradley, told *Imponderables* that the puzzle is even checked by eye for potential duplicate pieces. An eye check is far from foolproof, of course, but the best assurance of keeping out potential twins is that if everything is drawn by hand, duplication is virtually impossible.

Once a design is approved, a die is cut (by laser) from the blue-prints. Then the physical die is used to cut the pieces. The scene is printed on a cardboard backing and the die, inside a hydraulic machine, pushes down and cuts the puzzle in one shot. The whole process (including the creation of the box top, the closing of the box, and the sealing of the entire contents) takes seconds.

Another insurance policy for the manufacturer is that the same die is used throughout an entire product line. For example, Milton Bradley produces several different lines of puzzles. All the 550-piece Big Ben puzzles for a season will be designed from an identical die—only the image will differ. Morris adds that Milton Bradley changes the dies frequently, though, because "hard-core" puzzlers will recognize the die pattern "after a while."

At least one of Milton Bradley's competitors, Edaron, utilizes a comparatively high-tech solution to the duplication threat. You may not recognize the Edaron name, because it is a "contract manufacturer" that makes puzzles sold under the brand names of other companies. Edaron utilizes a proprietary computer pro-gram that designs the shape of the individual pieces and also checks to assure both that the pieces interlock and that the pieces are unique. The software creates a design from which the die is cut.

Edaron, like Milton Bradley, uses the same die across a given puzzle line. Edaron might have contracts with four different com-panies for 550-piece puzzles, so a separate die is used for each client, but the same die is used for all the 550-piece puzzles for that client.

One of the big advantages of this high-tech solution is that all the old designs can be saved conveniently as software. At any time, Edaron can recut a die with the same design. Edaron recuts the dies about once a year because the die loses its sharpness and be-gins to yield dull, unclean cuts. Fuzzy jigsaw borders can lead to just as much frustration among solvers as the scourge of duplicate pieces.

Submitted by Rory Sellers of Carmel, California. Thanks also to Howard Givner of Brooklyn, New York.

Why Do Many Restaurants Insist That You Take a New Plate Every Time You Go Through a Buffet Line?

We can't imagine some of the cheapo buffet establishments we've patronized actually encouraging patrons to increase their dish-washing load. So we assumed that local or state boards of health demanded that restaurants satisfy this policy, presumably for hygienic reasons.

We contacted a New York City Board of Health restaurant inspector and posed this Imponderable. She replied, "Huh? We have no such rule. I've never heard of such a thing." Of course, New York City is not exactly fabled for its fastidiousness, so we decided to poke around in other climes.

One of our favorite sources for information about restaurants, Elmhurst, Illinois, consultant Henry Verden, filed this report:

> "I can't speak for other states, but as for Illinois, it's not just a good idea, it's the law. I contacted Mary Beth Carlson of the Illinois Department of Public Health, who explained it.
>
> "You pick up your first load of grub from the buffet and sit

down to eat. As you transfer food in one direction from plate to mouth, you are also transferring germs in the other direction, from mouth to plate, on your eating utensils. If you then take that plate back to the buffet, the reasoning goes that you will then transfer said germs from the plate to the holding pan full of food on the buffet line by means of the serving spoons, tongs, etc.

"The logic behind this law is similar to that behind the law requiring sneeze guards. The concern is to keep your germs off everybody else's food."

A short conversation with Richard Siegel, manager of the District of Columbia Food Protection Program, revealed that D.C. also requires a clean plate for each trip through a buffet line, and for the identical reasons as Illinois. In fact, Siegel was astonished that New York City has no such rule. New Yorkers would probably consider the lack of a buffet "double-dipping" law among their least crucial problems.

Although we've occasionally seen a sign on a buffet line indicating that patrons should take a new plate for every trip, we are wondering exactly who is responsible for enforcing these laws. Can a patron be busted for sneaking an old plate into line? Will an unsuspecting busboy have a camera crew from *Cops* shoved into his face if a patron at his station is found piling some pancakes onto a plate that once held eggs Benedict? Or do diner-violators get thrown into a country club prison or get probation with the proviso that they go into a twelve-step program for repetitive buffet-plate syndrome?

Submitted by Mary Ellen Jelen of Akron, Ohio.

Why Don't Lizards Get Sunburned? Why Don't Other Animals Get Sunburned?

Look down on lizards if you want, but you must admit that they sure know how to cope with the sun better than we do. We stay out too long at the beach and our skin starts peeling and falling off. Next thing we know, our bodies look like a map on the Weather Channel (and not on a sunny day). All mammals shed skin as soon as their outer layer of skin (epidermis) dies.

But reptiles can hang out on rocks all day, basking in the sun. Reptiles, clearly, are different. As Dr. Norman J. Scott, Jr., of the Society for the Study of Amphibians and Reptiles told *Imponderables,*

> *"Reptiles keep the outer layer of dead cells on their skin until the next layer is ready. Then it is shed."*

Scott also points out that a lizard's epidermis, both the living and dead layers, is thick and cornified, making it far harder for ultraviolet rays to penetrate.

And as in humans, the pigment melanin helps protect lizards from harmful rays. Dr. R. Anderson, of the American College of Veterinary Dermatology, notes that heavily pigmented animals are protected from the sun, much as darker-complected humans are partially safeguarded. But many animals do exhibit ill effects from the sun, even critters with fur.

Just like us, many animals are subject to skin cancer. Dogs can and do get carcinomas, even ones with heavy fur. White-eared cats often develop carcinomas at the ends of the ears. "For some reason," Anderson observes, "bull terriers seem to love to sunbathe and can contract solar-induced lesions on their undersides."

Are we sensing a potentially booming market for "Sunblock for Pets"?

Submitted by Julie Peterson of North Carolina State University.

Why Do Bombs Create Mushroom-shaped Clouds?

Before we can explain the reason for the shape of these clouds, two common misconceptions have to be cleared up. Many people believe that bombs are dropped from planes, hit the ground, and explode in part because of the contact from the earth. Actually, bombs are designed to detonate in the air before they hit the earth.

And the "mushroom" is not composed of ingredients contained in the bomb. Rather, the cloud is a conglomeration of dirt, dust, and debris from the ground.

We talked to Todd A. Postma, a nuclear engineer at the Advanced Nuclear Engineering Computational Laboratory, who explained the formation of the menacing mushroom:

> *"In an atomic blast, such as the bombs dropped on Hiroshima and Nagasaki, the mushroom cloud develops because the blast lifts a tremendous amount of debris from the ground into the air.*
>
> *"The bomb blast is directed downward and reflects off the earth's crust. As a result, much soil is carried upward into the air. Initially, most of this soil motion is straight up [creating the 'stem' of the mushroom]; however, once the soil is up in the air and the vertical kinetic energy is spent, the horizontal wind force takes over and spreads the cloud out. Then gravity takes over, and the soil begins to drift downward [accounting for that weird phase when the cloud appears to be imploding].*
>
> *"The mushroom shape can be distorted somewhat if there is a strong prevailing wind at the time. Also, once the soil has had time to disperse, the cloud looks less and less like a mushroom.*
>
> *"Conventional explosions [such as TNT] create mushroom clouds, too. It's just that the effect is magnified with nuclear explosions because of the magnitude of the blast. There's nothing inherent in a nuclear blast, as opposed to a conventional blast, which causes the mushroom cloud."*

❦   **D**avid **F**eldman

The "horizontal wind force" that helps disperse the "cap" of the mushroom is to a large extent created by the blast itself rather than ambient weather conditions. When the bomb detonates, a fireball spreads out in all directions. Because this fireball is a hot gas, it tends to rise, creating a suction effect underneath that helps "suck" up the debris from below in a vacuum effect.

At the top of the fireball, the expansion meets some air resistance and tends to flatten out, creating the "flat top" associated with the cap of a mushroom, rather than the roundish top you might expect to see. If there were no gravity or air resistance (for example, if you set off the bomb in space), a bomb would presumably expand equally in all directions, creating a huge, inflating sphere.

When the blast hits the earth, a parabolic-shaped crater is usually formed (a parabola is the shape of satellite dishes and the reflectors below the bulbs in flashlights). The parabolic shape is crucial to the formation of the cloud, because no matter in what direction an incoming object hits a parabolic shape, be it a television wave in the case of a satellite dish, a light wave in the case of a reflector, or debris from a bomb, the reflected objects are sent back perpendicularly—all parallel to one another. In the case of the bomb, since the crater is located on the ground, the debris moves straight up, perpendicular to the ground, which results in what appears to be a perfectly straight, vertical "stem" on the mushroom.

When a smaller "conventional" bomb is set off, you often don't see the mushroom shape because of the smaller scale and blinding speed of the blast. An atomic bomb's speed might be just as great, but the cloud is so much larger that it takes longer to unfold.

And what happens if a bomb does not detonate until it hits the ground? The results are unpredictable—no consistent pattern is formed. The shape of the "cloud" would depend on the content of the target hit. It is likely to look more like a turbulent mess than any vegetable.

Submitted by Alexander Heppenheimer of Atlanta, Georgia.

How Do They Keep Soda in Soft-Drink Machines from Freezing in the Winter?

You will be pleased to know that the soda companies have resisted the urge to solve this problem by inserting a little antifreeze in their concoctions. Instead, they keep their drinks fluid by controlling the temperature inside of vending machines.

According to Larry M. Eils, director of health, safety, and technical standards for the National Automatic Merchandising Association,

> *"The cabinet [that] is so well insulated to keep it cold also prevents the soda from freezing under certain conditions."*

And what are those conditions? Coca-Cola's senior consumer affairs specialist, Melissa Packman, estimates that only in locations where the average temperature stays below twenty degrees Fahrenheit for weeks at a time is the insulation unlikely to keep the beverages stable, and she adds that along with the excellent insulation,

> *"the small amount of heat generated by the fan that circulates the air in the vender will prevent product from freezing."*

But if you encounter a soda machine outside a gas station in Montana, you'd be right to assume that insulation and a little fan wouldn't be enough to keep the beverage flowing. That's why in such cold locations, machines with two different systems are installed: a refrigeration unit to keep the sodas cold in warm or moderate weather; and a heating system to warm the drinks in cold weather.

Of course, "heating systems" can be high- or low-tech. In some cold-weather machines, the heaters are wired to a temperature sensor. When the electronic thermostats "tell" the heating unit that the temperature is below freezing, the heater is turned on, and cold, but not frozen, soda is available for guzzlers.

But our trusty representative from Pepsi-Cola, Chris Jones, told us that some vending-machine heating "systems" are not that elaborate, to say the least:

> *"In extreme conditions, such as Montana, a sixty-watt lightbulb is often placed inside the insulated compartment. The heat from the bulb is often sufficient to maintain temperatures in the machine above freezing. The heat from the sign light ballasts and electronics in the coin mechanism and bill validator is sufficient to keep these systems functioning properly except in the most extreme conditions. These kits have thermostats and can control temperatures very accurately, but most operators prefer the less costly and simpler lightbulb. Sugared products freeze at around 23 to 26 degrees Fahrenheit, depending on the sugar content, while diet products freeze at 32 degrees."*

Submitted by Terry Newhouse of Downers Grove, Illinois. Thanks also to Craig Townsend of Brooklyn, New York.

How Do Skywriters Have Good Penmanship? How Do They Know When to Start and Stop Letters While in the Air?

Those of us whose "John Hancocks" read more like "Jean Hedgehogs" even under the best of circumstances can only marvel at the penmanship of skywriters. Younger *Imponderables* readers probably view skywriting as a novelty, but before World War II, it was a prominent advertising medium. A day at the beach, before the advent of television, would hardly be complete without a skywriter touting the merits of a local used-car dealership or a favorite nationally distributed soft drink. Long before wide-screen message boards, a visit to the local ballpark often included a display of the skywriter's virtuosity. Alas, in this age when most skywriting businesses have converted to the less expensive and less soulful banner towing (or disappeared altogether), there are probably only about twenty folks in the United States who earn a substantial part of their income from skywriting.

We enlisted the help of three veteran skywriters to learn their trade secrets. All three indicated that skywriting is a high-pressure occupation, in which a mistake is visible to all. As one of them told us, "You can't correct a mistake. There's no eraser."

Skywriting is sometimes referred to as "smoke writing," but that term is misleading. What you see is not smoke at all. The "smoke" is created by pumping (at a rate of three or four gallons per minute) a nonpolluting paraffin-based machine oil into the exhaust stream of the plane. The oil vaporizes from the heat of the exhaust, but it does not ignite or burn.

A line from the pump is run up near the controls of the plane, and the pilot "writes" with a switch or button that turns the pump on or off. While the pilot is deciding whether or not to "drop smoke," the plane is normally moving at somewhere between 80 and 150 miles per hour, usually between 8,000 to 12,000 feet off the ground.

Our three professional skywriters outlined the four biggest problems in achieving "good penmanship" and shared their secrets for overcoming the problems. One consistent theme that all repeated was the importance of meticulous planning. Skywriters make a detailed "flight plan" before they go up in the air; they know exactly when they will turn the smoke on and off.

1. Visualization. The individual letters usually range between 2,000 and 4,000 feet high. It's impossible for the skywriter to see the "big picture" while flying "inside your work." Remember, too, that skywriters are working upside down and backwards. They are laying smoke "above" where the letters will be formed, whereas viewers of the skywriting have an opposite vantage point.

Dan Gramann, head of Aerial Banner Towing and Skywriting, is based in Milwaukee and the only skywriter left in his area of the Midwest. Dan uses a decidedly low-tech solution to the "upside down and backward" problem. To map out his route, Gramann takes two sheets of paper with a carbon in between. On the top sheet he writes the message he's going to skywrite. The back of the carbon, if flipped 180 degrees, then displays the message as he will see it when he is skywriting. He then writes this "reversed" image on a piece of paper and tapes it to the dashboard of his plane.

Milo Tichack, of Aerial Advertisers, who is based in the Oakland area, literally paints the message he's going to write (as the viewer would see it) on the windshield of his plane from the outside. When he hops into the plane, the message *from the inside* appears the way Milo will have to write it from the sky.

Dan Gramann emphasizes the importance of keeping up a constant speed while up in the air, as it's one of the most important tricks to writing consistent, good-looking letters. Instruments in the cockpit help assure that the pilot maintains a constant "heading" (traveling in a straight line, important for crossing those *T*'s and making the vertical lines in the *H*'s perfectly parallel) and banks smoothly so that curved letters like *P*'s don't end up looking like *F*'s.

The pilots use ground markings as aids, too. Milo likes to use roadways to line up vertical lines. Sometimes, natural phenomena can be used as landmarks, and even as cheat sheets of sorts, according to our third skywriter, Greg Stinis, head of Skytypers, Inc., located in Los Alamitos, California. Greg's father, Andy, a decorated World War II Navy aviator, was one of the pioneers of skywriting. Andy started skywriting in 1932 and flew around the country for ten years, full-time, promoting Pepsi-Cola in the sky. Greg, who learned to fly solo before he could drive a car, told *Imponderables* that when conditions are perfect, he can sometimes see the shadow of his plane on the ground, most commonly on the beach.

But just as often, a pilot's eyes can fail him. Parallel lines, such as those on an *H*, can be difficult to draw if a pilot relies on the naked eye. The lines are more than 2,000 feet long and, when observed from the plane, seem to converge in the distance (not unlike the way railroad tracks in the distance seem to converge). That's why all three skywriters prefer to depend upon rigorous planning rather than what they can see out of their rearview mirror (yes, they do have rearview mirrors).

2. Time. Skywriters are under tremendous time pressures. They may be artists, but they produce disposable art. Their writing evaporates quickly and is subject to wind drift. For this reason,

part of the planning for each trip consists of determining how to minimize banks and turns in order to finish the job as quickly as possible.

Not only do the pilots feel pressure to perform their task quickly, but maintaining a constant speed is required to make the letters look uniform. All three skywriters said that they did not have time to look at their watches while in the air; they are too busy consulting instruments and looking ahead for visual cues. Instead, they "time themselves." Dan told us that when he is writing the capital letter *I*, he gets in position at the top or bottom of the line and then flips the smoke switch on. He then counts to ten in his head and flips the smoke switch off. That draws a line of about 2,000 to 3,000 feet long, depending upon the air speed. He then immediately executes a slow turn bank to get in position to form the horizontal line that matches where he has just finished the top (or bottom) of the smoke he has just laid. Skywriters become so proficient at counting that the letters are remarkably uniform in height.

3. Disturbing Your Own Writing.

Not only do skywriters not have erasers at their disposal, but they have the means to destroy their own masterpieces as well. If a pilot tempts fate and flies repeatedly into smoke that has been laid down, the meticulous lettering will end up looking like a cumulus cloud.

Dan Gramann and Greg Stinis both share a favorite trick to eliminate this problem: They often write each letter at a slightly different altitude. Even varying the altitude by 50 to 100 feet per letter not only has the advantage of minimizing turbulence, but also allows the skywriter a better vantage point to see what he's already written. From the ground, it's impossible to notice the altitude shift, although from the air, the actual writing might look like "it's going up or down a staircase."

4. Weather.

The clearer the day, the clearer the smoke letters will appear to the targeted customers. But the skywriters have other preferences, too. The less windy the weather, the less chance there is for the message to deteriorate before the skywriter is finished.

Stinis adds that the more hazy and humid the air is, the longer the message will remain intact. But direct sunlight tends to evaporate the smoke. So the ideal day features a cloudless, blue but overcast sky, with high humidity.

Even the most skilled skywriters can't change the weather. If a skywriter anticipates poor visibility or high winds, the pilot might take a banner along with him as a backup. A skywriter doesn't always have the luxury of choosing when to drop smoke.

The weather isn't always the enemy of skywriters, though. Greg Stinis told us a true, weather-related story about a job he once did for Continental Airlines. The airline asked him to write "Continental Flies to Hawaii," a message that Stinis considered "insanely" long. But Greg managed to write the "Continental Flies to Hawaii" (on three lines) in the skies of Ft. Worth, Texas.

After finishing the job, Stinis landed and started to refuel, for his contract specified that he write the same message in Dallas, approximately fifty miles away. Greg received a call on the ground from his client, who asked how he had managed to skywrite in Dallas already. Innocently, Greg replied that he, unlike Debbie, had not done Dallas.

"*Au contraire,*" his client responded (although possibly not in French). "I'm looking up in the [Dallas] sky and the message looks beautiful."

You guessed it. Greg's message had drifted the fifty miles from Fort Worth to Dallas and had remained perfectly intact. The client said,

"We'll pay you for it. Don't do it again. You couldn't do it any better."

So Mother Nature, for once, made Greg's job a little easier.

Submitted by Elaine Murray of Houston, Texas.

Why Does Some Skywriting Feature Squarish Letters?

That's not sky*writing*, Terry. You're seeing sky*typing*, a technique invented by the father of Greg Stinis, Andy Stinis. And you are seeing the penmanship of five pilots, not one.

All five pilots fly simultaneously, wing tip to wing tip to wing tip (separated by approximately three hundred feet). From the vantage point of the ground looking up, the five planes are in a straight line vertically and all move horizontally from left to right. If they all drop smoke in a coordinated way, they can write a message quickly in *one* horizontal pass, far more efficient than old-fashioned skywriting.

Of course, the difficulty is coordinating the writing of five sky-typers. When Andy Stinis pioneered the field, he used a transmitting device that looked something like a player piano roll, with a turning steel drum. The drum had five channels, one for each plane. In each channel, little troughs and mountains corresponded to when smoke for each plane should be off or on. Each channel was rigged with a transmitter at a frequency for each plane. As the drum turned, the signals to drop smoke were sent to the five planes.

Now, everything is computerized. Software has been designed specifically for this purpose, and onboard computers in each plane read data files—nothing is left to chance. The lead plane flies in the center of the five. His plane has a transmitter, which sends radio-control signals to the other planes. These signals automatically turn the smoke on and off in each plane. Whereas skywriters must perform banks and worry about when to lay the smoke down, a skytyping pilot's only job is to fly in a straight line at a constant speed.

To type an *L*, for example, all five pilots would simultaneously drop smoke, forming the vertical line. Then only the bottom plane drops smoke for a few seconds, forming the smaller horizontal line. A *T* is a little more complicated: only the top plane would drop smoke at the beginning, then a simultaneous puff from all five planes forms the vertical line, immediately followed by the top plane finishing the horizontal line at the top. Curved letters are more complicated yet, for they require staggered puffs from the various planes to create the illusion of curvature. Unfortunately, the letters formed by skytyping have the cold look of LED calculator displays: none of the gorgeous rounded *O*'s and *B*'s a skywriter (with good penmanship!) can produce.

Skytyping is a much faster process than skywriting. Greg Stinis says that skytyping is seventeen times faster (each letter in skytyping takes four seconds, compared to sixty to ninety seconds in skywriting). Greg's skytyped letters are 1,200 feet tall—although smaller than skywritten letters, still higher than the Empire State Building. A twenty-character skytyped message stretches out about five miles in the sky and can be seen for fifteen miles. In a populous area, according to Stinis, as many as two or three million people will see the advertisement.

Submitted by Terry Johnson of New York, New York.

Why Are Most Perfumes Yellow?

We know that longtime *Imponderables* readers, accustomed to our discussions of why things are the color they are, will be awed and dumbstruck, but the answer to this Imponderable boils down to the not illogical conclusion proffered by Annette Green, president of the Fragrance Foundation:

> *"The reason that fragrance is usually yellow is because that is the natural color of the essential oils [in perfumes] when they are processed."*

Actually, the perfume concentrates, the collection of scores, hundreds, or sometimes thousands of raw materials (essential oils) that are later diluted with alcohol to make cologne or perfume, can vary quite a bit in color. Some of the common essential oils in perfume, such as oak moss, start out with a strong green or brown color. But many of these oils are amber in color, and according to Peter Gesell, vice president of creativity at International Flavor and Fragrances, will take on a yellowish cast when diluted.

If the natural ingredients don't yield a pleasing hue, the perfumer can tint it with federally approved colors, as long as it will be labeled on the bottle as one of the ingredients. According to Gesell, it is difficult to turn an extremely dark mixture light, or to make drastic changes, so the end result is usually not profoundly different from the ingredients' natural color.

Not all perfumes are yellow, of course. Some perfumes with other colors are packaged in opaque bottles, to hide the actual cast. Bright "designer colors" are trotted out as marketing tools, although one perfumer we spoke to said, off the record, that he thought the "natural" yellow color appealed more to the upscale customer, and that the popularity of perfumes with "weird" colors was confined mostly to teenagers; these products' popularity tends to be as ephemeral as the fragrance's scent.

Submitted by Betsey Hemphill Pollikof of Towson, Maryland.

How Do Judges in Long Racewalking Competitions Determine Whether Contestants Have Violated the Rules by Running?

In a rare burst of good physical fitness intentions, we once learned how to racewalk. We focused on extending our legs, quickening our normal walking strides, and pumping our arms efficiently. Yet as casual joggers passed us in the park, the temptation to burst into a run (or trip those trotters) was overwhelming. One definition of frustration must be the attempt to move as fast as possible using one technique when it is as easy as pie to move much faster using another. We can only imagine how frustrating sticking to racewalking must be for serious competitors, who could gain an edge by running a bit, presumably out of the sight of officials.

Racewalking judges serve as deterrents to any walker tempted to break into a sprint—it is the judges' duty to identify when a walker has broken into a run. What differentiates running from walking? According to the USA Track and Field association (US-

ATF), "The racewalker must maintain constant contact with the ground (violation of which is called 'lifting')." If the right foot has been raised to start a stride, the left foot must already be on the ground.

But a second, more stringent rule separates racewalking from power walking or fitness walking: the dreaded "straight-knee rule":

> *"The advancing leg must be straight as it hits the ground and remain straight as the body passes over it (violation of which is referred to as 'bent knee' or 'creeping')."*

Racewalking aficionado Justin Kuo told *Imponderables* that this rule prescribes that the advancing leg must be fully extended 180 degrees: 175 degrees just won't do.

In most road races, a chief judge assigns six to nine judges to observe at strategic intervals along the course site. Obviously, on a ten-kilometer course, six judges can't keep tabs on every walker, as officials concede. However, there are techniques to make a few judges more effective. Most courses involve some form of "looping," in which competitors either walk up and back the same route, or walk around the same course at least twice; either way, stationary judges will see each walker more than once.

But judges don't have to remain in one place. We spoke to Chuck Bryant, a racewalking competitor and certified judge, who is on the board of directors of the Miami Runners and Walkers Club. Bryant indicated that although the chief judge assigns him a position on the course, Bryant will sometimes change stations, especially in road races:

> *"I'll judge maybe a half-mile or so from the start, watch the pack get past me, then drive around to another point, get most of the pack again, and return to my original space or near the finish line for a third observation. That's not always possible or practical."*

The judges have no electronic or mechanical aids in making their decisions. All observations must be made by the naked eye, and most offenses are far from flagrant, as Bryant bemoans:

"It's the instantaneous lifting [of a leg] for maybe a half-inch, or the two-degree bent knee in a fraction of a second that is difficult to detect. Judging takes a very trained eye and that comes only with time and practice. But it's not much different from any NFL or NBA game—officials don't catch every offense, and sometimes they disagree. That's frustrating and infuriating, but nothing's perfect. We're only human."

Because it is so easy for a racewalker to violate one of the two cardinal rules, racers aren't disqualified the first time they are cited for an infraction. According to Ken Mattson, a USATF racewalk judge, if a walker is spotted breaking a rule, the walker is issued a warning (often, the judge flashes a white paddle indicating the nature of the offense). If the walker continues to commit the same infraction, the judge can give him or her a red card (an official citation). If three different judges issue a red card, the walker is disqualified, and the chief judge then alerts the competitor that he or she has been disqualified. The walker must leave the course immediately. If a walker is thought to be flagrantly violating the rules (trying to get away with a brisk jog, for example), a red card can be issued without warning.

How much cheating goes on in racewalk competitions? The consensus seems to be that intentional cheating is relatively rare. As Chuck Bryant puts it:

"It varies, of course. I'd say most of us on the common roadrace circuit are pretty honorable. Most of us are diligent; a few of us are not. The 'cheating' usually comes from power walkers or fitness walkers who simply don't understand. They think: 'Hey, I'm not jogging, so I must be walking.' They're not stupid; they just don't see the point. They sometimes think we judges are too picky. But we're no more picky than a baseball official who calls a runner

out who sprints six inches from third base but does not touch the bag—it's illegal, it doesn't count. That's the rule."

Judge Mattson agrees:

> "Overall, most walkers don't try to break the rules, but when you're pushing yourself to the limits (like the world's best walkers, who go about six minutes per mile for 12.5 miles), sometimes form breaks down."

Form breaks down especially often in longer events and in the final sprint near the finish line (which is why more judges are ordinarily placed there).

Alas, one racewalker, Mike McNamee, reports that not all walkers conform to the tenets of good sportsmanship:

> "The only limits on cheating are the judges' eyes. Competitors here in Washington, D.C., tell tales of walkers whose gaits undergo mysterious transformation when they pass behind hedges along a course. Judges are supposed to move around to cover the entire course. But they can't cover it all at once. And only a judge can spot a violation—or maybe I should say, only judges can call 'em."

Unfortunately, the rare deliberate cheater might be sighted only by fellow competitors. And although Chuck Bryant indicates that occasionally a runner will report a miscreant, little can be done to punish the offender:

> "Only event judges have the authority to call offenses and disqualify participants. If the judges don't see it, there can't be a disqualification. Same as any other sport."

Submitted by Joanna Parker of Miami, Florida.

Why Does Soda Fizz Up So Much More When Poured into a Glass Containing Ice Than When Poured into an Empty Glass?

Before you open a can of soda, carbon dioxide gas (CO_2) has been dissolved in the liquid. The drink is actually "supersaturated" with CO_2, holding the maximum amount of CO_2 under high pressure. Without the pressurization, the CO_2 wouldn't have dissolved and the liquid wouldn't normally be able to hold as much gas—the pressurization traps the CO_2 and keeps the bubbles dissolved in the drink.

When you open the can, all hell breaks loose. The pressure inside the can drops quickly to the ambient pressure of the room, and the CO_2, suddenly free to roam, jumps out of the solution, bursts into the fluid equivalent of the lambada, and frantically forms bubbles.

Why does the escaped gas turn into bubbles? Physicists call this process "nucleation." In nucleation, several CO_2 molecules cluster together to form the bubble. Because the bubble is lighter than the liquid it's immersed in, the bubble rises (gains buoyancy) to the top of the drink. Nucleation has to occur *somewhere*, and these places are called "nucleating sites." When you pour soda into an empty glass, you'll see nucleation occur in many places on the sides and bottom of the container as well as throughout the liquid.

The more nucleation sites there are available, the more likely bubbles are to form. But not all nucleation sites are created equal. The rougher the surface that comes in contact with the carbon dioxide, the more bubbles will form. And as Janet Ivaldi, scientific information specialist for Pepsi-Cola told *Imponderables,* ice is a particularly salutary choice for generating bubbles, because it has a rough surface. Compared to the smoother surface of a glass, ice is full of microscopic irregularities and pockets of air, all places that promote bubble growth.

But even glass is not as smooth as it appears. Without ice, soda

∞ **David Feldman**

has no trouble finding imperfections in glass and using them as nucleating sites. Pepsi-Cola's Christine Jones adds that many customers mistakenly believe that it is the coldness of ice (and the differential between the temperature of the ice and the beverage being poured on it) that creates the fizzing, but explains: "The same phenomenon would occur if the glass had any other solid substance in it."

Fluid mechanicist Jim Eninger points out that nucleation occurs not only along the sides of the container but also throughout the drink itself:

> "Many people think that if you shake an unopened can of soda, you increase the pressure inside, and that's the reason such a can will fizz much more when opened (compared to an unshaken can). But this is not so. Shaking the can does not change the pressure.
>
> "Actually, the shaking disturbs the liquid and creates many more nucleation sites within the liquid itself. When the can is opened, the bubbles become more ferocious simply because there are an increased number of nucleation sites in the system."

Submitted by John Kominek of Waterloo, Ontario.

Why Do Carbonated Drinks Seem to Bubble More in Plastic Cups? Is There a Scientific Basis for This?

If you've read the Imponderable above, we think you can work out the answer to this one! In his book *Rainbows, Curve Balls, and Other Wonders of the Natural World Explained*, Ira Flatow explains that at the point at which bubbles form, the nucleation sites are actually tiny nicks in the surface of the container. Simply, plastic contains many more and larger irregularities than glass.

When the drink is being poured, air bubbles get trapped in these crevices. Explains Flatow:

> *"The air pocket begins to attract molecules of carbon dioxide which leave the liquid and stick to the air. The molecules of CO_2 are caught in a tug-of-war. They are attracted both to the liquid and to the air pocket. But in the end the attraction of the air is stronger, so they pile up along the surface of the air pocket. As more molecules join in, a bubble grows. The growing bubble soon becomes too buoyant to be held down, so it breaks away and rises to the surface. The whole process is repeated, resulting in a steady stream of bubbles."*

Submitted by Mrs. Edward Carr of Overland Park, Kansas.

David Feldman

Why Does Adding Ice Cream Make Soda Fizz More?

Yep. Ice cream is another substance festooned with nucleation sites! If the ice crystals in ice cream were any more irregular, they would have to take Kaopectate on a regular basis.

We have a friend who recently tried to liven up a champagne punch with two cups of sugar. It did liven up the drink, but unfortunately not in the intended way—the liquid roiled so much that most of the punch ended up on her carpet. The crystals in sugar (or salt) are superb nucleation sites. In fact, an old trick among beer drinkers to regenerate the head of a glass of beer that's gone flat is to pour in a little salt.

Vanderbilt University physicist Chris Ballas adds that another effect helps create and retain a big head of foam when you make a root beer float: Ice cream increases the viscosity (or stickiness) of the soda. The higher viscosity causes the surface tension of the bubbles to increase, so the bubbles resist bursting more than they would if you added plain ice.

Submitted by Bill Doo of Daly City, California.

Why Does Sticking Your Finger into the Foam of Carbonated Soft Drinks Drive the Bubbles Down?

If the tiny irregularities in a glass or ice cubes are sufficient to promote more fizzing, you might think your hand would create a frenzy of bubbling. But it seems to have the opposite effect; indeed, we've seen more than a few overeager pourers of soft drinks and beer trying to stanch the overflow of beverages by putting one of their digits into a glass of burgeoning bubbles.

The physicists we spoke to about this Imponderable were quick to say that the answer to this question was "surface tension." But what does that mean?

The surface of a given liquid has a "strength" determined by the bonding capacity of its molecules. Insects such as water boatmen and some mosquitoes can literally walk on lakes and ponds without sinking—the molecular structure of the water is strong enough to support admittedly light creatures (Chris Farley: Do not try walking on ponds).

When water freezes, it seems self-evident that the surface of the ice bonds and possesses strength; but the molecules in water form less rigid, less strong, but still demonstrable bonds. A classic classroom demonstration of surface tension is to carefully place a razor blade on top of the water. It floats, not because it's buoyant, but because the blade is being supported by the surface tension below it. It takes some exertion to break the bonds of this surface tension, but of course it can be done. Place the blade in the middle of the water and it will quickly sink to the bottom, because the surface tension, logically enough, exists only on the surface of the water.

Surface tension also explains how soda bubbles stay intact. Without surface tension, the bubbles would burst as soon as they are formed. The more surface tension in a liquid, the bigger the formed bubbles are, and the more they resist breaking. Pure water has a lower surface tension than viscous liquids such as beer or soft drinks. So even though we can see water bubbles forming in noncarbonated water, they generally dissolve quickly.

We haven't forgotten the original question. Honest. What happens when we stick our fingers into our cola? As you might have guessed, our fingers break the surface tension of the soda, but perhaps not for the reason you might expect, as Vanderbilt University physicist Chris Ballas explains:

> *"Your fingers are loaded with oils and other secretions which, when placed in water-based liquids, such as soft drinks, will be released into that liquid. All liquids have a surface tension. Some chemicals increase this surface tension (like soap—that's why you blow bubbles with soapy water) and some decrease this surface tension (like oil or grease—that's why greasy dishwashing water loses its bubbles). So, in essence, the grime on your finger acts like an antifoaming agent by reducing the surface tension of the soft-drink bubbles."*

Loaded down with the grease from our fingers, bubbles pop more quickly, and the burgeoning head of foam turns into a meek, receding conglomeration of bubblettes.

Submitted by Chuck Flagg of Houston, Texas. Thanks also to Dr. Steven Mintz of Winnipeg, Manitoba, and James Evans of Cincinnati, Ohio.

Why Do Divers Spit into Their Scuba Masks Before Entering the Water?

When we conjure up images of the underworld of Jacques Cousteau, we tend to linger on the splendors of the iridescent colors of tropical fish, the subtle beauty of the coral reefs, the fierce determination of sharks, and the vastness of the oceans. But upon closer inspection, we note that whenever he dives, Jacques Cousteau can be seen spitting into his mask and rubbing the spittle around the inside of the lens. Ewwwww! Blecch!

We've written at length before about why men spit so much. Often spitting seems to serve no physiological purpose; we have pondered the possibility that spitting is a way for members of the male persuasion to mark territory. But divers are spitting into a mask that they are putting on their own faces. And, surprise of surprises, women do it too.

No, the predive ritual is one of the few socially sanctioned rationalizations for spitting, for this is expectoration with a cause:

---

spitting helps defog mask lenses. Even casual divers are aware of the problem of lenses fogging up on them in the water, and no one prefers to dive into murky waters.

What causes the fog? During a dive, the air inside the mask becomes more and more humid (full of water vapor). In very close quarters, you are continually breathing, expelling water vapor, plus you are perspiring. Inside the mask, the water vapor turns into liquid water (condensation), leading to fogging.

Why condensation? The air in the mask can become oversaturated with water vapor. But another reason is that the inside of the mask gets cooler as you continue to dive. The lens of a mask is cooler than the air inside the mask because the outside of the lens comes in constant contact with the water, which is considerably colder than the temperature of your breath (unless you are diving in a hot tub). Cooler air has a lower relative humidity than warmer air, so condensation occurs.

If the air inside the mask is saturated with water, it must find something to condense onto. As air hits the lens, it condenses onto the lens itself, forming microscopic "sweat beads," which are tiny droplets of water. These droplets refract light in all directions, making the lens appear opaque: instant fog.

Most of the diving experts we spoke to indicated that dirty lenses exacerbate the problem. Small specks of dirt lend tempting spots for water to condense onto. Even irregularities in the glass are effective sites for condensation.

So how does spitting help (after all, you're adding more water to the inside of the lens)? Water molecules are "dipoles," molecules with a small positive charge on one end and a small negative charge on the other end. They tend to want to condense onto a charged particle or attach themselves onto large molecules (which may also be charged). As a result, you have clusters of microdroplets that are spread out. These microdroplets refract light in unpredictable directions.

When you spit on the mask, you coat the inside of the lens with many diffuse charges. This increases the number of nucleating sites exponentially, so that the water condenses in a uniform manner. Instead of the sweat beads that normally form, you've created a smooth "sheet" of water. Once this "sheet" is formed, when new water molecules get added to the lens, they join the continuous sheet rather than clustering up at one site; as a result, the forces of gravity cause the water to run off the mask in a sheet. Because the water that remains adhered to the lens is a continuous sheet itself, it doesn't refract light in all directions—we can see through it— it's transparent. This "sheeting action" is the same process used in dishwasher detergents designed to remove water spots. It doesn't clean the glasses any more than other products, but it coats the glasses and disperses the charged molecules so that imperfections don't cluster at one site.

Alas, spitting is not a cure-all. Jay Black, a scuba-diving instructor who works at Blue Cheer Dive Shop in Santa Monica, California, told *Imponderables:*

> "*Many divers do spit into their masks, and rub the spit around before diving. This prevents the mask from fogging, at least for a while. However, the mask will still tend to fog up eventually.*
>
> "*When it does fog, you can clear it out underwater. You must remove the mask, let the seawater slosh around the mask, and maybe wipe the lens. Then put the mask back on. You clear the water out of the mask by blowing in air. However, this tends to work for only about fifteen minutes. Then the mask will tend to fog up again.*"

Is there an alternative to spitting as a defogger? Divers have been experimenting for eons. Black indicates that toothpaste, liquid soap (Joy detergent seems to be a particular favorite), chewing tobacco(!), and even kelp have all been used. But all pose problems. The abrasiveness in toothpaste that helps clean your teeth can also scratch the dive mask. Dish detergent works well but can irritate your eyes. Kelp isn't always readily available. And the surgeon general would not approve of your using tobacco.

So two better alternatives have surfaced. The most popular are commercial defogging products. We spoke to Bob Heck, product manager at McNett Corporation, which produces Sea Drops, the industry's leading no-fog product. Sea Drops comes in a small bottle and costs approximately five dollars. A diver simply squeezes two drops onto a dry lens. Although the instructions specify that you rub the product on both the inside and outside of the lens, Jay Stone indicated that rubbing the product on the inside only seems to work just as well.

Rodale's *Scuba Diving* magazine recently (February 1996) published an article, "Spit or Squirt," written by John Francis, that compared various methods of defogging mask lenses. Francis concluded that the commercial products do a better and longer-lasting job than our saliva, and one of the two highest-rated products was 500psi Mask Defog. We spoke to the president and creator of the product, Brad Ogle, who told us that one of the advantages of his product is that it comes in the form of a thick gel, not a liquid. Because it is denser than seawater, 500psi can be applied underwater and will still stick to the lens because the defogger won't float away.

The second alternative to spitting is to buy no-fog lenses. We spoke to Don Patten, manager of technical services at Scuba Pro, the company that manufactures and distributes the largest line of scuba and diving gear and accessories. In the last few years, Scuba Pro has been selling no-fog lenses, and Patten claims that they work well. The lenses are treated with a special no-fog agent (the agent is *so* special that Patten refused to share its ingredients):

> *"The lenses are tempered glass, but they are treated with special antifog coating. The coating is applied to the masks with a polycarbonate adhesive. The coating causes the condensed water to disperse evenly around the lens. To activate the mask before a dive, all you do is submerge the mask in water prior to a dive."*

Some divers seem almost to relish the challenge of sticking with normal lenses and fighting the good fight against fog. We asked some divers for their opinions about spitting on the mask, and the opinions range from the antagonistic:

"There are definitely downsides to spitting in a mask. One, it is simply gross and nasty. Two, it is potentially dangerous. There is at least one case of a Herpes infection resulting in partial blindness caused by transferring the virus from a cold sore in the mouth, via spit, into the eyes. There is nothing wrong with using one of the commercial defog agents on the market today."

to the zealous:

"I started diving last summer. At first, I used commercial defoggers, but I kept losing the little bottles. By the end of the season, I was a confirmed spitter. It works great!"

Submitted by John Paul Vaudreuil of Ooltewah, Tennessee. Thanks also to Rosemary Lloyd of Elberon, New Jersey.

Why Do Blank Videocassettes Slide Out of the Backs of Boxes, While Prerecorded Cassette Packages Open at the Bottom, Where They Can Fall Out?

The two innocent *Imponderables* readers who posed this perfectly logical question are assuming that the companies who manufacture the cassettes care about whether or not your cassette might drop to the floor every time you pick up its case. We're not so sure.

We once conducted a round of research on why audiocassette packages are impossible to open. The representatives of the tape companies, off the record, were more than willing to concede that even if you can find the spot on the cellophane that supposedly unravels the wrapping, human fingernails don't seem to be sufficient to pry it open. The answer, ruefully acknowledged, was that cassette packaging was convenient from *their* point of view, allowing the manufacturers to pack and store the tapes efficiently and satisfy retailers' desire for neat packaging on their shelves.

So we weren't surprised to find that the different configuration of prerecorded and blank videotapes had far more to do with commercial pursuits than consumer convenience. Once again, our sources in the cassette industry were a little shy about speaking on the record, but they confirmed what production mixer Jim Tanenbaum wrote:

> *"The blank videocassettes will normally be recorded at home and are provided with a blank adhesive label, which fits on the back edge (opposite the edge inserted into the VCR). Since the box (called a 'sleeve') is printed with the manufacturer's name and tape type on all sides, leaving a long edge open, it allows the label on the cassette to still be read when it is in its sleeve and stored on a shelf.*
>
> *"Prerecorded tapes have the title of the picture or subject printed on all sides, and leaving the bottom open ensures that the title will always be visible when the tape is on the store shelves."*

Placing the opening on the bottom of prerecorded tapes also forces video stores to store the cassettes vertically. If they are laid on their sides, as Tanenbaum points out, the tape on the bottom tends to bend, and will not contact the head properly during playback. Stacking the sleeves vertically assures the stores of a longer life for the cassettes they rent out.

Some prerecorded tapes do come packaged in fully enclosed sleeves, with flaps on the back, or top and bottom, that must be opened to remove the cassette, but the function of these more elaborate sleeves is not so much to protect the cassette as to draw attention in video stores, and add "perceived value" to the product.

Submitted by Leigh Ann Mazure of Grant Town, West Virginia. Thanks also to Gary Gawel of Clarence, New York.

Why Did Pirates Bother Making Prisoners or Enemies "Walk the Plank" Instead of Just Chucking Them Overboard?

Try as we might, we couldn't find any pirates to talk to us, on or off the record. Instead, we had to rely on a librarian and historian, Toby Gibson, at the University Library at the University of Illinois at Chicago (who has made a lifelong study of pirates, and maintains an entire web page devoted to pirate lore at http://tigger.cc.uic.edu:80/~toby-g/pirates.html, and on more than twenty books about pirates. Pirates have always captured the imagination of writers, both nonfiction and storytellers, and it has become difficult to separate the myths about pirates from serious documentation.

The reader who posed this Imponderable rightly wondered why pirates would bother with the elaborate ritual of forcing a victim to walk on a wooden plank with eyes blindfolded and hands behind his back, when it would have been far easier simply to throw the poor guy overboard. Either way, the victim would end up as shark food.

The stories about "walking the plank" usually refer to the "Golden Age" of piracy, from approximately 1690 to 1720, when such legendary (but flesh-and-blood) pirates as Blackbeard, William Kidd, and Stede Bonnet terrorized the oceans. But accounts of piracy have been documented as long as there have been ships, including tales of skullduggery in the Mediterranean in ancient Roman and Greek times.

We are lucky that many contemporaneous accounts of piracy written in the seventeenth and eighteenth centuries still exist. Many purport to be firsthand reports, but unfortunately exaggerated and outright fabricated adventure stories often masqueraded as nonfiction in those days, so much of the information therein must be taken with more than a few grains of salt. Several pirates were tried and executed for their crimes, however, so court records exist, including minutes of the proceedings for many of them.

The bottom line: There is little, if any, proof that walking the plank existed. Three other forms of punishment are clearly documented:

1. Flogging. Miscreants were beaten with a whip, the dreaded cat-o'-nine-tails.

2. Marooning. Offenders of the worst variety (murderers, rapists, despised captains) were given the clothes on their backs (and sometimes were even stripped of those), a bottle of water, a pistol, a bottle of powder, and a handful of shot, and were abandoned on an inhospitable island. They were never left on a romantic island with abundant vegetation, as depicted in Robert Louis Stevenson's *Treasure Island*. Marooning was a nonviolent but nevertheless torturous death sentence.

3. Throwing Overboard. This form of punishment, while not common, *has* been amply documented.

Some historians maintain that walking the plank did exist. In his book *The Age of Piracy*, Robert Carse claims that

> *"The story about prisoners being forced to walk the plank is almost complete fiction. Examination of the record gives only a single example. Men were thrown in over the side, though, and strung up from the yards for musket practice, pistoled point-blank."*

Carse's "single example" is a reference to Major Stede Bonnet, a soldier rather than a seaman, who in the early eighteenth century forsook a comfortable life as a gentleman in the West Indies to become a pirate. Carse writes:

> *"Bonnet died with two distinctions as a pirate. He was the first man ever in recorded history to have bought a ship with his own funds and then to have gone forth deliberately on a piratical venture. He was also, by the record, the only captain of his kind to make his victims walk the plank."*

Perhaps the most famous real-life pirate was Blackbeard, whose real name was Edward Teach. In his 1935 book, *Sinbad's Book of Pirates*, author A. E. Dingle claims that Teach tortured the skipper of a captured ship:

> *"Blackbeard laid a plank across the brig's open hatch, dragged the skipper toward it, and promised him that if he could walk across it blindfolded he would be set free and his brig given back to him. He was even permitted to walk across the plank with his eyes unbound, and he performed this part of the task with agility. He was much astonished to land safely on the other side of the deck, unhindered, and submitted to the blindfolding with a little laugh of returning confidence . . .*
>
> *"But the pirates turned him about, shoving him here and there while the bandage was being tied, a dozen of them vowing that it was not well fastened, shifting him about until when at last he was set with his feet on the plank he never noticed that it now projected*

out through the gangway and over the sea instead of across the hatch."

The victim's wife, mad at her husband for surrendering to Blackbeard so easily, protested, and was sent below into the cabin:

> *"There she saw her husband tumble past her open window from the end of the plank."*

Neither of these two stories is substantiated in any way, and the second, at least in the manner of expression, "feels" like fiction. Most of our sources discounted the reality of walking the plank. In his 1951 book, *The Great Days of Piracy in the West Indies,* George Woodbury argues that pirates' ferociousness has been greatly exaggerated. Pirates made most of their money from kidnaping and holding wealthy shipowners as hostage. There was every reason to keep such valuable booty alive. On the other hand,

> *"Those of poorer estate were usually invited to jump overboard, encouraged, and finally coerced, to do so."*

In general, though, pirates did not injure, let alone kill their captives, unless the victims provided physical resistance. In fact, it was common for pirates to recruit their prisoners, often offering them equal rights, although some were forced into indentured servitude. Even if violence was a byproduct of their work, Woodbury describes pirates as less than bloodthirsty:

> *"Ordinarily, too, pirates did not scuttle or burn ships just for the fun of it. If they wanted the ship for their own use, they took it; if they didn't, they let it go. The mere fact that there are so many tales about pirates is pretty good evidence that they did not follow the practice of 'Dead men tell no tales,' generally ascribed to them.*
>
> *"Only one atrocious practice, marooning, seems to be really characteristic of piracy. Marooning was a form of punishment usually meted out to backsliders from their own numbers . . ."*

        David Feldman

Even stronger in his "defense" of pirates and the denial of the reality of walking the plank is perhaps the most prestigious historian to write extensively about pirates, Patrick Pringle. In his 1953 book, *Jolly Roger, The Story of the Great Age of Piracy,* Pringle notes:

> *"I have ransacked official records, reports of trials, and much other documentary evidence without being able to discover a single case of walking the plank. I do not mean merely that I have not found an authenticated case. In all the documentary literature on pirates I could not find even an accusation or suggestion that the practice was ever used. The very expression seems to have been invented many years after the Age of Piracy."*

Pringle argues that it was to the advantage of pirates to have potential victims fear them. And seamen of merchant ships had little reason to resist—who would want to risk their lives to protect the merchandise of the ship's owner?

And although Bonnet is the one famous pirate often "credited" with having prisoners walk the plank, Pringle discounts the contention:

> *"Bonnet's career is even more fully documented than Blackbeard's, for a full report of his trial has been preserved. The evidence against him was considerable, yet not one of the witnesses accused him of ill-treatment of prisoners. It seems as if this is another myth."*

So then how did these myths begin? They began with early "classics" of pirate literature, such as *Bucaniers of America* (1679) and *A General History of the Robberies and Murders of the Most Notorious Pyrates* (1724), which contained facts mixed in with hyperbole. The latter book, written by "Captain Charles Johnson," is widely suspected to have been the work of Daniel Defoe, author of *Robinson Crusoe.* Pirate stories remained popular in the nineteenth century. Several of the most popular, Stevenson's *Treasure Island* and Gilbert and Sullivan's *Pirates of Penzance,* had no mention of walking the plank.

But Howard Pyle, a popular author and illustrator who worked in the last half of the nineteenth century into the beginning of the twentieth, used pirates as one of his most common subjects. And one of Pyle's most popular pictures depicted a man walking the plank, along with this commentary by the artist:

> *"With Blackbeard, we have a real, ranting, raging, roaring pirate who really did bury treasure, who made more than one captain walk the plank, and who committed more private murders than he could number on the fingers of both hands."*

Probably totally untrue, but even folks in the nineteenth century needed goose bumps, too.

When we first asked Toby Gibson about walking the plank, he answered,

> *"There's little doubt that pirates threw people overboard, especially enemies. We also know that Hollywood has turned walking the plank into a pirate tradition."*

Perhaps no Hollywood rendition is more famous than in *Peter Pan*, in which the nefarious Captain Hook forces Wendy to walk the plank. Luckily for Wendy, Peter Pan just happens to be hiding under the plank, eager and able to snatch her and fly away, with Hook none the wiser.

Even if pirates were not the brutes they have been commonly depicted to be, they are without a lobbying organization to better their image. In cartoons, they remain evil and merciless. And even though they sing beautifully, a ride through the Magic Kingdom's "Pirates of the Caribbean" will try to convince you that forcing prisoners to walk the plank was part of the "pirate's life for me."

Submitted by John Little of Coquitlam, British Columbia.

Why Did Pirates Wear Earrings?

*A*nother famous portrait of Howard Pyle's depicts the notorious Captain Kidd, clearly wearing an earring. And movie pirates usually don them, too. Did they wear them in real life?

Evidently so. Our resident pirate expert, Toby Gibson, writes:

> *"While I'm sure Hollywood was trying to make leading men such as Errol Flynn and Douglas Fairbanks, Sr., look suave and exotic, real pirates were piercing their ears for a more practical purpose. It was believed that piercing the ears with such precious metals as silver and gold improved one's eyesight. This was the main reason pirates performed such a ritual. It must also be noted that most other seafaring men also indulged in this practice.*
>
> *"While for years this was considered an old wives' tale, today the art of acupuncture lends some credence to the practice of ear piercing. The earlobe is an acupuncture point for several eye ailments. It is quite possible that the practice of ear piercing may have been brought to the West from the Oriental trade routes."*

History confirms that pirates increasingly worked Asian waters after the Caribbean and "New World" prospects "dried up" in the early to mid-eighteenth century. This would also explain why the graphic depictions of pirates in the earliest books we described in the previous chapter do not picture pirates sporting earrings.

We decided to speak to some acupuncturists, to determine whether practitioners, then and now, believe in a relationship between piercing the ear and improved vision. When we asked Dr. Steve Given, an acupuncturist who also teaches the art at Emperor's College in Santa Monica, California, he gave us a shock. We asked him about the ear-eye connection, and before we could broach the subject, he brought up pirates:

> *"There are reports of people enjoying vision improvements after having their ears pierced. In fact, when I studied acupuncture, the*

subject of pirates piercing their ears just for this reason was discussed."

Given doesn't dispute that pirates pierced their ears for this reason. He discussed how the ear is often used in acupuncture as a focus point for eye problems in general, and vision problems, in particular. A point on the ear, called the "eye point" or "vision point" corresponds to the area on an earlobe where piercing might take place. But he doubts that any *lasting* vision improvement could be attained from piercing:

"If they did get a benefit by puncturing the master sensorial [yet another name for the 'eye point'] in a fortuitous manner, it certainly wouldn't be a lasting thing. Once the ear is pierced, scar tissue forms around the hole. This will block any further beneficial effects."

Given's arguments were corroborated by two other acupuncturists we consulted. Timothy Chen, of the Acupuncture Clinic of Pasadena, told *Imponderables* that he has found nearsightedness and conjunctivitis to be conditions helped by acupuncture on the ear, but doubted whether piercing could help general vision on a long-term basis. Dr. Michael Apelian, of the Acupuncture Therapy Center in Santa Monica, has heard of cases of vision being harmed and helped by ear piercing:

"I've heard it go both ways. I've also heard because you're damaging that area by piercing, it can inhibit vision. I think that most of the more ancient beliefs (and Chinese literature) felt that it would stimulate vision rather than hinder it."

We asked Dr. Apelian if *he* treated people on the ear for vision problems:

"Sure. However, I think that other body points, especially on the face and feet, are stronger."

Maybe pirates pierced their faces and feet, too. But it would be hard to find rings underneath the bushy beards and salty footwear.

Submitted by Lauren Kuehl of Levittown, Pennsylvania. Thanks also to Amy Kelly of Cleburne, Texas; and Douglas Watkins, Jr., of Hayward, California.

Why Do Phone Companies Charge Customers Extra for Unlisted Numbers?

Imponderables is pleased to announce a change in policy. As you know, we have always sent a free, autographed book to any reader who is the first to send in an Imponderable that we use. And we will continue to do so. However, because of added overhead costs, we have reluctantly decided that we will now charge all readers who haven't sent in an Imponderable that we use a small service fee of two dollars per month.

That's right! For less than the cost of buying a daily newspaper for a week, you can have all the privacy attendant on not being published in our books. You can hardly afford *not* to pay a mere twenty-four dollars per year for this luxury. Sorry, no credit card orders can be accepted. But for your convenience, we'll call you with this offer when we know you'll be home—dinnertime. There's no way you can afford *not* to avail yourself of this service, offered exclusively to *Imponderables* readers.

Well, we tried, anyway.

The phone company has been getting away with charging us for *not* being listed in the phone book (and directory assistance) for a long time. Do they have any rationalization for the practice?

Officials from phone companies were reticent about speaking on the record about this topic, but we've been able to piece together the story with off-the-record interviews and discussions with telephone consultants. Engineering consultant Douglas A. Kerr, of Dallas, Texas, wrote us:

> *"The original rationale for this surcharge was that, first, the telephone company needed to take special clerical steps to keep that subscriber's entry out of the database system from which directories were compiled. Second, a person's having an unlisted number inflated the volume of inquiries made to directory assistance, which was a free service at the time."*

Historically, unlisted numbers weren't handled the same way as listed numbers. Phone companies maintained an "unlisted number bureau" to provide access for police and fire departments.

But the bigger expense, as Kerr indicates, is the increased volume to directory assistance. A disproportionate percentage of "information" calls are for unlisted numbers. The calling party doesn't know that the number is unlisted but is more likely to call because the desired party is not listed in the phone book. James Turner, who worked at Pacific Telephone from 1974 to 1983, explains the problem he faced when the company charged fifteen cents per directory assistance call (it now costs approximately fifty cents in most localities; in the 1960s and before, it was *free)*:

> *"I don't know if any studies were ever made about the true cost of an unlisted number to the telephone company, but I would suspect that it exceeds the revenue brought in. As a former service rep, I can tell you that we spent a great deal of time explaining to callers who wanted someone's unlisted number that we couldn't give it out.*
>
> *"And I'm sure that operators had a much harder time with it than service reps ever did. Then there's always the customer who insists that it's an emergency, so the operator has to call the unlisted party and relay a message to call the other party back."*

Of course, providing unlisted numbers also lessens the total number of phone calls, for the few folks who can't find the phone number of the intended party will never make that revenue-generating call. The phone company also derives income from selling "names" to phone directories; every unlisted phone number is one entry "missing" from the White Pages.

Still, we think the most compelling explanation for the current policy was voiced by many of our sources: The phone company charges more for unlisted numbers because the phone company can get away with it! Steve Forrette, of Seattle's Walker, Richer & Quinn, Inc., put it this way:

> *"Telephone services in many cases are not priced in relation to their cost, but rather the perceived value to the consumer. Take, for example, TouchTone dialing, which actually reduces the telco's cost, but is often surcharged because the customer perceives that they are getting an extra service."*

Most telephone companies now offer "nonpublished" as well as unlisted numbers. Even though the term would seem to mean the opposite, other parties *can* obtain a nonpublished number, even if it doesn't appear in the phone directory.

With current technology, a few key strokes by a service rep can process inquiries about listed, unlisted, or nonpublished numbers with ease. And with the current pricing for making directory assistance calls, the telcos might even be turning a slight profit on the service. We can think of no truer statement to close this chapter than the wisdom tendered by Douglas Kerr: "Telephone surcharges have a way of never evaporating."

Submitted by William F. McGrady of Vallejo, California. Thanks also to Curtis Kelly of Chicago, Illinois; Dennis David Thorpe of Appleton, Wisconsin; and Jeanie Vance of Hyannis, Massachusetts.

How Did Candlestick Park Get Its Unusual Name? And Why Would the Giants Put Their Ballpark in Such a Cold, Windy Place?

Candlestick Park is located at the southeastern tip of San Francisco, at a point that juts out into the bay. This would have been a considerably shorter chapter if this protrusion were shaped like a candlestick, but alas, it is not.

Even before Candlestick Park was constructed, the swampy marshland upon which it was built was known as Candlestick Point. Thus, the Park was named after the Point. In 1958, the city ran a contest to name the new Stadium, and on March 4, 1959, "Candlestick Park" was officially declared as the winner.

A more intriguing question is how Candlestick *Point* got its name. When we contacted the San Francisco Giants, Blake

Rhodes, of the office of public relations, told *Imponderables* that before the development of the park, the marshland was inhabited by birds known as "candlestick birds," and that the Point was probably named after these feathered denizens of the area. Unfortunately, consultation with several California birding experts proved fruitless. No one has ever heard of any birds being called "candlestick birds," officially or colloquially, which leads us to believe that the Point gave the name to the birds, not vice versa.

More likely, Candlestick Park was named after some unusual rock formations that resembled a candelabra. Faun McInnis, of the San Francisco Historical Room at the San Francisco Public Library, cited several books that confirmed this theory. Evidently, the rock formation was on the bay side, so it was more easily seen from the water.

Yet, as with any good mystery, the evidence is cloudy. The rock formation collapsed (or was destroyed) long before ground was broken for the stadium.

Speaking of cloudy, the problems with determining the origins of the name Candlestick Park pale in comparison with trying to catch a fly ball in Candlestick Park. To say the least, the location is not ideal.

The New York Giants moved to San Francisco in 1958, without a major league ballpark in place. They played the first season in California at Seals Stadium, a minor-league park with a capacity of only 18,500. The voters of San Francisco approved a five-million-dollar bond issue to help finance a new stadium in or near downtown. A maelstrom of politics ensued, when a local builder, Charles C. Harney, "came to the rescue." Harney owned most of the property at Candlestick Point, including 60 percent of the land under "Bay View Hill," a large hill above the Point.

From the start, there was vocal opposition to the site of the new stadium. Local citizens were aware of the fog, cold, and stiff winds in the area, but Harney convinced the city that Bay View Hill would form a natural windbreak. To counter concerns about cold, Harney offered to build heaters throughout the stadium. Best of all, Harney assured the city that he could complete the stadium in time for the 1959 season.

Of course, he couldn't. The Giants came close to winning the pennant in 1959, blowing a big lead, while Harney struggled to finish the stadium in time for the World Series. Instead, the Dodgers beat the White Sox in *their* temporary stadium, the L.A. Coliseum, which held more than 100,000 fans.

Although Harney did finish Candlestick Park in time for the 1960 season, all the fears about the stadium proved to be true. Fielders manhandled routine plays; fans sought hot cocoa instead of cold beer. Bay area citizens were furious, none more so than the litigious litigation lawyer Melvin Belli. Belli bought a six-seat box for the 1960 season at a then-expensive $1,597 price tag. As Art Rosenbaum and Bob Stevens recount in their book, *The Giants of San Francisco,* Belli sued the city to get his money back, stating:

> *"Even with long underwear and an Alaskan parka, the same one I wore to Siberia last year, I couldn't keep warm in Box J, Section 4."*

A two-day trial convened in 1962, in which Belli claimed that the Giants had promised an effective radiant-heating system would keep his bottom warm during ball games and cited a yearbook article in which the Giants claimed the boxes were heated to 85 degrees. The owner of the Giants, Horace Stoneham, countered that all the Giants owed fans was a seat and nine players on the field.

For those who think that grandstanding in trials started only when cameras were in the court, let it be on the record that Belli presented a long stream of witnesses, including a man who had swum in San Francisco Bay for forty years but had never felt more like a "frozen mackerel than when at Candlestick Park."

But no jury of San Francisco peers could side with Stoneham

on this issue. The jury voted eleven to one for Belli, who promptly announced that he would donate his winnings, $1,597, to the city for trees, "but not at Candlestick because they would freeze out there."

Submitted by Lynn Carlson of Yakima, Washington.

Cow Palace Hall of Fame

Queen Bossy I

Queen Flossie

Princess Clarabelle

Candidate Goldwater

TOURS →

Why Would an Arena Be Called the Cow Palace?

They don't build 'em like the Cow Palace anymore. Whereas most complexes are designed for specific purposes, this multipurpose arena, built on the outskirts of San Francisco in the mid-1930s, has hosted everything from rock concerts to wrestling matches, from trade shows to hockey games, from rodeos to the 1964 Republican National Convention (and the disastrous Barry Goldwater acceptance speech).

But originally, its primary business was hosting livestock expositions. While the building was being constructed, a San Francisco newspaper columnist dubbed it a "palace for cows" and an anonymous headline writer transposed the expression to "Cow Palace," so the nickname of the building existed before the structure was even completed.

With a less than mellifluous official name of "First Grand National Livestock Exposition and Rodeo," the arena was known

𝕯avid 𝕱eldman

as the Cow Palace from the start. Not until the 1950s were the words *Cow Palace* painted on the building's exterior, and only in 1963 did the building's name legally change to Cow Palace.

Submitted by Lynn Carlson of Yakima, Washington.

Auntie's Insect Killer — Really Works! — KEY

Auntie's Oven Cleaner — Really Works! — KEY

Auntie's Paint Thinner — Really Works — KEY

Auntie's All-Purpose Solvent — Really Works!

Auntie's 100 Proof WHISKEY

Auntie's Cough Mixture — Really Works! — KEY

Auntie's Floor Wax Remover — Really Works! — KEY

What Did Liquor Distilleries Do During Prohibition?

During the nearly fourteen years of Prohibition (the Eighteenth Amendment went into effect on January 17, 1920), most of the distilleries in the United States were put out of business. Many distilleries were small, family-run operations with colorful names that were forced to shutter their operations: The Chickencock distillery was converted into a seed company; Rolling Fork became a stockyard.

Some distilleries were a little luckier. According to Matthew J. Vellucci, library director of the Distilled Spirits Council of the United States, some distilleries were given reprieves by the federal government—they were licensed to produce industrial alcohol or whiskey for medicinal purposes.

But enterprising entrepreneurs found all kinds of ways to get booze to a parched America. The government demanded that industrial alcohol be denatured so that citizens would not drink what could easily blind or cripple them. Industrial alcohol was usually mixed with soap or lavender, but many included more dangerous agents, such as wood alcohol or carbolic acid. Some thrill-seeking alcohol cravers still bought the smuggled, adulterated liquor, and many paid for it with their lives.

The larger bootlegging outfits hired chemists to remove the poisons from industrial alcohol, according to Lynwood Mark Rhodes, who wrote "That Was Prohibition" for the August 1974 *American Legion* magazine. After the toxins were removed, to form a substance called "washed alcohol," the bootleggers added caramel for coloring and oil of rye or bourbon for flavoring. With luck, the final product tasted not unlike real whiskey:

"All such mixtures were offensive to the taste, but so what? They had unmistakable wallop. The thumbnail test was devised. Stick your thumb in your drink and if the nail stayed on it was safe. If you think I am being flip, this is exactly how those who drank the stuff spoke of it."

Obviously, alcohol consumers could not be fussy during Prohibition. Indeed, several large distilleries tried to make the best of a bad situation by producing new, nonalcoholic or low-alcoholic drinks. Many breweries tried to market "near beer," with only occasional success. Anheuser-Busch was forced to diversify out of the beer business during Prohibition but also foisted a legal, nonalcoholic drink called "Bevo" on the public as a way of utilizing its otherwise moribund breweries. Another company produced "wort," the cooled boiled mash that would ordinarily be the stage of the brewing process before the beer became alcoholic. The company was kind enough to package the wort with a cake of yeast, which promptly turned the wort into a spirit, but of course such a suggestion was not stated on the label.

Another alternative for lucky distilleries was to manufacture "medicinal spirits." Sean Thomas, of the Seagram Museum, wrote:

"Some companies, such as the Frankfort Distillery, remained open to produce medicinal spirits, which were available by prescription to treat various illnesses."

Suddenly, Americans were beset with maladies that could be treated only by a nip or two. And of course, the poor sufferer wasn't consuming illegal liquor to obtain a cheap high—it was medicine.

According to Rhodes, doctors wrote eleven million prescriptions for alcohol per year ("for medicinal purposes") during Prohibition. Theoretically, a "patient" was only allowed one half-pint every ten days, but drugstores became havens for the dispensing of spirits. Counterfeiters produced fake prescription pads and sold them for two dollars apiece, while motivated "sufferers" learned the fine art of forgery.

Even though the production of spirits by big distilleries was severely curtailed during Prohibition, Americans, displaying characteristic Yankee ingenuity, found ways to consume the stuff.

Submitted by David Bang of Los Angeles, California.

Why Do Bees Buzz? Do They Buzz to Communicate with One Another?

Most of the bee buzzing that we hear is nothing other than the vibrations of their flapping wings during flight. When bees are flying, their wings are usually cycling more than two hundred times per second. Entomologist Lynn Kimsey, of the Bohart Museum of Entomology in Berkeley, California, notes:

> "In my experience, even a bee flying slowly makes a buzzing sound. However, many bees are small enough that the human ear simply isn't capable of hearing the sound they generate. The speed that a bee is flying does alter the sound quality to the human ear to some extent.

"The buzzing sound in bees is generated by the architecture and deformation of the thorax by the flight muscles. Because of this, larger bees produce a lower-pitched sound than smaller ones. Needless to say the buzzing sound continues as long as a bee flies."

Before we generalize about bees, entomologists tend to get a tad waspish when the term is thrown around indiscriminately. The "bee" is actually a member of a superfamily (Apoidea) of the order that includes many other insects, including wasps. Only approximately five hundred species of the twenty thousand or so bees are the social bees (e.g., honeybees, bumblebees) that form colonies and seem to have a fifty-fifty chance of being followed by camera crews from documentary nature shows.

In this chapter, we're talking about the social bees because the communications needs of solitary bees are quite different. As Kimsey puts it:

"You have to realize that 90 percent of the bee species are solitary and have no reason to communicate with other individuals except to find a mate. Only the social bees (honeybees, stingless bees, and bumblebees) need any kind of specialized communications among individuals. In all bees, mating 'communication' is done either using visual or olfactory cues."

Leslie Saul-Gershenz, insect zoo director of the San Francisco Zoological Society, adds that bees are also capable of other forms of nonvocal communication, including creating vibrations by tapping a substrate, and touch or tactile signals (honeybees use their antennae to communicate with one another).

Bees can't hear the way we do (if they could, they'd probably knock off that annoying buzzing) for one simple reason—they don't have ears. They detect sound by "feeling" the vibration through their antennae or feet.

Nowhere is the bees' potential for using vibrations from buzzing to communicate more evident than in their "waggle dance." In 1973, Karl von Frisch won the Nobel Prize for unlocking the mystery of how worker honeybees "tell" their companions at the hive about nectar sources. Frisch discovered that bees perform two distinct dances. One is a "circle dance," which seems to indicate a food discovery, but not its specific location; and a tail-wagging dance, which pinpoints the treasure. While the dancer is tail-wagging, the bee is also madly beating its wings, generating a distinctive buzzing sound.

Although the other bees can't hear the buzz, they can feel the vibration through their feet. Successors to von Frisch have confirmed the validity of his discovery by creating a "robot bee" that is capable of transmitting information that other bees can successfully interpret. Kimsey reports that the vibrating wings of the dancer also help to disperse the aroma of the flowers visited by the worker, which helps the other bees locate the same resource.

According to Mark Winston, associate professor of biological sciences at Simon Fraser University, the beating of the wings during the waggle dance is considerably slower than during flight, so the buzz would be at a much lower pitch, more like a "low-pitched drone":

> *"The tone would be comparable to that produced by the lowest notes on a piano. Most of the bee buzzing that we hear is certainly at much higher tones."*

The other most common form of buzzing is what Doug Yanega, of the Illinois Natural History Survey, refers to as "body-buzzing." Unlike wing-buzzing, body-buzzing is executed with the wings folded, with the bees using their thoracic muscles to produce the vibrations. Whereas wing-buzzing seems to be merely a coincident byproduct of flight (although it might, possibly, scare off potential nonbee predators), body-buzzing, according to Yanega,

> *"can be relevant in a number of biological contexts, depending on which bees are involved. Virtually all bees will buzz if provoked while they are in burrows (bear in mind that most of the thirty thousand bee species live in burrows in soil or twigs) or when held.*
> *"Bumblebees will buzz to warm up their bodies, and to produce*

heat to warm young brood. Male bees of many species will vibrate during mating, and presumably the buzzing is part of the ritual, performed in a species-specific manner."

We have heard of only one other use of buzzing in bees, and from a far-flung place. Pia Bergquist, a graduate student in chemical ecology at Göteborg University in Sweden, is currently researching bumblebees and pollination. Bergquist told *Imponderables* that while most flowers' anthers (the part of the stamen that contains pollen) open longitudinally and are relatively easy for bees to extract nectar from, some flowers have only tiny holes or channels. Bees have found an extraordinary way, though, to bring home their equivalent of the bacon:

> *"In these flowers, the bees can't just brush and groom to get pollen, so they use the buzzing technique. Usually, the bees hang from the flower holding on to the anther with all six legs. While hanging like this, the bee buzzes. This causes vibrations, which sonicate the flower and cause the pollen to fall out from the anther and onto the bee's belly."*

Submitted by Amy Bagshaw of Las Vegas, Nevada. Thanks also to Scott Robinson of Bay City, Michigan.

Why Do You See Spinning Blades on the Tops of Some Billboards?

For those of you have never seen them, these blades spin horizontally (parallel to the ground) along the top of a billboard. Usually, you'll see the entire top edge of the board covered by the span of the "wands." Many billboards are exactly twenty-four or forty-eight feet across. With the shorter configuration, you'll see two twelve-foot wands; with the longer, four twelve-foot wands.

We have long passed these slowly but constantly moving blades, found in profusion in southern California, and mused: "What are they for? To keep pigeons from roosting on the billboards?"

Guess what? That *is* why those blades spin. The device is called the "Bird Whacker" or "Pigeon Whacker." They were invented in 1987 by Rodney Wales, who had worked in the outdoor advertising field for thirty-five years, and he soon established Wales

Whacker Works to market them. Although Wales died a few years ago, the company, under the stewardship of his son and daughter, is still going strong.

The blades run on a standard outdoor, 110-volt electrical line and don't use that much energy, as Gilbert Steadman, electrical superintendent of Eller Media, explains:

> *"It's just a motor with a blade on top. The blades are real thin and very light. The blades look like rejected fishing rods. They turn near the top of the board and keep the birds from landing on the top of the board."*

As we were learning about how the Bird Whackers worked, a niggling thought popped into our otherwise unoccupied cranium: Why do the billboard companies care if birds roost on the tops of their billboards? Let's take the worst-case thesis: Birds roost atop the billboards all day and poop to their hearts' content. It's not as if consumers could see the unsightly accumulation that would pile up on top of the board.

Alas, the whackers aren't there to satisfy the advertisers, but rather the landowners. Billboard space is leased from the folks who own the land below the board. We discussed this issue with Mike Jensen, operations manager of the biggest outdoor advertising company, Gannett Outdoor, and he confirmed that

> *"usually the biggest problem is with the tenant or property owner that lives with the pigeon mess below the board. Even if it doesn't work perfectly, at least we're cutting down on the problem and helping with the pigeon mess.*
>
> *"The big problem is not the birds themselves, but the mess they create. Defecation is the worst problem, but also the feathers, nest scraps, and so forth. Pigeons are definitely* not *the cleanest of birds. Pigeons represent about 95 percent of the problem. Sometimes we have troubles with blackbirds and a few others."*

Gannett installs whackers only on an "as needed" basis. Occasionally, a board that has been pigeon-free all of a sudden turns into the avian equivalent of Fort Lauderdale on Spring Break; if so, it's a relatively easy matter to install whackers on already existing boards.

Eller's philosophy is similar, but he stressed that the type of location is as important as the number of birds using the billboard as a nesting site:

> *"It's only standard procedure to install whackers if we foresee a problem. We want to keep our lessors and the public happy. There's no need to use the whackers when the board is in the middle of a field, or along the freeway. The birds only come to a board when there's a food source nearby—donut shop, deli, restaurant, or grocery store where there's trash out back. Even a dog's bowl might have food in it."*

Do whackers work? Our sources tended to agree with Debbie Wales Murillo, daughter of the inventor, who said:

> *"Yes. Usually just the movement of the wands is enough to deter the birds from landing."*

But whackers may not be a panacea, as Jensen elucidates:

> *"They work where they are—that is, the spot on the board where they're installed, especially the visible spots on the top of the board. They don't do much for where they aren't. There are a lot of other places for the birds to go on a billboard besides the top. If you keep the birds from landing and roosting on their favorite place [which does tend to be the top], it does help keep them from landing on the rest of the structure.*
>
> *"At some locations, if the whackers scare the birds away, they never come back. At other locations, they land on other parts of the billboard. But at least we're doing something about the problem."*

Gil Steadman told us that in his experience, whackers work most of the time. But occasionally, you can find a small bird sitting underneath them "and ducking every time the blade comes around." That's what we call living dangerously. But larger birds, Steadman reports, occasionally use whackers as theme park attractions: "A couple of times, we found some birds actually riding the whackers."

Wales Whacker Works has an exclusive patent on the whacker, so it has no competitors. Still, of course, WWW is looking for ways to grow sales, especially because many localities are prohibiting the installation of new billboards. Debbie reports that whackers have been sold for boats and yachts in marinas. Sea World in San Diego bought about 100 units to use on the buildings around their eating areas, and even have a couple above the shark tank.

Whackers have been sold to as far-flung places as Japan and Antarctica. Antarctica? Please, please don't tell us that there is such a thing as a "Penguin Whacker."

Submitted by Michael Rusak of Sun Valley, California. Thanks also to Sam Williams of Canoga Park, California; and Jason Niedle of Cypress, California.

Why Are College Basketball Games Played in Halves, While the NBA Plays in Quarters?

Baseball, football, and hockey all share not only the same scoring structure at the professional level as the college level but also play for the same amount of time. College basketball players run up and down the court for a "mere" forty minutes, while the pros must toil for an extra eight minutes to earn the sneaker endorsements that constitute nearly 1 percent of the American gross national product. Why the difference?

The college game preceded pro hoops. While the origins of baseball are shrouded in some mystery and considerable controversy, we can credit the invention of basketball to one person, Dr. James Naismith, a physical education instructor at the YMCA Training School (now Springfield College) in Springfield, Massachusetts. He developed the sport because his boss asked him to invent a game that could be played indoors during the winter. In 1892, Naismith published a rule book in the school magazine, so we know that the earliest basketball games consisted of two fifteen-minute halves with five minutes of rest in between.

Geneva College became the first school to organize a basketball team, in 1892, followed by the University of Iowa in 1893, Ohio State and Temple in 1894, and Yale in 1895. The first college game (with *nine* players on a team) was played in 1895. Hamline (of St. Paul, Minnesota) squashed the Minnesota State School of Agriculture by the mammoth score of nine goals to three.

Intercollegiate basketball became popular quickly, but there were regional variations in the rules until the early twentieth century. Once the NCAA became a unifying force, after World War I, all college games were played in two twenty-minute halves.

Professional and semipro basketball leagues were formed as early as the late nineteenth century, but none was national in scope and the players did not earn enough to quit their day jobs. Bill Himmelman, proprietor of Sports Nostalgia Research in Norwood, New Jersey, provided us with fascinating information about these early leagues.

One of the prominent pre-NBA leagues was the American Basketball League, based in New York. Formed in the 1920s, the ABL rules designated three fifteen-minute periods, presumably a holdover from hockey, for the games were played in hockey arenas. The National Basketball League, formed at the end of the nineteenth century, was based in Chicago and in its last days (in the 1930s and 1940s) had forty-minute games divided into four ten-minute periods.

After World War II ended in 1945, a group of hockey team owners got together to figure out how to wring more money out of their hockey stadiums when their teams were on the road, and how to better exploit the entertainment needs of a suddenly booming economy. The ABL had just folded and the owners saw an opening. In that meeting, they hatched the Basketball Association of America (BAA).

Although they "borrowed" the rules from college, the BAA lengthened the season to increase revenue; earlier basketball leagues generally scheduled games only on the weekends. They decided to try sixty-game seasons and a playoff format similar to hockey's.

However, the basketball association faced the opposite problem that fledgling professional baseball faced: The game of amateur basketball, as it had been played, wasn't long enough to suit paying customers. So they lengthened the playing time of the game to forty-eight minutes, with the goal of providing what hockey fans had come to expect: two hours of entertainment.

The owners could have divided the forty-eight minutes into two twenty-four-minute halves, but by instituting four twelve-minute quarters, they gained two advantages: the evening was lengthened, but more particularly, the transitions between periods provided more time for fans to hit the concession stands.

After two years of play, the BAA merged with the remnants of the failing NBL and formed the National Basketball Association.

The first NBA season, with seventeen teams, was played in 1949–50. According to John Neves of the NBA, the league has never varied from the twelve-minute–quarters format.

In the spirit of full disclosure, we must add that the NCAA did tinker once with its timing structure. For two seasons (1953–55), the college game was divided into four ten-minute quarters. At the time, the NCAA was under a cloud because of point-shaving scandals in the early 1950s. Himmelman indicates that collegiate basketball needed a public-relations makeover, so they "borrowed a bit" from the NBA, which was flourishing at the amateur game's expense, by going to quarters. After the 1955 season, the college game reverted back to two twenty-minutes halves, reducing concession revenue but restoring this Imponderable, so that the public could be confused and so we could have something to write about.

Submitted by Brian Adams of Carmel, Indiana. Thanks also to Michelle and Mitchell Szczepancyzk of Grand Rapids, Michigan; and Frank Norman of Manhattan Beach, California.

Why Are There Nine Innings in Baseball?

Does each player in the starting lineup get "his" inning? Does each Muse have an inning named after her? One inning per cat's life? Alas, the genesis of innings in baseball has more than a passing similarity to the story of basketball's quarters and halves.

Like basketball, baseball was first an amateur game. In its earliest incarnations, baseball was known as "town ball," "goal ball," or "old-cat," and only by the 1840s was it known as "base ball." We'll skip the fight over whether Abner Doubleday or Alexander Cartwright was the "father of baseball" and simply state what we know to be true: Alexander Cartwright, a bank clerk, convinced a group of amateur players to form the "New York Knickerbocker Base Ball Club," and in 1845, the club laid down a set of rules that resemble today's baseball game in many ways: the game was played on a diamond-shaped field; the bases were placed ninety feet apart; an inning consisted of three outs, etc.

But the Knickerbockers' game had a few "striking" differences from the modern version. For one, there were no *called* balls and strikes—the only way to strike out without hitting the ball was to swing and miss three times. And most important, for our purposes, there was no inning limit to the games; the winner was the first team to get twenty-one runs (provided that each team received an equal number of times at bat).

The Knickerbockers (and their rule book) helped base ball spread rapidly throughout New York City and into other urban areas. By the mid-1850s, base ball mania had arrived. Compared to today's game, base ball then was a high-scoring affair, mainly because pitchers (who stood a close forty-five feet from the plate) threw underhand in a stiff-armed motion. They threw softly to a "batsman" (a term borrowed from the English game of cricket), who was supposed to be stopped by the fielders. But according to baseball historian and writer Bill Deane, within ten years, pitchers started developing pitches that were difficult to hit. Some even worked on a "speed ball," what we would now call a fastball, and more deviously, a curve.

Whereas in the early game of base ball, scores of 21–19 were not hard to rack up, as pitchers improved, it became harder and harder for a team to attain the goal of 21 runs. Games took longer and longer.

By the late 1850s, although baseball clubs were nominally amateur organizations, talented players were recruited with under-the-table payments. Betting among players and fans was common. In the late 1850s, the National Association of Base Ball Players was formed not only to codify the rules and organize the burgeoning club competition but also to try to make a few dollars from the popular game. Not unlike the hockey owners who met to see how they could exploit the game of basketball, the new association saw the potential for base ball as a spectator sport and foresaw a problem with the length of the game.

In the early 1850s, it was not uncommon for games to last two days, but the association realized that paying fans wouldn't settle for not seeing the resolution of a game before nightfall. By 1858 the National Association of Base Ball Players dethroned the Knickerbockers as the overseers of the game, and it set the nine-inning rule. The goal was to make the competition last approximately two to two and one-half hours. The average game takes longer now, but then they didn't have to contend with commercials and preening prima donnas in the 1850s.

The Civil War helped to spread baseball throughout the rest of the country. In 1869, four years after the war ended, the Cincinnati Red Stockings became the first all-salaried baseball team. And the National League arrived in 1876. From the start, the pros played nine innings a game.

Submitted by Rick DeWitt of Erie, Pennsylvania. Thanks also to Douglas Watkins, Jr., of Hayward, California; Jena Mori of Los Angeles, California; Joe Dagata and sons of Parma, Ohio; Steve Kaufman of New York, New York; Melissa Hall of Bartlett, Illinois; and Scott Ball of Chico, California.

How Did Folks Wake Up Before Alarm Clocks Were Invented? How Did They Make Specific Appointments Before Clocks Were Invented?

Imagine an average guy during the Dark Ages, let's say in the ninth century. After a hard day's work, he decides to meet a pal for a cappuccino or a grog. Was there an awkward pause after, "Okay, why don't I meet you at my place at . . . "?

Or he got a new gig as an apprentice carpenter. His boss says, "Be here right on the dot of . . ." How did he know when to show up? And how did he make sure he awakened in time to make it on the dot of an undisclosed time?

Although the Egyptians and Chinese used water clocks much earlier, the mechanical clock was not invented (in Italy) until the mid-fourteenth century. Presumably, before clocks, most folks reckoned the time by following the progress of the sun. On clear days, following the shadows on trees or on "noon marks" etched on buildings would indicate the approximate time.

David Feldman

Before then, people were forced to rely on natural events to wake them up. Although approximately 90 percent of the European population lived in rural settings, even most town dwellers had animals, such as chickens, that made it abundantly clear when the sun had risen.

And it's not as though medieval peasants had much leisure time, as Martin Swetsky, president of the Electrical Horology Society, explains:

> *"Life was casual, yet demanding. The workman or farmer was awakened by the rising sun, performed his day's duties until the sun set, and thus ended his day to retire until the next morning."*

Presumably, just as most of us don't need an alarm to wake up every day, folks had the same "biological clock," the same circadian rhythms, that we do today.

Even centuries after the invention of the mechanical clock, most folks couldn't afford them. In early America, roosters, the sun, servants, the town crier, church bells, and factory whistles were all more likely to wake up the average person than an alarm clock. In his fascinating book *Revolution in Time*, David S. Landes speculates that these signals were likely irregular:

> *". . . dictated by nature, weather, and the varying requirements of agriculture, conforming not to schedule but to opportunity and circumstances. They were not so much a sign of punctuality as a substitute for it.*
>
> *"The pattern of work in the cities was a little different. There, too, the craftsman awoke with the dawn and the animals and worked as long as natural light or oil lamps permitted. In the typical household workshop, one person, usually the newest apprentice, would 'sleep on one ear,' wake before the others, start the fire, get the water, then get the others up; and the same person would usually shut things down at night. Productivity, in the sense of output per unit of time, was unknown. The great virtue was busyness— unremitting diligence in one's tasks."*

When tower clocks were installed in villages, they often provided wake-up service. But in the Middle Ages, clocks reflected the casual approach to time: The earliest mechanical clocks had neither minute nor hour hands; their bells rang on the hour, occasionally on the quarter hour.

The Chinese were the first to experiment with timepieces devoted to waking up their owners. Milton Stevens, executive director of the American Watchmakers-Clockmakers Institute, provided *Imponderables* with a glimpse of some of the primitive alarm clocks:

"The Chinese are credited with using the first rope clocks. The 'clock' consisted of a rope saturated with an oil to support combustion. Through experimentation, they learned the length of rope that burned in an hour. With this knowledge, they tied a knot at the proper length for each hour. To awaken at a given time, the rope was tied to the toe. Thus, when the proper time to awaken arrived, the individual felt the heat on the toe and had little trouble waking up.

"With the candle clock, by experimentation it was learned how far down a candle would burn in one hour. Hours, then, were marked on the candle at the appropriate locations. To make this serve as an alarm, the candle was mounted in a large metal dish. A small hook with a small bell was inserted into a location on the candle, which indicated the time to be awakened. When the candle burned to that point, the bell fell into the metal dish, which made a noise—with luck, enough to arouse the sleeper."

The demand for more precise alarm clocks came, not as one might expect, from the world of commerce, but from religion. Moslems traditionally prayed five times a day, and Jews three times a day, but early Christians had no set schedule. The emergence of monasticism, a full-time vocation, established the need for routines. And these monks, devoted to the service of God, were methodical in organizing their prayer schedule.

Although different orders varied, many monasteries divided

David Feldman

the day into six segments, mandating prayer six times a day. This demanding schedule included nighttime vigils, which required the monks to be awakened after they had gone to sleep. Before alarm clocks, one person was often designated to stay up while other monks slept; the "waker" had the unenviable task of rousing the others for prayer.

The mechanical alarm clocks created by the monks were more akin to today's egg timers than the devices on today's bedstands, as Martin Swetsky explains:

> "The first alarm clocks were primitive devices, without hands or dials. They were mechanical contrivances intended to ring bells at the desired time, with this accomplished by a peg placed in a hole nearest the hour and a linkage system connected to this mechanism that provided the bell-ringing service."

Subsequent clocks were set to strike at the six (later seven) canonical hours, with varying numbers of bells indicating which prayer service was to begin.

And how did folks, before the advent of clocks, make that heavy date or crucial job interview on time? Most likely, they played it safe, arriving for appointments long before they needed to. If courtiers needed to be at the palace for a predawn ceremony, they arrived at midnight and waited for the drums to beat and the gate to open, rather than risk oversleeping. Time, as we know it, "belonged" to the wealthy, and peasants were forced to play by their "betters' " new rules. And just as most appointments today are set for round numbers (few make reservations at restaurants for 7:38 P.M.), many times were set to coincide with natural events ("Meet you when the sun sets!").

Eventually, many towns had clocks on the towers of their tallest buildings, giving more folks access to precise times. But this access was a double-edged sword, allowing the wealthy to rigidify, and in some cases increase, the already taxing workloads of peasants and craftsmen. Later, the proliferation of clocks and watches (which were invented in the early sixteenth century) helped fuel the efficiency and regimentation of the Industrial Revolution.

Submitted by Steven Zelin of Scottsdale, Arizona. Thanks also to Danny Cheek of Swainsboro, Georgia.

W h.y Are Blue Jeans Traditionally Sewn with Orange Thread?

Did cowboys want the threads in their 501 jeans to match the color of Bozo's hair? Was House of Fabrics running a sale on orange thread more than a century ago? Highly unlikely.

When you're talking about the history of jeans, you're talking about Levi Strauss, so we contacted the company's crack archivist, Lynn Downey. Lynn reports that company legend is that the orange thread was designed to match the copper rivets that have graced Levi's blue jeans from their inception. Unfortunately, even an archivist can't prove this theory, because all the earliest records of Levi Strauss were destroyed in the big San Francisco earthquake of 1906.

Other jeans companies copied the Levi's orange-thread formula for their blue jeans, but according to Levi Strauss publicist Jill Lynch, even Levi doesn't use orange thread in some of their jeans, such as on the more fashion-oriented Silvertab line.

Submitted by Renee Sebestyen of Durango, Colorado.

Why Do Many Cable TV Companies Rearrange the Location of Over-the-Air VHF Channels (2–13) on Their Cable Systems?

Despite the proliferation of cable television and remote controls, it is still a huge advantage for any station to be located on the old VHF band, channels 2 through 13. Viewers without cable must fiddle with a UHF antenna to ensure good reception for channels higher than 13. And research indicates that even folks with remote controls still tend to surf more along the lower-numbered stations—this proclivity is one of the reasons why the Fox Network has been aggressively courting CBS affiliates. Originally, the Fox Network was cobbled together with many low-powered stations on the UHF band, even in big cities.

Technologically, there is no reason why a cable system couldn't rearrange the channel numbers of all the over-the-air stations, but why bother? It's terribly disconcerting for the average TV addict to find channel 8 on cable station 26. Are ruthless executives of cable networks bribing system operators to garner better positions? In some cases, the "golden slots" are given to cable networks that just happen to be owned by the parent companies of the cable system, but there is no evidence of widespread tampering.

In fact, usually a technical problem motivates the reallocation of channel positions of over-the-air VHF stations. The usual culprit, Wendell Bailey, vice president of science and technology for the National Cable Television Association, told *Imponderables,* is signal interference from the over-the-air transmission of the same channel. Occasionally, a significant number of subscribers' TV tuners are incapable of rejecting the *non*-cable signal.

How does this happen? Marvin Nelson, of the Society of Television Engineers, explains:

> *"Anytime a cable system operates within close proximity to a TV broadcast tower, there is a strong potential for the off-air signal to ingress the cable plant or the customers' equipment. In most cases, the cable company can and should prevent this ingress of signal. However, customer equipment is often not shielded to a high enough level to effectively prevent the ingress of signal. This results in ghosting in the subscribers' pictures for the local channels.*

> *"The ghosting phenomenon can be understood when you consider the fact that the shortest distance between two points is a straight line and that is the path taken by the off-air signal. The cable signal, on the other hand, must be received at some central point and then distributed along streets and alleyways to the TV set.*

> *"Therefore, while the cable signal will generally be stronger than the off-air signal, it will arrive later in time. Thus, the image on the subscriber's set will show a leading ghost in the picture. That's why many operators have opted to relocate the off-air channel to another spot on the cable system."*

Submitted by Jim Burgan of Columbus, Indiana.

Why Is There an Expiration Date on Many Bottled Waters?

Pepsico recently attracted much media attention when it announced that it was going to start putting expiration dates on its soft drinks. Consumers, who have been scared repeatedly by warnings from health officials about the dangers of virtually everything in the supermarket, suddenly had a new anxiety to confront: Is there something dangerous about "old" soft drinks?

There is no health hazard in an old Pepsi-Cola, let alone in bottled water. Pepsi chose to stamp expiration dates on its drinks to assure consumers that the product they purchase is wholesome (and, no doubt, to gain a competitive edge versus its main rival, Coca-Cola), and the same is true for the bottled-water industry. As C. E. Gostisha, corporate manager of packaging services at G. Heileman Brewing Company, put it, the expiration date is there to designate that the purchaser has bought a "fresh-tasting product."

In reality, the only serious degradation in water is likely to be the loss of carbonation in fizzy water. Sally Berlin, in quality control at Perrier, told *Imponderables* that most bottled water is given a two-year expiration date because some containers "break down" at that time. The water doesn't deteriorate so much as that the container itself, especially plastic bottles, will lend an off-taste.

A secondary advantage of expiration dates is to assure consumers that carbonated water will not be flat when opened. Plastic containers also allow carbonation to migrate through the container wall, reports Ruth A. Harmon, consumer affairs representative at Miller Brewing Company, and this problem is one of the key reasons why beer is sold in aluminum cans and glass bottles rather than plastic.

Some local regulations have led to expiration date stamping, too. Lisa Prats, vice president of the International Bottled Water Association, told *Imponderables* that New Jersey requires that all bottled waters, whether carbonated or still, must be stamped with an expiration date (two years after the bottling) in order to be sold in the state. Prats considers the regulation to be arbitrary and contends that if kept away from extreme temperatures, bottled water has an indefinite shelf life.

As we reported in *Why Do Clocks Run Clockwise?*, you'll find "Registered by the Pennsylvania Department of Agriculture" on virtually every prepackaged baked good sold in the U.S. because Pennsylvania doesn't allow any product sold in the state without such an inspection and this notice on the label. It's cheaper for national bakery and snack-food chains to include the notice on all its products than to make separate packages for Pennsylvania.

Although New Jersey doesn't demand credit on the label, the effect is the same. Any bottled-water company that intends to distribute its product in New Jersey will stamp all its bottles with an expiration date, as it is not feasible to separate out Jersey-bound bottles from the others.

Submitted by Mark Kramer of San Diego, California. Thanks also to James Marino of New York, New York.

David Feldman

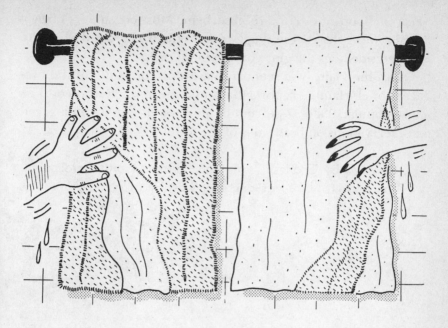

Why Do Many Towels Have One Smooth Side and One Textured Side?

Some towels are two-faced. The "smooth" side is sheared—the terry loops are extricated by a machine that has cutting blades similar to an old-fashioned push lawn mower. According to W. G. Hamlett, vice president of research and quality control at towel behemoth Fieldcrest Cannon, the smooth side is sheared purely for aesthetic reasons: many consumers like to put the smooth side out on the towel rack, displaying a velour or crushed-velvetlike look and feel.

Towels with special designs display them on the sheared side, so that the motifs will stand out more obviously in relief, according to Tim Jackson, manager of bath marketing at Fieldcrest Cannon. Putting the designs on the unsheared side (also known as the "terry" or "loop" side) would be akin to setting a design on a shag rug or the fur of a wolfhound.

But lurking on the other side is the workhorse. It might not have the glamour and pretty looks of the sheared side, but the unsheared "loop side" is more absorbent. Most consumers of two-faced towels relegate the shaggy side to the background while the sheared side hogs the glory on the towel rack.

Alas, the Plain Jane seems to have won the battle of the two-faced towel. Hamlett reports that while sheared towels used to be more popular, 93 to 97 percent of most towels now manufactured have terry loops on both sides of the towel.

Submitted by Charles L. Lyle of Charlotte, North Carolina. Thanks also to Terry M. Gannon of West Hills, California.

Is There Any Logic to the Arrangement of Numbers on a Dartboard?

The dartboard you see above, the "clock" board (occasionally known as the "London clock" or "English clock") is today the international standard for all darts tournaments. The board itself is eighteen inches in diameter, with a scoring diameter of $13^3/_8$ inches. The center of the board contains two small circles: the inside bull, called a "double bull" or "double bull's-eye" is worth 50 points; the outer bull, called simply a "bull's-eye," scores 25.

Each pie-shaped wedge is worth the number of points indicated on the board, but the outer circumference of the scoring pie contains a concentric ring, about three-eights of an inch wide, the double zone, that allows you to double the value of the wedge in which it is hit. The triples ring, located halfway between the center of the board and the outside circumference, allows you to triple the value (so hitting the triple ring on a 20 gives you more points than landing on the double bull's-eye).

Dartboard patterns and numbering schemes were not always so uniform. Undoubtedly, darts were originally used as weapons rather than as game equipment. Legend has it that the first darts were made for a Saxon king who was too short to use a bow and arrow. He solved the problem by sawing off the ends of arrows, leaving projectiles about a foot long.

The sport of darts dates back to England in the fifteenth century, when military men sawed off arrows and threw them against the ends, or butts, of wine casks. The game was called "the butts," and the shortened arrows were called "dartes." Henry VII was an aficionado of the sport, and Anne Boleyn gave her king a set of jewel-encrusted darts as a birthday gift.

As the sport grew in popularity, warriors looked for better targets than wine casks. They began using round slices from fallen trees, particularly elm trees. The concentric rings of the trees formed natural divisions for scoring purposes (they looked not unlike an archery target's rings), and the cracks that appeared when the wood dried out provided radial lines for more scoring areas.

Puritans brought darts and dartboards to the New World on the *Mayflower*, but the proliferation of new patterns on boards stayed in England, where various regions claimed their own patterns. By the early twentieth century, some boards featured as many as twenty-eight different wedges; some as few as ten.

Eventually, standardization of the boards became inevitable, if only because of the affinity between beer and darts. Darts became *the* popular game in English pubs during the late nineteenth century. The elm dartboards had to be soaked overnight to keep them from drying out and developing cracks. Often, the boards were soaked with the most available liquid, beer, so the boards tended to drip all over the floor, creating a smelly mess.

To the rescue came Ted Leggett, an analytic chemist, who just after World War I created a modeling clay that had no scent, unlike other clays of that time. He called his product (and company) Nodor (a compressed version of "no odor") and quit his job to market the clay. According to Leggett's daughter, Doris Bugler, one day the chemist threw some darts at a lump of his clay, and the darts held. Eureka! Ever since, Nodor has been the most esteemed brand name in dartboards.

The Nodor dartboard was first marketed in 1923; it sported today's "clock" pattern but also many other regional patterns. As darts increased in popularity, Leggett decided that a ruling body should be formed to regulate interdistrict competitions—Leggett became the first president of the National Darts Association in 1935. It was at this point that the "clock" pattern became standard.

Was there any particular reason for the ascendancy of the "clock" board? *Imponderables* contacted many experts to find out who invented the English clock board, but to a person, they repeated the words of Barry Sinnett, of Anglo-American Dartboards, Inc., who has worked in the darting business for thirty years:

> *"No one seems to know. It's known to be unknown. I have taken a couple of trips to England and have talked to several of the old-timers from the English dartboard companies. No one knew (and that includes people at Nodor) . . ."*

Even a casual glance at the numbers on the dartboard indicates that there is some method to the numbering scheme on a dartboard. Note that high and low numbers alternate around the board. So in games where players are solely trying to score the most points possible, why not always aim for the 20? There are two good reasons why one might not, as Mike Courtenay, a devoted darter and manager of Darts and Things, a Van Nuys, California, store, points out:

> *"Many people just try to throw at the 20 segment because it's the highest score on the board besides the bull's-eyes. But that's often a mistake. The numbers on either side of the 20 are only 1 and 5. A higher scoring area is near the bottom left, where 16, 7, and 19 are adjacent."*

The clock board constantly forces players to make strategic decisions. After all, it might occur to the neophyte always to aim for the double bull's-eye. The problem with this approach is that when you miss, as you usually will, you have no idea what wedge you will land in—you are just as likely to land in 1 as 20.

Submitted by Daniel Farber of Kingston, New York. Thanks also to Jon Hyatt of Boise, Idaho; Susan Hurff of Linden, New Jersey; Erica Luty of Redmond, Washington; and Jon Wearley of Augusta, Montana.

What Keeps the Water in Lakes and Ponds from Falling Below Ground?

Let's say you happen to spill a can of soda on your kitchen floor. The liquid remains on the floor's surface, doesn't it (unless you happen to have a dog handy to lap it up)? Spill it on the front lawn of your house, though, and the earth will absorb it.

The same principle applies when it rains. Gravity carries the raindrops down, and the precipitation "wants" to soak into the ground, and will, unless something prevents it. Assuming the rain goes below ground level, it will continue its progress downward until it hits something that stops it. Most commonly, the moisture encounters bedrock, which can consist of basalt, shale, slate, and many other substances that water simply cannot permeate. Eventually, if enough water collects on the bedrock, the soil starts to fill up like a sponge. When the soil becomes saturated with water, the upper surface is referred to as the "water table."

But the water table is not a static line; it is a dynamic and ever-shifting entity, as Seattle, Washington, physical oceanographer Karl Newyear explains:

"The water table is not found at a constant depth at any location. Plant and tree roots are always drawing water out of this reservoir, and the groundwater may 'flow' sideways. When it rains, more water is added and the water table rises.

"Sometimes the soil layer is very thin or lots of precipitation has fallen. Then the water table may actually be at or even above the ground surface: this is when puddles form. The water stands on top of the mud because all the ground beneath is saturated.

"The water table is not necessarily a horizontal surface. When the water table is tilted, you would expect the water to 'flow downhill.' This is indeed the case, but usually it happens quite slowly. To move in any direction, water needs some sort of pathway: earthworm holes or empty spaces between clumps of dirt. Different soil types have different porosities; soils with large particle sizes, like sand, have high porosity, while soils with small particle sizes, like clay, have low porosity. The higher the porosity, the easier it is for water to flow through it."

As Arved Sandstrom of the Physical Oceanography Group of Memorial University of Newfoundland puts it: "Ponds and lakes don't permeate because the space is already occupied by other water." In this sense, the presence of the lake or pond is a manifestation no stranger than the puddles found on a bathroom floor when the tub has overflown with water.

But as all the oceanographers we spoke to insisted, the accumulation of water in lakes and ponds is more complicated. In some cases, bodies of water are simply the exposed portions of the local water table. But a pond can appear well above the water table if rain is falling faster than it permeates the ground, a natural manifestation of "standing water" not unlike the bathwater that refuses to leave the basin because of a "slow drain."

Submitted by Tammy Kurilko of Dillmar, Pennsylvania.

In a Box of Assorted Safety Pins, Why Are the Small Pins Gold and All the Other Pins Silver?

We have spoken to the representatives of more than ten safety-pin manufacturers over the past few years and have come to one conclusion: Folks in the safety-pin industry don't spend much time worrying about the origins of their customs. Everyone to whom we posed this question mulled it over and kindly offered theories. But none of them had a ready answer and little consensus was formed.

We spoke to several folks at Pym-Dritz, a pin company in Spartanburg, South Carolina. They all noted the fact that those "gold" pins are made out of brass, while the "silver" pins are usually nickel dipped into a stainless-steel solution or steel dipped in a nickel solution. Nickel is far cheaper than brass; if brass were used in the larger pins, the price of safety pins would skyrocket.

But that kind of begs the point, doesn't it? Why can't the smaller pins be made out of nickel, too? John Badas, of B&S Wire in Beacon Falls, Connecticut, argues that the problem is that most consumers use the small brass pins on their garments. Steel pins tend to rust, and users don't want rusty pins on their clothes.

Of course, "silver" pins can be made rust-free, too, but at a price. Pam Handley, in customer service at Battle Creek, Michigan's, Keyes-Davis Company, notes that her company sells stainless-steel safety pins at far more cost than brass pins. Her theory is that brass pins are prized for garments (by sewers, in particular) because brass is more pliable and easier to bend; steel is stiffer and tends to break.

We asked the safety-pin companies who the customers were for their products. To our surprise, the U.S. military is a major buyer, as are hospitals (safety pins are sometimes used to hold down IVs, fasten gowns, etc.). Alas, the diaper market, in this era of Pampers and Huggies, is not a growth area. The biggest buyer of safety pins seems to be the dry-cleaning industry. Most dry cleaners are content to tag clothing with steel pins. Note that all these customers would use the pins for short enough stretches not to require non-rusting metals.

But many clothing manufacturers and retail stores buy pins to tag merchandise, and many of them favor brass pins to avoid the rust problem. Karen Kussell, of Jonathan A. Meyers Co., indicates that some clothing companies prefer the "aesthetics" of the gold color, too.

Individual customers of safety-pin assortments tend to be either home sewers or women who use the pins for remedial work on garments (shortening lingerie straps, replacing buckles, and, in particular, fastening shoulder pads seem to be among the most popular uses). In most of these cases, the users desire an inconspicuous pin, arguing for the tiny variety. But as for why the tiny pin should be gold, only Handley's "pliability theory" seems to make any sense.

A few representatives of the safety-pin manufacturers tried to argue that safety pins are cool replacements as tie tacks for men. From a casual survey, we respond: We don't think so. In fact, none of the ten men we asked could remember ever buying safety pins or, for that matter, the last time they used one.

Submitted by Marsha Nation of Harrah, Oklahoma.

Why Do Kids Get More Runny Noses Than Adults?

The most common causes of runny noses are nasal infections, allergies, and the common cold. Kids tend to suffer from these conditions more than adults. As Dubois, Wyoming, ear, nose, and throat specialist Keith M. Holmes wrote:

> *"Perhaps it is safe to say that children are more susceptible to nasal infections. This susceptibility gradually clears as the child ages."*

Stephen C. Marks, of the American Rhinologic Society, notes that research shows that

> *"the average child contracts up to six colds per year, while the average adult has only two colds per year.*
> *"The reason for this may be that children have a less well developed immune system than adults. Alternatively, it may be that*

each time a person gets a cold, he or she develops some degree of immunity toward a subsequent infection by the same virus. Therefore, as time goes on, the immunity to different viruses becomes greater and greater, leading to fewer episodes of infection. A third possibility is that due to the close interpersonal relationships of children compared with adults, viral infections tend to be passed from child to child more readily."

Dr. Ben Jenkins, an ENT specialist from St. Mary's, Georgia, notes that many serial runny nosers suffer from problems with adenoids, an affliction adults are spared.

But we cast our lot with Richard O'Brien, an osteopath from Berkeley, California, who observes that children don't have the same obsessions about hygiene and aesthetics that their elders do. Although he concedes all the foregoing, he reminds us that kids have less awareness of their runny noses than adults. Smaller kids haven't learned that they are supposed to blow their noses when they start running. And children, who are prone to assorted hijinks and hyperactivity, often don't feel the drip on their faces. Or they do feel the drip, and they just don't care.

Submitted by Jennifer Martz of Phoenixville, Pennsylvania.

Why Do Migrating Birds Bother to Fly Back North?

Bear with us while we anthropomorphize for a bit. We can totally understand why a bird living in the tundra of western Canada might find it considerably more pleasant to spend the winter in Mexico. Why shiver in your feathers, looking for nonexistent insects, when you can go down south and drink piña coladas at the beach?

But why bother going back? The "sunbird" New Yorker who comes back from Florida every winter, only to head south the following November, is "programmed" every bit as much as the birds, but the human need not suffer for his migration. There is considerably less labor involved for the humans—we have jets to do the flying for us.

Much to our surprise, coldness is a relatively minor factor in dictating migration to temperate zones. Birds are actually hardy creatures and adaptable to extreme temperatures. The northern grouse, for example, lives in the Arctic all year round and survives temperatures well below zero degrees Fahrenheit. Penguins, of course, face extreme cold in the Antarctic and hatch their young while standing on ice.

The authorities we spoke to indicated that there are several reasons why migration might benefit birds. As Kimball Garrett, director of the ornithology section of the Natural History Museum of Los Angeles County, put it:

> *"Migration is rooted in the exploitation of seasonally available resources, whether it be food, nest sites, or safety from predators."*

But all the experts agreed that by far the most important reason why birds "bother" flying back in the winter can be stated in one word: food.

There are at least four solid reasons why "the north" is superior as a food source during the spring:

1. **Abundance of Insects.** Many insects lay eggs in winter, while adults either die or hibernate. Many birds, such as swallows, swifts, and flycatchers, feed on flying insects that disappear completely from Arctic regions in North America during winter; other birds feed on hibernating insects, so they have no need to fly south in the first place.

In the spring, eggs are hatched and the insect population is laid before birds like an all-you-can-eat smorgasbord. As birds try to nourish their youngsters, an abundant food supply is crucial to the birds' health.

2. **Less Competition for Food.** While there is a smorgasbord up north, back down in the tropical climes, it's more like a buffet dinner with more guests than entrees, as Erica Dunn, a field ornithologist for the Canadian Wildlife Service, explains:

> *"In the north, there is a seasonal flush of insects that is much bigger than the supply that is available in the wintering area at any one time. This makes the north a great source for raising youngsters.*
>
> *"Moreover, on the wintering ground, you have resident birds that are native to the areas, as well as northern-nesting migrants, so there is a lot of competition for food. When you migrate north in spring, you find relatively few other birds keying into the same resources."*

In some wintering areas, there can also be a crucial competition for space for safe nesting sites, as well.

3. **Facilitates Breeding.** What do birds do when they fly back north? They don't just eat. They breed. As Rebecca Irwin, an ornithologist and assistant professor of biological sciences at the University of Tennessee at Martin, explains, even birds that don't normally eat insects use the critters to benefit their young:

> *"When birds migrate to the north in the spring, they are doing so to breed (they don't breed in the tropics during the winter). The*

David Feldman

more northern latitudes have longer days in the spring and sum-
mer, and an abundance of emerging insects. Most birds feed insects
to their young, even if the adults feed on seeds or fruit. Most babies
apparently need the high protein content of insects in order to grow
rapidly and to develop feathers, which are made of protein.

"So birds that migrate to the north are going to conditions
where there is lots of food to feed their young, and long days during
which they can be finding food to feed their young."

4. "Northern" Birds Have More Kids. Tropical-nesting birds tend
to have fewer youngsters with each nesting than northern-nesting
birds (who nest more often). In general, in tropical climes, food
supplies are stable but with relatively low volume. Erica Dunn
elaborates:

> *"Northern-nesting birds (songbirds, at least) tend to have large*
> *clutches, breed only once a year, and are relatively short-lived (that*
> *is, they 'put all their eggs in one basket')."*

Nothing like ornithology jokes.

Lest we give the wrong impression, we must point out that we have
grossly simplified the migratory habits of birds. Not all birds do
migrate (many New Yorkers and Venetians wish that pigeons *did*
migrate), and some flocks of the same species might migrate,
while other flocks do not. But even among migratory birds, the
differences can be astounding. The Arctic tern, for example, gives
new meaning to racking up frequent-flier mileage: It breeds close
to the North Pole and then winters in Antarctica! On the other
hand, some birds fly only as little as a few hundred miles.

And not all migration is in the same direction. Some birds
have east-west migration routes, and others breed in the south
and fly north in the winter. But because we're as xenophobic as
the next guy, and since it kills the humor of the question if we
don't, we've talked about it from a North American point of view.

Essentially, then, migratory patterns tend to be the birds' "rational" if instinctive response to shifting supply and demand for food: another example of the beautiful, yet cunning, balances of nature. Los Angeles birder Phil Feldman put it this way:

> *"Whenever resources are available, different species will develop strategies to exploit those resources. In the case of migratory birds, you can think of them as 'living' in the south. But then a resource develops in the north during spring/summer, in which a temporary abundant food supply becomes available (hatching insects) and nesting territories are prevalent. So it would be expected that certain species would develop a strategy—migration—to exploit these resources.*
>
> *"It's just like economic supply and demand. Although most cab drivers would exploit a rich source of revenue (airport traffic, for example), some will find niches getting fares in less well-traveled areas. If a niche is available, someone, or some animal, will develop a strategy to exploit it."*

And from Mother Nature's point of view, what's the use of developing resources if they aren't exploited? Sure, the North American tundra might seem dead in winter, with flora and fauna blanketed in snow, but in spring, nature miraculously comes back to life. What a pity it would be for these resources to be wasted? And what better use for a flying insect than to be put into the mouth of a young songbird?

Submitted by Nathan Trask of Herrin, Illinois.

Why Do Beer Steins Have Lids?

When we first started researching this Imponderable, we posed the mystery to the partisans of "rec.beer," the Internet newsgroup devoted to the love of lager. Soon we were offered all sorts of plausible theories. These are the four we liked the most. Which do you think makes the most sense?

1. *The lids keep the beer from overflowing.* As Tim Harper put it:

> *"A good hearty pour down the middle, as you know, often results in suds runneth over. A quick capping, however, would keep all the nectar in the stein, to settle back down without a drop being wasted."*

Ray Shea added that light, "hoppy" beers have a particular penchant for overflowing.

2. *It keeps insects out of the beer.* Bernie Adalem wrote:

> *"Without a lid, you'd be picking flies off the top of the rich, creamy, foamy head of your favorite beer. Drinking a full Mass on a hot day outdoors in the farm country will attract all manner of flying vermin that are drawn by the sweet malt aromas of a fine beer."*

3. *The lid helps keep the beer cool.*

4. *The lid keeps the beer fresher for a longer time, and helps retain its head.*

So, what do you think?

Believe it or not, the correct answer is number two. Although all the theories *might* have helped explain why lids were put on steins, the precipitating event was a law passed in Germany in the late nineteenth century that mandated lids on all steins. Fred Kossen, a collector who maintains a website devoted to steins (http://net-gate.com//~fkossen//steininf.html) wrote *Imponderables:*

> *"I asked the same question when I first got into stein collecting more than twenty years ago. I found out that it was because of lack of sanitary conditions of the time and the common belief that insects, predominately flies, caused disease. After Europe experienced the plague, many steps were taken to minimize the spread of diseases.*
>
> *"Germany had many drinking establishments, a good portion of them outdoors, especially during the Oktoberfest in Munich. Therefore, Germany passed a law prohibiting stein makers from producing them without lids."*

Another cyberspace beer expert, John Lock ("The Beer Info Source" at http://www.beerinfo/com//~jlock), notes that folks often enjoyed their beer outdoors in gardens, under the shade of a nearby tree. Unfortunately, Murphy's Law seemed to dictate that various flora and fauna floated straight into the suds. Lids proved to be effective in eliminating problems with plant, as well as insect, infestation.

The German law mandating lids caught stein makers unprepared. Most manufacturers were not equipped to make their own lids. Even the most renowned stein maker, Villeroy & Boch of Mettlach, Germany, realized that stoneware was their specialty and chose local pewterers to furnish their lids. Villeroy & Boch and most stein manufacturers offered consumers a choice of lids at many different price ranges. But even the humblest of lids did a fine job of keeping thirsty flies at bay.

Submitted by Marie Beekley of Casper, Wyoming. Thanks also to Myron Meyer of Sioux Falls, South Dakota.

David Feldman

Do Pole-Vaulters Do Anything Differently When Trying to Clear 18'0" Than When They Try to Clear 18'4"?

In the long jump, an athlete is given six tries to jump as far as possible. The one who jumps the farthest wins. Simple. But pole-vaulting (and the high jump) works differently. Although the winner is indeed the vaulter who clears the highest height, one contestant might vault far more often than another.

Each vaulter may attempt to clear a given height three times before he or she is eliminated; but each has the option to "pass" at any given height and attempt a higher height later. Of course, if you choose not to attempt to vault at a certain height and then cannot clear the next height you try, you will be placed below contestants who cleared the height you passed. In serious international competition, the bar is moved up 10 centimeters (approximately 4 inches) at a time, until 5.8 meters (approximately 19 feet and $3/4$ of an inch), at which point the bar is raised 5 centimeters at a time.

We've always wondered, given the fast sprint, the long poles, and the excruciating leverage that pole-vaulters must contend with, how vaulters would vary their technique between one try and another. Why don't vaulters capable of clearing 20 feet ever clear 17 feet by a yard? Are vaulters truly capable of fine-tuning their performances to a matter of 2 or 4 inches?

To answer this Imponderable, we assembled a group of experts on pole-vaulting, who agreed that there are three main physical adjustments that vaulters can make to try to jump higher:

1. *Change poles.*
The vaulters we spoke to bring between two and six poles to a meet. Although the dimensions of different competitors' poles might vary, the poles of any one contestant are usually uniform in weight, length, and diameter. The only significant difference among the poles is their varying flex strength.

Surprisingly, the poles that are stiffest (i.e., bend the least) are used for the higher heights, while the more flexible poles are used earlier in the competition at the lower heights. Most competitors take their first jump at approximately 18 inches below what they think they can clear. Less stiff poles (also known as "softer" poles) afford the vaulter more of a feeling of control. But once the vaulter gets within a foot or so of the target height, the stiff pole usually comes out.

We spoke to Scott Huffman, the American record holder in the pole vault (with a jump of 5.97 meters or 19'7"—only three men have ever jumped higher). We are writing this before the 1996 Atlanta Olympics, but with luck, Scott will be a medalist for the U.S. team. At 5'9", Huffman is the shortest top pole-vaulter in the world. He uses eight-pound, 16'5" poles rated to carry 185 to 200-pound athletes, even though Scott weighs only 165 pounds.

Huffman often only changes poles once during a meet: "For me, the idea is to get on my biggest [stiffest] pole as soon as possible." Another top American vaulter, Jim Drath, uses longer poles but has the same philosophy of switching poles as Huffman.

2. *Change the grip height.*

Perhaps just as crucial as the height and stiffness of the pole is where the hands of the vaulter are placed on the pole. All vaulters seem to change their grip heights as the bar ratchets up. The grip height is measured from the end of the pole that is planted in the box on the ground to the top hand where it grasps the opposite end of the pole. The greater the grip height, the higher a vaulter can leap.

Huffman moves his grip height from about 15'8" to 15'10" in the course of a meet. By the time he's attempting 19', he's always at the maximum grip height. The taller Drath varies between 15'9" and 16'3". Drath emphasizes that changing the grip height only works for him if he doesn't change the way he vaults. He makes no attempt to alter his technique when he moves his grip up later in the meet.

3. *Change the run up to the bar.*

The three obvious ways a vaulter can change his run at greater heights is to run faster, take a different number of steps in the approach, or take different-sized steps. We were surprised to find that none of the vaulters changed their run in any way. Drath told us:

> *"In competition, I always use the same 18-step stride regardless of the height I'm attempting. In the pole vault, you don't want to change too many variables because the event is so technical. I never try to run slower at lower heights. If I jump at 17 feet, I will still approach with acceleration and the best takeoff I can do. I would rather clear the bar by a foot or more with good technique . . ."*

Huffman's technique involves exactly 18 strides at 142 feet, but he finds that as he "gets into it" and "gets pumped," he adjusts the approach distance up to 143 feet, and his running speed increases a bit.

Several of the pole-vaulters we spoke to indicated that they've practiced their run so many times that they don't even think about it consciously. And some warned that when they've let up a little on the effort, injuries tend to occur and technique starts to break down. Only one top American vaulter that we know of, veteran Joe Dial, does vary his technique from jump to jump, and he has the tendency to just clear the bar, even at lower heights.

Indeed, we were surprised at the relative lack of physical adjustments that the vaulters make from jump to jump. As Huffman put it:

> *"Basically, my technique remains the same at 17, 18, or 19 feet. Same run, same rhythm. What varies are the pole size and my grip height somewhat. I always go all-out. I'm not holding back on any particular jump."*

For Drath, the desire is to reach what he calls the "technical zone," in which his mechanics are flawless, his mind is clear and unobsessed, and his mental state is calm:

"Some meets involve two to four hours of performance, rest, performance, rest, and so on. You have to learn to regroup and stay focused. Yes, I try to do as few vaults as possible. It really only takes one [to win the event]. In early attempts, I feel it's important to conserve energy by being relaxed, however, I never *vault with less effort. The pole vault is one sport that is completely ballistic— if you don't go 100 percent, you won't be vaulting."*

All the vaulters we spoke to said that the mental adjustments were far more arduous than the physical ones. Eric Jolpat, a former collegiate vaulter for Ohio State University, told us that vaulters know that early in the event, they can get away with mistakes without hitting the bar. But as the event proceeds, the vaulter worries whether a less-than-perfect effort will work on the next leap.

These mind games can affect even the best of vaulters, and Scott Huffman has not been without his demons. Huffman developed a reputation for missing more than his share of heights that he should have cleared easily (and this is significant—if the two last vaulters fail at the same height, the competitor with the fewer misses wins the event).

Scott has worked extensively with a David Cook, a sport psychologist at the University of Kansas. Huffman now uses a five-point checklist for visualizing each successful vault (e.g., "explode out of the start," "good high plant"). Scott credits Cook for helping him in at least three ways to keep his cool as the bar steadily rises:

1. Realize that all the other competitors are facing the same problems and pressures that he is, whether they be crosswinds, injuries, or fearing the "last chance" with two misses. Before, Scott used to let these factors bother him; now he welcomes them as challenges to be overcome.

2. Before big meets, Scott feared choking and that the nervous energy would get him down. Now he harnesses this energy and channels it toward increased performance.

3. Scott learned how to focus on the task at hand and not be

bothered by the extraneous stuff. In one meet, where Huffman missed two chances at 18'10", he passed the third jump and opened successfully at 19'.

We wondered whether fatigue played a role in the adjustments necessary to scale greater heights, but Scott said that physical fatigue is not a problem for him:

> *"I do extensive fitness training and except occasionally for meets at high altitudes, I almost never get fatigued to the point where that accounts for misses. In fact, the adrenaline kicks in and I usually get stronger as the meet goes on."*

If the lack of significant changes in technique at different heights suggests that pole-vaulting is a bit random, the athletes themselves would not disagree. When Huffman first cleared 19 feet in 1990, at a time when his personal record was several inches below 19 feet, he says:

> *"I think that jump was the best jump I ever made, even higher than when I set the American record of 19' 7" some four years later. I had no clue that such a tremendous jump was coming. Everything just clicked."*

Huffman thinks, then, that he exceeded his personal best by more than a foot. Yet he's not aware of why the jump was superior. Similarly, when he broke the American record in Knoxville, Tennessee, four years later, he had "no clue" that would be his big day.

Why Don't Women Pole-vault?

This is a rare, time-dated Imponderable. We hope this question intrigues you as this is written in February 1996. But if you happen to be reading this in the next millennium, we hope you are shaking your head in disbelief and wondering what we're talking about. For although currently the women's pole vault (WPV) has not been recognized as a championship event by the biggest high school and college federations, or the USATF (USA Track and Field association), barriers are falling faster than you can say "Bubka."

According to Phil Johnson, USATF's National WPV Coordinator,

> *"Women have been pole-vaulting for some time. I have a picture from 1905 that shows a lady vaulter at a New England women's college. However, in those days, it certainly wasn't considered 'ladylike' . . . In our modern era, the Masters [senior]*

David Feldman

women pole-vaulted first. They have been vaulting in competition for about ten years."

The International Amateur Athletic Federation has just recently sanctioned the WPV for the world championships, and it's likely the event will be part of the 2000 summer Olympics. The development of WPV is moving so fast that world records are falling on almost a weekly basis. At present, the finest female vaulter in the world is Australian Emma George, whose world record is 14′5″. By the time you read this, the record will surely be eclipsed.

The greatest battleground has been at the high-school level, and *Imponderables* was lucky enough to speak to Shannon Walker, the first female to mount a challenge to pole-vault competitively with boys (there was no girls' pole-vault event) in the Northeast. With the support of coaches and teammates, she quickly excelled at pole-vaulting, but the Massachusetts Interscholastic Athletic Association (MIAA) would not allow Shannon, the best pole-vaulter on her team, to compete at a regional class meet. The boys' team was threatened with disqualification if Shannon vaulted. Shannon says:

> *"This was obviously gender discrimination, because there is no girls' pole-vault event, and had I been a boy, I would have been allowed to compete because I reached the qualifying height. My family retained a lawyer who went to the MIAA and said that if they didn't give me permission to compete by a certain date, we would go to court . . . The MIAA did grant me a waiver to compete but they included in that waiver a stipulation that named two coaches who would be responsible for ensuring that I didn't 'disrupt the men' in any way."*

Ironically, most of the boys that Shannon competed with did not give her a hard time—the officials were the main culprits.

What justifications were given for preventing girls or women from pole-vaulting? Our panel of experts, none of whom could conjure up one legitimate reason for excluding women, shared some of the most cited excuses for banning WPV:

1. *Females don't possess sufficient upper-body strength.* It's true that most females can't bulk up their upper body as much as men, but females also tend to weigh less. Many female pole-vaulters have other athletic experience that makes them strong. For example, Lisa Kirchner, a seventeen-year-old high-school vaulter in Virginia, who has struggled with school officials to obtain permission to vault competitively, took gymnastics for nine years, so she has unusually great leg and arm strength.

Jan Johnson, the bronze medalist in the pole vault at the 1972 Olympic games and coach at his "Sky Jumpers" club in northern California, notes that many of the younger girls are more qualified to vault than boys of the same age, as they tend to be more mature physically. Indeed, girls in the fourteen to sixteen range generally vault higher than boys. Although upper-body strength is crucial to success in pole-vaulting, it isn't everything, as Johnson observes:

> *"The physical traits for a good pole-vaulter are running speed, jumping ability, and being strong for your body weight. Athleticism is key. Women can have these things just as well as men. If you aren't blessed with these traits, you can still pole-vault, you just won't go as high."*

2. *Safety.* Sanctioning bodies often cite "safety" as their main concern in approving WPV, yet no one we spoke to knew of the slightest reason why pole-vaulting is more dangerous for women than men. Dan Koch, a downeast Maine high-school coach who teaches several girl pole-vaulters, echoed the sentiments of others we spoke to:

> *"To me, the safety issue is bogus. I've lost more athletes to hurdling than to pole vaulting."*

Insurance is not a factor, either, as most athletic programs are covered by a universal policy that wouldn't require special provisions or costs. We suspect that most stated "safety" concerns are really obfuscations about the fear of the next reason,

Ᏸavid Ᏺeldman

3. *The Insides Arguments.* Lisa Kirchner was not initially allowed to vault because her high-school coaches told her

> *"that it messes up a girl's insides. A coach from a college team told me that girls vaulting made a woman's reproductive organs get out of joint from the way the body is positioned when the muscles are used in that way."*

Perhaps the most pointed response to the "insides argument" was made by our old pal, vaulter Rick Baggett:

> *"Girls can not get hurt worse than boys! We had a very important old man say that girls couldn't vault because it damaged their ovaries. What a crock! What about the boy who gets hit in the groin?"*

4. *There isn't enough interest.* Female pole-vaulters find themselves in a bureaucratic Catch-22 situation. Many federations won't add any event to competitions unless there are enough athletes to compete. But if girls aren't allowed to pole-vault in high schools and colleges, how will the athletes be developed?

Jeff Robbins, Shannon Walker's former mentor and a vaulting coach for nearly thirty years, has been trapped in these Catch-22 situations before and notes that many school districts take a reactionary, wait-and-see position:

> *"I've heard it all: 'If the NCAA doesn't have pole vault for women, why should we?' 'Call me next year.' Many institutions wait and see what their peer organizations will do."*

5. *There aren't enough coaches.* Here's another Catch-22 situation. There aren't enough good coaches to go around, but how can coaches be developed if programs aren't allowed to add pole-vaulting?

As we learned in the last chapter, pole-vaulting is perhaps the most technically daunting event in track and field. Says Jeff Robbins:

> "*Some schools and federations vote against WPV (and some-times male pole-vaulting) because they just don't have the coaches for it. For some, the coaches are already overworked, having to coach thirteen or more events already.*"

6. "*WPV will hurt our program.*" Jeff Robbins presented us with two scenarios he has personally seen unfold. In one, coaches vote against WPV because they fear that the pole vault will weaken their team's scoring chances, mainly because the best female vaulters tend to be stars in other events. The grueling pole vault, they fear, will weaken the athlete's overall performance.

Frequently, the decision is even more crass. Robbins mentioned a college federation consisting of eight schools: four with decent female pole-vaulters, four with none. When a vote to allow WPV came up, guess what the vote was? In another case, one school had two good female vaulters. The vote of the athletic directors was, as you no doubt have surmised, one for, eight against.

Many of our sources had no doubts what was behind the prohibitions against WPV, and they were quite willing to call it an ism that starts with "sex." Dan Koch's sentiments were typical, if a little more colorful than most:

> "*I've heard all the 'reasons' why women shouldn't vault (it's too dangerous, women lack upper-body strength, etc.). It's hog-wash. The coaches don't feel this way—they're all for it. The opposition tends to come from the principals and the athletic directors. They're typical old males [watch it Dan, we're approaching old maledom ourselves!] who, unfortunately, control women's access to sports. It's the same reason that women weren't allowed to do the marathon in the past, and the triple jump, hammer throw, and de-cathlon now.*"

If there is more than a little anger from most of our sources about the past of WPV, there is unanimous optimism about its future. Not only is the WPV likely to be an official event in the 2000

Olympics, but the women's decathlon is likely to displace the current heptathlon. The pole vault is part of the decathlon, but not the heptathlon. Every major female track program will need coaches to instruct in WPV for the decathlon alone.

What surprised us the most is how enthusiastic the male pole-vaulters and coaches were about the progress of WPV. American record holder, Scott Huffman, told us he was very supportive and quite excited by the development of WPV, and his sentiments were echoed by Jeff Robbins, who recently took five women whom he coaches to a pole-vaulting "summit" in Reno, Nevada, that attracted about seventy-five female and two hundred male vaulters from all over the world. Men and women were vaulting at the same time, in different pits. The audience, reports Robbins, seemed to cheer more for the women than the men.

Meanwhile, girls like Lisa Kirchner and young women like Shannon Walker are blazing trails for their female successors. Lisa is still the only female pole-vaulter in her county, and she has only recently been given the okay to start competing for her school. Shannon was denied the right to compete in an intercollegiate meet, even though several of the boys failed at heights more than a foot below what Shannon can vault.

It's easy to scoff at "nuisance" civil-rights lawsuits, but until some athletic officials work on the "insides" of their *brains*, women can't pole-vault.

Submitted by Sue Costa of Independence, Kansas.

Why Don't We Ever See Left-handed String Players in Orchestras?

We posed this Imponderable to reader-cellist Craig Kirkland, who responded:

> *"I know two lefty violinists and both were taught as youngsters to play the same way righties do, so it's never been an issue for them. 'Backwards' instruments may exist, like those lefty electric bassist Paul McCartney uses, but I've never seen a string equivalent."*

Precisely, Craig. Although there were isolated lefty sightings (Jeannine Abel, secretary of the American Musical Instrument Society, spotted a left-handed violinist in the St. Luke's orchestra), they are few and far between, and for a perfectly logical reason. Imagine two violinists bowing furiously during the crescendo of a symphony: The bows would be moving in opposite directions. The applied pressure on the strings would be different, and the bows would look as if they were engaged in a duel rather than a musical enterprise. Furthermore, left-handed bowing would ruin the visual symmetry that is part of the concertgoing experience.

We spoke to William Monical, a violin restorer and dealer in New York City, who emphasized the difficulty in retrofitting high-quality violins for left-handers. Although the violin might be symmetrical on the outside, the inside is not. For example, there is a bass bar (a long, vertical piece of wood) glued to the inside top of the violin that runs along the G-string. A sound post lies behind the bridge near the D-string (in layman's terms, this is a dowel held in place by the pressure of the D-string). These pieces must be moved with great delicacy to accommodate left-handers. Likewise, the strings cannot simply be reversed for left-handers; the finger board would also have to be changed as well.

And how would a left-hander know if it was worth making the change? Monical suggests it would cost several thousand dollars to make the adjustments. Some of the valuable seventeenth- and eighteenth-century violins were made slightly asymmetrically to accommodate the sound post, adding even more difficulties (and costs) to the process.

Monical has a half dozen or so clients who are left-handed, and two of them have asked for left-handed modifications. But others fear harming the sound of their instrument and have decided to make the best of the fate that the right-handed world has bestowed upon them: accommodation to the dominant right-handed style of playing.

Submitted by Solomon Marmor of Portland, Oregon. Thanks also to Phyllis Diamond of Cherry Valley, California; and Sean Campbell-Brennan of Middleton, Idaho.

Why Do Lobsters Turn Bright Red When Boiled?

Wouldn't you get flushed if you were dumped into a vat of boiling water?

But seriously, folks, before the lobster gets boiled, it has a dark purplish-bluish color. But hidden in the exoskeleton of the lobsters (and shrimp) is a pigment called astaxanthin, in a class of compounds called carotenoids.

We spoke to Robert Rofen of the Aquatic Research Institute, and Ray Bauer of the biology department at the University of Louisiana at Lafayette, who explained that astaxanthin is connected to a protein. When you boil lobsters, though, the pigment separates from the protein and returns to its "true color," which is the bright red associated with drawn butter, white wine, and hefty credit-card bills.

Submitted by Douglas Watkins, Jr., of Hayward, California. Thanks also to Laura Cannano of Englewood, Colorado; Kathleen Beecher of Naples, Maine; Jay Vincent Corcino of Panorama City, California; Emily Durling of Glens Falls, New York; Melissa and Dan Morley of Yelm, Washington; and Louis Lin of Foster City, California.

David Feldman

Why Do Ceiling Fans Get Dusty?

You'd think, says reader Loren Larson, that the constantly turning blades would throw off any incidental dust that accumulates on a ceiling fan, particularly the blades of ceiling fans. But you'd be wrong. Ceiling fans seem to be dust magnets.

Your house or apartment, we say without insult, is full of dust. In the hair-raising first chapter of the marvelous *The Secret House*, David Bodanis notes that tens of thousands of human skin flakes fall off our body *every minute*.

"Luckily" for us, there are millions of microscopic mites in our abodes, insects that dine on the skin that we shed. Bodanis estimates that just within the average double-bed mattress, two million dust mites live on our discarded skin and hair. Each mite defecates perhaps twenty times a day; their fecal pellets are so small that they float in the air, circulating around the house. Despite the millions of insects who depend upon our shedding skin for their survival, human skin and hair is by far the largest component in the dust found on ceiling fans and throughout the house. Makes you want to run out and get an air filter, doesn't it?

Ceiling fans create a tremendous amount of air flow, and dust *is* thrown around the room. But much lands on the fan and its blades, and just seems to sit there. Charles Ausburn, of Casablanca Fan Company, pleads guilty, but with an explanation:

> *"The air always has a great deal of dust in it—larger particles that you can see, and also microscopic ones. Over time, a large volume of the circulating air hits and collects on the blades of the fan. People often ask why spider webs and dust can be seen on the fans. But they must understand that there is a lot of dust in the circulating air."*

But the accumulation of dust on a given object is not random. Most dust particles carry an electrical charge and therefore can be attracted to one another (a dust ball is simply an accumulation of charged dust particles that have a fatal attraction). Physicist Chris Ballas, of Vanderbilt University, explains:

> *"The charged dust particles are attracted and cling to any surface that develops a charge. This can be electrical equipment, which directly carries electric current, or a surface subjected to frictional forces, which result in a static electricity buildup. The latter is the case for ceiling fans. As the blades rotate, they experience frictional forces as they 'rub' against the air; this knocks electrons around, causing the blades to build up a net charge. The charged dust particles then stick to the charged areas of the blades.*
>
> *"The leading edge [the edge first cutting the air as the blade spins] of the blades usually develops the thickest layer of dust. That's because the leading edge encounters the most friction and develops the largest charge.*
>
> *"So the dust doesn't collect on the blades simply by 'falling' or landing on them. The electrical-attraction effect also plays a large part. This same effect explains why some vertical surfaces also get quite dusty (television and stereo equipment, for example). The*

David Feldman

dust doesn't just fall off these surfaces—it sticks due to the electrical attraction."

Submitted by Loren A. Larson of Orlando, Florida. Thanks also to Crystal Lloyd of Perryville, Kentucky.

Why Are You Supposed to Run Ceiling Fans Clockwise in the Winter and Counterclockwise in the Summer?

Ceiling fans can't change the mean temperature in the room, but they can make you *feel* more comfortable. Because cool and hot air don't mix well, the more buoyant warm air naturally rises in any indoor setting; in a room with a high ceiling, the temperature difference is considerable. In the winter, even if you have the heat on, it's frustrating to know that you are heating the ceiling rather than your BarcaLounger.

So the purpose of the ceiling fan, in the winter, is to make sure that some of the hot air that has risen to the ceiling is sent back down. In the summer, even though the cooler air in the room tends to gravitate toward the bottom, a ceiling fan can still make you feel cooler by recirculating the warmer air above. Why? The wind-chill effect, as Vanderbilt University physicist Chris Ballas explains:

> *"Direct air flow has a cooling effect on our bodies. If you stand in front of a fan that is blowing directly on you, it feels cooler even if the air being blown on you is a bit warmer than the air you are standing in."*

To obtain optimal heating or cooling, the most convenient solution is to mix up the warm and cool air.

As if fending off dust weren't enough to induce anxiety in ceiling fan owners, why should it matter which direction the fan blades move?

The answer lies in the construction of the fan, itself. Charles Ausburn, of Casablanca Fan Company, told *Imponderables* that the fan blades are tilted at fourteen degrees, the "optimum angle to create the maximum air flow." This tilt enables the fan to position where it is sending the air. In the summer, Casablanca suggests spinning the blades at the highest speed counterclockwise (as seen from below). In this direction, the air is blown directly downward toward the floor in a concentrated stream. The wind-chill effect cools the people in the room.

In the winter, you are instructed to spin the blades clockwise at a slower speed. The warmer air that is recirculated by the fan is nudged slowly upward, bounces off the ceiling, and gently heads downward to warm the room. Because the air comes from a wider area, you get a smaller-velocity flow than from the direct, faster flow in the summer mode, thus minimizing the wind-chill effect. Running ceiling fans in winter can cut heating bills anywhere from 10 to 30 percent, so it behooves ceiling fan owners to know in which direction their blades are moving.

Submitted by Gloria Rosenthal of Valley Stream, New York. Thanks also to Michael Overstreet of Chesapeake, Virginia.

Why Are Potato Chips Curved?

Potato chips themselves, let alone their shape, were a fortuitous accident. The most popular of all snack foods was invented in 1853 by George Crum, a Native American, who was a cook at Moon Lake Lodge, an exclusive resort in Saratoga Springs, New York. A guest complained that the fried potatoes that Crum had cooked were too thick (in many accounts, this guest is said to be Commodore Cornelius Vanderbilt, the railroad magnate), and in retaliation for what he considered to be a supercilious request, the chef sliced potatoes paper thin and fried them.

The practical joke "backfired." Vanderbilt, or whoever Crum's intended "victim" was, loved what soon became known as "Saratoga Chips," and the new dish became a staple at the resort. Other restaurants in the East borrowed the idea, but potato chips were not produced for home use until William Tappenden of Cleveland, Ohio, started the first potato-chip factory in a converted barn in Cleveland.

The shape of Crum's and Tappenden's chips was the result of slicing the potatoes in the most efficient way possible. Marsha Mc-Neil Sherman, technical director of the Snack Food Association, told *Imponderables* that from the very beginning of the product until today, all the technology involved in washing, peeling, slicing, frying, and packaging potato chips has revolved around avoiding waste by gearing equipment to take advantage of the natural, rounded shape of the potato:

> *"The more uniform in size and shape the potato is, the less trimming is required to achieve chips that are similar in size and shape, and that result in a greater yield of finished product. Round or oblong-shaped potatoes that are about 2.5 inches in diameter are ideal for chip production . . ."*

If the shape of the finished potato chip is dictated by nature, so is the curl at the edges of potato chips. Potatoes are composed of approximately 25 percent solids (mostly starches and sugars) and 75 percent water, but that ratio is not uniform throughout the spud, as Sherman explains:

> *"Generally, more of the solids' content is concentrated near the surface layers of the potato from the peel to the center of the potato. Frying is a drying process, which means that potatoes with a high water content require more time and energy to cook than potatoes with a high solids content. Potato chips are cooked to a moisture content of about 1.5 percent. The area of the slice with less moisture will fry faster than the area with more moisture. Therefore, the edges of the slice will fry faster than the middle and will curl."*

Although a consumer representative at Frito-Lay assured us that nothing can be done to keep the chip from shrinking unevenly, our folks at Pringles want to remind *Imponderables* readers that their reconstituted chips share none of these irregularities.

We will stay neutral about what shape is preferable, but we do have one reminder. Curls can have their advantages: they do a wonderful job of propping up heaping portions of onion dip.

Submitted by Kristofer McDaniel of Holyoke, Massachusetts.

Why Are Potato-Chip Bags So Hard to Open? And Why Are They Unsealable Afterward? Can't the Potato-Chip Companies Do Better?

We discussed a similar question in our first book, *Imponderables*. Milk cartons are similarly difficult to open and then impossible to make airtight after opening.

And we're dismayed to reveal that not much has changed in the packaging industry in the past ten years. Sure, our sources concur, there would be no problem developing a superior package, one much easier to open and, more importantly, reseal so that the chips would remain fresh after the first use. But this new kind of packaging would come at a cost, a cost consumers would not be willing to shoulder, according to their research.

The requirements for potato-chip packaging are many. The first worry for packagers is that potato chips are very fragile and consumers hate opening packages of crushed chips. The package must be tightly sealed, because any exposure to air tends to turn the oil rancid and the chips absorb any moisture in the air, turning the texture to mush. According to Dick Botch, vice president of business development at Atlanta, Georgia's, Print Pack Company, a potato-chip package must also keep out light and be able to withstand the changes in air pressure during long-distance shipments.

All these requirements lead to a package that is composed of three or four layers of different materials (to add rigidity to the package to eliminate crushed chips, as well as to shield the chips from light) and more complex structurally than it might appear— but not complex enough to make the package sealable.

The perfect technology for potato-chip bags would be a Ziploc-like contraption, which could be burst open easily and yet sealed airtight. We spoke to a representative at potato chip behemoth Frito-Lay, who told *Imponderables* bluntly that consumers prefer to pay less money than to pony up for a (re)sealable bag, and no one has come up with one that wouldn't cost the consumer a few extra cents.

Dick Botch emphasizes that snack-food customers tend to be very price conscious, and potato chips are often discounted in supermarkets, so the cost is critical. A better mousetrap is available, but no one seems to want to build it, although the folks at Procter & Gamble might argue that they already have found the solution—dehydrate U.S. Idaho potatoes; remoisten them; turn them into a paste; cut them so that each is an identical size; shape them in a machine; put them in a can that is easily resealed; and call them Pringles.

Submitted by Brian J. Sullivan of Chicago, Illinois.

How Were the Various Colored Belts in Judo, Karate, and the Other Martial Arts Assigned, and What Do They Signify?

Although the martial arts have existed for at least four thousand years, and in structured disciplines for several centuries, the belt system originated in judo, a modern style developed by Dr. Jigoro Kano in 1882, about the same time basketball was invented in the United States. Kano, a Japanese educator, had studied the older jujitsu and other martial arts for more than twenty years and wanted to create a competitive sport that emphasized athleticism rather than combat.

"Judo" stems from *ju,* which means "gentle" or "to give way," and *do,* the Japanese word for "way" or "principle." "Jujitsu," sometimes spelled "joujitsu," means "gentle practice," while "judo" is usually translated literally as "the gentle way."

What's so gentle about judo? Remember that the early martial arts were used for actual combat, and the participants had considerably more to worry about than the color of their belts: the loser of a kung fu fight often lost his life. The sport of judo, from its inception, emphasized self-defense and turning the attacker's force against the opponent. Kano also stressed the health and philosophical side of the martial arts, including morality, diet, social interaction, and of course, physical fitness. Kano promoted his beliefs in his Kodokan school, which opened in Japan in 1882.

Before Kodokan, the traditional Japanese martial arts student wore a *gi,* a loose-fitting robe, usually tied around the waist with a cloth belt. The gi was all-white, including the belt. Kano hit upon the idea of differentiating the experience and skill levels of his students by awarding different belt colors. This not only enabled students to find suitable sparring partners and to differentiate teachers from students but also introduced a tangible status symbol, a recognizable "trophy" of accomplishment.

Kano's original belt system was relatively simple. The beginner wore a white belt and advanced to green, brown, and finally black.

Within each of these rankings were various degrees of achievement. For example, there were ten *dans* (categories) within black belt, ranging from the first to the tenth degree, but all wore the same black belt.

Kano's belt scheme eventually spread to many of the other martial arts, and to the profusion of subschools of judo. No overseeing body or federation mandated any consistency in color schemes, so that variations from Kano's model were common. There is still no international organization that specifies universal color schemes or any exact measure of proficiency necessary to achieve any belt color.

In some schools, a promotion of belt color can be achieved only in competitions. In others, demonstrations of technique are emphasized. One teacher can award a promotion in some schools, while others employ committees to judge progress.

The lack of consistency in the awarding of belts has led to strange anomalies, even among serious judo practitioners. Some schools have lax standards, essentially allowing students to "buy" a black belt. The Olympic Games judo committee has tried to monitor different schools, in order to make competitions fair, but it isn't always possible, as *Bruce Tegner's Complete Book of Judo* illustrates:

> *"The Olympic Games judo committee recognizes a number of judo associations whose members are permitted to wear their rank belts in contest; other players must wear the white belt of the novice, regardless of their level of skill. The recognition of an organization means only that there is a formal relationship, but it does not mean the judo clubs or groups without 'official' recognition are incapable of producing tournament judo players."*

Several martial-arts students we contacted indicated that their particular school employed eccentric coloring schemes. One mentioned that the founder of his school did not like black, so that dan belts in Tang Soo Do are midnight blue, instead; another, a practitioner of Northern Shaolin (a Chinese style), indicated that all students wear a black sash, except for the grandmaster, who wears a saffron (yellow) sash. In some schools, only the tip of the belt is colored.

Swiss Master Zurg Ziegler (the "Lightning Fist"), a lofty eighth-dan black belt, who specializes in kung fu (Chinese) and Hapkido (Korean) and owns several martial-arts academies throughout the world, told *Imponderables* that before the advent of judo, belt coloring schemes were unnecessary:

> *"In the olden days, there was no grading at all: there were only students and teachers/masters. Your title was [given] according to your 'age and generation' in martial arts and your name was upheld with your skill. There was no belt level or color differentiation. It just wasn't necessary because most styles were only taught to a very few—often within a single family."*

If we have established that there is no consistency or uniformity in the awarding of belt colors, most judo and karate schools have a scheme not dissimilar to that used by Raymond L. Walters, president of the USA-Korean Karate Association and proprietor of the Jade Dragon Martial Arts Academy in Great Falls, Montana. Here is the summary of belts used in Walters's school:

> White—No knowledge
> Yellow—Learning the basics
> Orange—Building on the basics
> Green—Developing your skills
> Purple—Testing your skills
> Blue—Reaching for knowledge
> Brown—Refining new knowledge
> Red—Understanding yourself
> Red over Black—Guided self-direction
> Black—Now a true student

How were these colors chosen to represent the various skill levels? Perhaps the most common explanation is that before judo was invented, martial-arts students were issued an all-white robe. According to Zurg Ziegler, in those days a student was expected to fold his uniform in a precise way after each class, forming a small, tight package tied with the belt. The perspiration of the student started discoloring the belt, but students were not allowed to wash their uniforms:

> *"After some time, your belt started to have a different color, yellow-greenish at first. Then you started working on throwing techniques and ground fighting so your belt/uniform became slowly green-brownish colored . . . After some months of intensive training, the color of your brownish belt slowly turned into some blackish shade—that's how these colors came along."*

Others, such as martial arts student Gary Donahue, emphasize the spiritual meaning behind the colors:

> *"White is the pure state of being. You have no knowledge of any martial abilities. When you have a black belt, your soul is stained with the knowledge of how to maim and kill. You must constantly practice and achieve higher understanding of your art, thus achieving a point at which you will never need to use your art, for you are at peace with the universe.*
>
> *"By the time this point is reached, you have so worn your old black belt, that it starts to fray and become discolored yet again, attaining the original white color. At this point, the circle is complete, and you again return to pure innocence."*

Several martial-arts practitioners employ metaphors about nature to explain the meanings of the belt colors. Raymond Walters writes about how his school of TaeKwonDo views the color scheme:

> *"A student in TaeKwonDo is considered to be a constantly growing individual, much like a tree grows from a seed that is planted in the ground . . ."*

For example, the white belt signifies the potential growth of a seed before it is put into the ground; the yellow belt indicates the seed has sprouted and can see the sun for the first time; a brown belt means that the tree's roots have spread in the soil to give it strength and stability; and a black belt signifies that the seed that was planted is now grown and has the potential to start new trees of its own.

But some of our sources claim that these spiritual and poetic explanations for the belt colors are nothing but hooey. The most vocal is John Soet, editor of *Inside Karate* magazine:

> *"The myth is 'the old belt starts white and gets dirtier with practice, and so the belts turned black after time and became a symbol of proficiency.' However, the reality is much more mundane. Mr. Kano, the developer of modern judo, was a teacher. He was looking for a way to distinguish (symbolize?) the level of achievement his various students had attained.*
>
> *"He hit upon the idea of using various belt colors to denote the various levels of achievement. He simply borrowed from what he was already familiar with. In the athletic programs of the Chinese schools at the time, students at various class levels wore uniforms of different colors to indicate what year they were in. In particular, swimming students wore the following colors (white—first year; green—second year; brown—third year; black—fourth year). Mr. Kano simply borrowed those colors to develop his original four-color belt system, ranging from white for a beginner, through green and brown, and finally black for a master.*
>
> *"Many disciplines have modified and embellished the colored-belt system. The U.S. added the myriad of colors you see now; this stems from Ed Parker of Hawaii [a karate teacher], who developed the first American styles in the late 1950s and 1960s."*

Our favorite response to this Imponderable came from Jim Coleman, the executive editor of *Black Belt* magazine, who advanced the "belt gets black from years of use" theory. When we asked him if he thought this story was true, he replied: "Well, it's as good as anything."

Submitted by Adam Frank of Canoga Park, California.

Why Do Glasses Sweat When Filled with Cold Beverages?

On a warm summer's day, a tall glass of iced tea is likely to sweat more than Rodney Dangerfield during a particularly badly received comedy routine. What's the deal?

Elementary physics, dear readers. The answer is "condensation." The "sweat" doesn't sneak from the liquid inside of the glass to the outside; rather, it immigrates from the ambient air.

The cool liquid (and ice) in the glass *cools the glass itself,* in particular the outside of the glass, and this slightly cools the air just outside of the glass. Cooler air cannot hold as much water vapor as warmer air, so the water vapor in the cooled air immediately surrounding the glass condenses into liquid form. The water molecules in the air surrounding the glass lose thermal energy to the cool surface and convert from a gas to a liquid.

Condensation is thus the opposite process of evaporation, in which water is absorbed into the air. We see the same principle at work in nature, as Chris Ballas, a doctoral candidate in physics at Vanderbilt University, explains:

> *"Dew forms for essentially the same reason, so in a way the 'sweat' on the glass is a miniature dew. You may notice that the 'sweat line' on the glass forms precisely at the cold beverage line."*

Dr. Tom LeCompte, research assistant professor of physics at the University of Illinois, told *Imponderables* that the colder the outside of the glass gets from the ice or drink inside, the more condensation occurs:

> *"The [amount of] cooling depends on the material of the glass. An aluminum can, a good conductor of heat and cold, filled with cold pop, will sweat more than a Styrofoam cup. [Styrofoam is a poor conductor of heat and cold, which is why it is slow to change temperature whether containing scalding-hot coffee or the coldest beer]. It is possible to get a Styrofoam cup to sweat but it takes effort—filling the cup with liquid nitrogen (at minus 196 degrees Centigrade) will do the trick."*

No thanks, Tom. We'll stick to coffee and Diet Coke.

The only other significant variable in determining the quantity of sweat is the relative humidity in the air. The more humid the ambient air is (i.e., the more water vapor there is in the air), the more the glasses will sweat. This explains why glasses, as well as humans, tend to sweat more in summer.

Submitted by Holly Smith of Grosse Pointe Woods, Michigan.

Why Does Water Drawn from the Tap Often Seem Cloudy at First? And Why Does Hot Water Tend to Have More "Clouds"?

Earth might be experiencing global warming, but this book certainly seems to have its share of Imponderables about water. And bubbles.

The cloudiness that you see in just-drawn-from-the-tap water is nothing more than air bubbles. Many of these bubbles are created as the water hits the metal aerator just as it is about to be released out of the faucet. Even more bubbles are created as you pour "new" water into a container that already holds water. The just-poured water creates turbulence in the container as the onrushing tap water "churns up" the existing water in the container; the inevitable sloshing and intermixing traps more air bubbles in the water.

The cloudiness disappears quickly because the bubbles, less dense than the water, rise to the surface and burst, while other bubbles dissolve lower down in the water before they reach the top. In the last Imponderable, we observed that warm air can hold more water vapor than cold air. But hot water cannot hold as much *air* vapor as cold water. Cold water dissolves trapped air bubbles faster than warm water does, so hot-water cloudiness not only might be more pronounced but also tends to linger longer.

Because cold water tends to dissolve more gases, cold water tends to taste better than hot water, which is why most recipes and coffeemaker instructions urge you to use cold water when preparing other foods. Why does gas taste so good? We'll save that for another book.

Submitted by Herbert Kraut of Forest Hills, New York. Thanks also to Katherine Burger of Tridelphia, West Virginia.

Why Are Home Radiators Invariably Placed Below Windows?

*A*re there any practical advantages to placing radiators under windows? There sure are, as C. Wayne Parker, P.E. (Professional Engineer), of Knoxville, Tennessee, explains:

> *"When the temperature in a room is comfortable, say 70–75 degrees Fahrenheit, a great deal of heat can be lost through the average window. In order to plan for this loss, a heat source can be placed on the floor at the window. By providing a heat source directly at the loss path, the effect of the cold window on the rest of the room would be minimized and the entire room would stay more comfortable for the occupants. Of course, there would be more heat loss overall since this would create a 'hot spot' near the cold window, but paying for the increased heat loss has to be weighed against the desire for comfort.*
>
> *"In houses without radiators, the designer typically places air*

supply registers near the outside walls, even in front of windows, primarily for comfort. Keep in mind that the heat of the radiator would also help to counter the effects of, not only heat loss through the cold window, but also the effects of any cold drafts caused by air being cooled on the cold window surface or of outside air infiltrating through cracks around the window. Also, by warming the window, radiation heat loss from warm-blooded occupants to the cold surface of the window would be minimized and provide additional comfort."

Engineer Matt Moran adds that not only do window radiators help kill uncomfortable drafts, but they also

"promote warm air flow across the glass (due to natural convection), which reduces condensation on the window . . . Excessive condensation on interior windows is both an eyesore and a potential source of water damage to the window frame."

Dave Nelsen, of the National Association of Oil Heating Service Managers, told *Imponderables* that there are some historical reasons for the placement of radiators that have little to do with technical engineering considerations. The "oldest reason," according to Nelsen, is that when central heating was introduced, around the 1840s, Americans considered it to be unhealthy to sleep with windows closed, so heating systems were designed under the assumption that windows would be cracked, even in winter. A heating source would thus be required under windows in all bedrooms (presumably, it wasn't considered healthy to roll around in bed all night with one's teeth chattering in the 1840s, either).

And under a window would be the last place to put a piece of furniture. Why place a comfy chair right next to the coldest spot in a room? Why block the view and the sunlight by placing a breakfront over a window? Usually, furniture is arranged to facilitate looking out of windows. So for the most part, the space under a windowsill was "dead space" anyway. In other parts of the room, a radiator would be "competing" with furniture for floor space.

All of the HVAC (heating, ventilation, and air-conditioning) experts we contacted agreed that the conventional placement of radiators provides a less drafty and more comfortable ambiance, even if it doesn't make the average temperature of the room warmer than placing a radiator away from the window. And they concurred with C. Wayne Parker that installing more energy-efficient windows, and making sure that they fit tightly, would be an even more important approach to solving the problem of heat loss near windows:

> *"These windows, in and of themselves, help provide for a more comfortable environment. The savings in not having to pay for the extra heat loss would help pay for the better windows anyway."*

Submitted by John Bickford of West Peabody, Massachusetts.

Why Is X Used as the Symbol of the Unknown in Algebra?

We can give most of the credit for the X-factor to René "I think, therefore I am" Descartes, the famed philosopher-mathematician-scientist who was literally and figuratively a Renaissance man.

No symbols were used in algebraic equations until the sixteenth century. For example, the general solutions to the cubic equation by Cardan and Tartaglia in the sixteenth century were all done without any symbols, just words.

David Joyce, math historian and associate professor of mathematics and computer science at Clark University, reports that

> "in the sixteenth century, symbols for plus and minus appeared. In Italy, the letters p and m were used, but in Germany + and −. Eventually, the German symbols became universal. Also, letters began to be used for quantities, both known and unknown.
>
> "François Vieta [a French mathematician who predates Descartes by a half century] was the greatest popularizer of letters for quantities, and the rest, consonants, for known quantities."

Descartes' greatest contribution to math was the development of analytic geometry, which allowed geometric shapes and concepts to be expressed with equations. Descartes also invented the system of using X (horizontal) and Y (vertical) axes when drawing the graphs on paper (presumably, Z was reserved for the third dimension).

But he used *X* differently in algebraic equations, as Joyce elucidates:

> *"In the seventeenth century, Descartes used a different rule to distinguish between known and unknown quantities. He used letters from the beginning of the alphabet for known quantities, and letters from the end of the alphabet for unknown ones. That's the general rule that caught on, but even today it is not a hard-and-fast rule."*

But if he chose a letter at the end of the alphabet, why did Descartes choose *X* instead of the last letter, *Z*? No one knows for sure. It could be because Descartes was used to working with *X* on his horizontal axis of graphs. Or it might be that the *Z* could be confused with the numeral 2. Lynn D. Yarbrough, head of the consulting firm Mathematical and Computational Sciences, offers an intriguing theory:

> *"He chose* X *because it's simple to draw on a blackboard or in the sand. It's the same reason that illiterate people use* X *to represent their name."*

Actually, in the Middle Ages, even the most educated aristocrats signed important papers with an *X*, for it was the sign of the apostle St. Andrew and implied a guarantee to live up to the promises in the document. The legibility and ease of writing were probably what led Descartes to decide that *X* should mark the spot.

Submitted by Alex Heppenheimer of Atlanta, Georgia.

In the illustration's speech bubble:

BY THE WAY, IN **THIS** BOWL WE DRESS FOR DINNER !!

Why Are Saltwater Fish More Colorful Than Freshwater Fish?

When we posed this Imponderable to Bruce Gebhardt, past president of the North American Native Fishes Association (NANFA), he was quick to say: "Whoa! Not so fast!":

> *"Some of the marine fish in a tropical-fish store are outstandingly colorful. They're more striking than freshwater fishes in the store from the same latitudes. I think part of the answer may be the particular environments some of those saltwater fishes come from rather than the colorful effects of sodium. If you compare fishes from other parts of the world, the balance might tip the other way.*
>
> *"If you go fishing the bays and ocean within 100 miles of New York, most of the fish you catch will be silver and bluish; if you go fishing in the creeks and streams within the same radius, especially in spring, you'll come up with a variety of colorful trout, green and yellow pickerel and perch with orange fins, and brilliant sunfish, not to mention the non–game fish like the common shiner that color up for a few months in spring and summer."*

NANFA's Robert E. Schmidt concurs with Gebhardt that many freshwater fish, such as the redbelly dace or *Notropis cardinalis*, both from North America, or the brilliantly colored South American tetras, display "incredible" colors:

> *"Our perception is that saltwater coral reef fish (note that it is not all saltwater fish that are considered colorful) are more brilliant—that is, the colors are more striking and the patterns tend to be bolder than freshwater fishes. Also, coral reef fish are colorful all the time, whereas our native fishes are colorful only during breeding season, and then usually just males."*

Both sources have alluded to the changeability of fish coloration. Many males adopt brilliant colors during mating season—presumably, flashy colors attract mates in the same way that a shiny red Corvette is intended to do for lucky owners. Some fish even vary colors from hour to hour, sometimes using the bright hues to attract breeding companions, at other times displaying duller colors to avoid predators.

When trying to figure out why tropical fish are more colorful than those from other climes, we have to contend with this very paradox: At times, colors seem to be used to blend in with other fish or the plant life; at other times, they are meant to attract other fish.

Other than luring mates, why would it be an advantage for fish to display bright colors? Glenda Kelley, of the International Game Fish Association, told *Imponderables* that the bright colors displayed by schools of foraging fish are a way of keeping individuals in contact with one another. Bright coloration can also function as a way of fish mapping territories or warning predators that they won't be easy or digestible prey. Some of the most brightly colored tropical fish are never eaten, which leads some researchers to believe that potential prey remember the colors of poisonous or spiny fish that aren't worth the effort to kill and eat.

But the coloration of just as many fish seems designed to allow them to blend in with their surroundings. The most obvious example of this principle is "countershading." Many of the fish that live near the top layers of the sea have dark coloring on their tops, with white or silver stomachs. The dark top helps shield them from potential predators from above, while the light coloration on the bottom helps them to blend in with the light from below. Bottom fish tend to have even more complicated countershading patterns, with their bottoms often matching the vegetation on the sea floor.

All these trends hold true for both saltwater and freshwater fish, as well as tropical and nontropical fish, so we can assume that the key to the answer to this Imponderable lies in the more complex nature of saltwater ecosystems compared to their freshwater equivalents. Tropical reefs, in particular, support even greater biodiversity, as Doug Olander, of *Sport Fishing* magazine, explains:

> "*More numerous types of fishes and more complex species inter-relationships seem to require more intricate schemes for interspecies identification (e.g., cleaner wrasse, with their bold blue-white striping to signal predators to open their mouths).*"

Kelley concurs with this thesis, noting that

> "*striking colors and patterns have evolved particularly in environments where there are many species living side by side (e.g., coral reefs)—perhaps recognizing and being recognized by one's own species is especially important there.*"

Coral reefs also tend to have ample supplies of warmth, hiding places, and food. The ecosystem is so benign that, again, biologists disagree about whether the main purpose of their vivid coloration is to blend in with the vivid hues of the plant life, or to draw attention to themselves. As Bruce Gebhardt puts it,

> "*They're colorful because they can get away with it. There's so much life, further, that bright advertising is almost a necessity to tell one's fellows and prospective mates from other species.*
>
> "*Moreover, many of these areas are very well sunlit, and sand*

and coral are white or multicolored; there's less of an advantage to being dark colored; though species that live in and on light substrates are liable to be sand colored.

"Tropical saltwaters are less turbid and that clarity may play some role in encouraging species' differentiation by colors. Many freshwater environments that produce tropical fish, by contrast, such as shady swamps and weedy banks, are sunless, and the substrates are muddy, which means they are dark. There's more of a survival incentive to have a dark coloration."

Several of our fish experts wanted to inform *Imponderables* readers that many of us have an unrealistic conception of the coloration of most tropical fish. We have a distorted viewpoint because most fish stores and aquariums we visit have no incentive to stock drab-looking fish.

Submitted by Karen Langley of Germantown, Tennessee. Thanks also to Nora Corrigan of Reston, Virginia; Anne Francis of Pittsburgh, Pennsylvania; and Andrew Cahill of parts unknown.

Why Didn't Chevrolet Produce a 1983 Corvette?

When we contacted the friendly folks at General Motors, several sources reported that the production of 1983 Corvettes was delayed until March 1983. Having fallen so far behind schedule, the company simply decided to call what was to be the 1983 model the 1984 Corvette.

We have been known to fall behind schedule ourselves. We can go to our editor and argue that *surely* the unlocking of the ultimate mysteries of the universe is worth the delay of a week or two. We remember even the sternest professors in college would usually give us an extension on a paper, or perhaps an "incomplete" grade if we couldn't finish our term project in time.

But in the 1980s, like clockwork, GM usually introduced new models the September before the model year. We can't imagine that the powers that be in Detroit casually noticed production delays and said, "Ah, what the heck! Let's skip a year!" So what explains the delay and the disappearance of the year 1983?

Many Corvette enthusiasts attribute the delay to the move of production facilities from St. Louis, Missouri, to Bowling Green, Kentucky. But 1981 was actually the transitional year. In 1980, all Corvettes were manufactured in St. Louis. By 1981, St. Louis produced 31,611 Corvettes while Bowling Green manufactured 8,955. We found no evidence that problems in transferring workers or technology from Missouri to Kentucky had anything to do with the nonexistent 1983 Corvette.

More likely, the complete redesign attempted for the 1984 Corvette was the culprit. The Corvette had maintained the same basic chassis since 1963 and the same body style since 1968, a remarkably long tenure for a cutting-edge sports car. But GM decided that a more significant change than the 1979–82 series was needed, and 1983 was supposed to be the year for it. According to Jen Gowan, of Chevrolet public relations, production snafus related to retooling and redieing for the new design were instrumental in creating the disappearing 1983 Corvette. Bugs are not uncommon during drastic redesigns, and Chevrolet rightfully feared foisting an inferior product on a demanding performance-car market.

But some Corvette devotees suggest a more conspiratorial explanation. Greg Ingram, the proud owner of a 1984 Corvette, notes that the Corvette was falling behind foreign sports cars in design and performance. And Corvette sales were showing it, too. While 40,606 1981 Corvettes were built, only 25,407 units were built in 1982, despite a six-months-longer-than-usual selling cycle.

Could the "production delays" have been bogus, a way of getting rid of unsold inventory? Probably not. Ingram points out that GM spent so much time on the redesign of the Corvette that it didn't have the new engine ready when production on the 1984 model first began. So the 1984 "'vettes" were all new, except for one big piece of equipment—the 1982 engine.

Another piece of evidence suggesting that the delays were unexpected is that Chevrolet did demonstrate the "1983 Corvette" to the trade press at Riverside Raceway in December 1982.

But accounts vary as to how many "1983" Corvettes were actually produced: the estimates range from ten to fifty. Presumably, these cars were not merely prototypes but were used for EPA testing.

And speaking of EPA testing, the most likely explanation for the timing of the introduction of the 1984 Corvette had to do with these government regulations. In his book *Illustrated Corvette Buyer's Guide*, Michael Antonick argues that when GM found out that the "1983" Corvette complied with all the *1984* federal regulations, the benefits of skipping the 1983 model year became obvious. Chevrolet avoided all the costs associated with changing models and was able to beat other manufacturers' launches by six months.

The strategy worked. More than twice as many 1984 Corvettes as 1982 models were sold.

Today, you can see a 1983 Corvette. There's one on display at the Corvette Museum, right next to the factory in Bowling Green, Kentucky.

David Feldman

Why Are Most Glow-in-the-Dark Items Green?

What makes, say, a glow-in-the-dark toy glow?

Phosphorescence.

What is phosphorescence?

It occurs when a substance continues emitting light for more than a second or two after the original light source is taken away. The outer electrons in the atoms of the substance get excited and jump to higher orbits. When the electrons eventually settle back to their original state, visible light is emitted; the stored energy can phosphoresce for a few minutes or much longer.

Does the toy have to appear green with the light on to glow green with the light off?

Absolutely not. Many rocks that look dull in bright sunlight emit dazzling color when the "lights go down."

So are we going to keep avoiding the central question, here?

No.

Then why are most glow-in-the-dark items green?

Because the active phosphorescing chemical in virtually every consumer glow-in-the-dark item is zinc sulfide.

Does zinc sulfide exist in nature?

Yes, but it's rare. Chemist John Vinson of Parma, Idaho, told *Imponderables* that he's seen zinc sulfide in the Ozarks.

So if it's rare in nature, how do manufacturers get ahold of it?

They manufacture it in a laboratory. Zinc sulfide is the phosphor, and it's usually "doped" (mixed) with other chemicals. It's actually quite cheap to make, which is one of its advantages. And it naturally glows the green color that you see.

What's so great about green?

We asked the very same question of Alan Schwartz, an industrial organic synthetic chemist who has quite the home page (http://www.com/adsint/freehand/uncleal/):

> "The human eye is maximally sensitive to green. Thus a phosphor emitting a given optical power in the green will be perceived as being brighter than a phosphor of any other color with the same emitting power."

Another way of looking at Dr. Schwartz's point: If you had various colored lights all emitting the same power, the yellow-green light would look like the brightest color to our eyes, which as we've discussed before, is why you find yellow (or amber) and green on our traffic lights.

Any other advantages to zinc sulfide?

One huge advantage for consumer products: Unlike some phosphors, it is nontoxic and not radioactive. And zinc sulfide is stimulated by ordinary visible light, such as that from a lightbulb. ZnS is also remarkably stable; A phosphorescent glow ball will work for a long time and doesn't deteriorate with age or easily decompose into other chemicals.

Can zinc sulfide be used to create colors other than green?

Another great quality of ZnS is how well it combines with other substances. For example, it mixes well with acrylics and is thus an ingredient in glow-in-the-dark paint. It's also used to make phosphorescent tape. And when mixed with other chemicals, the "dopants" can act as a catalyst to alter the energy levels that the excited electrons attain. So when the blended chemical phosphoresces, new colors are emitted.

So is green going to, pardon the expression, fade in popularity?

It could happen. But so far, it hasn't. We spoke to Jeff Pinsker, vice president of marketing and product development at Great Expectations, one of the leading marketers of glow-in-the-dark items such as the star and space stickers you can plaster the plaster on your walls with:

> "In the last few years, we've had a breakthrough in technology that lets us produce items that glow in various colors. The product

will look a certain color and also glow in that same color. Before, we could make products that had other colors in daylight, but they still glowed green.

"We sell a number of products, which are identical products, except for the glow color. For example, we sell packages that contain thirty glowing adhesive stars, which you can stick on a wall or ceiling. We market one such package in which the stars are a variety of colors—a blue, an orange, a reddish pink, the traditional green, and a yellow. We also market the same package, but with all the stars in the traditional yellow-green color. Both packages cost the same to the consumer. When the products are sold side by side in stores, the yellow-green package outsells the assorted colors, often by two or three to one. That's astounding to me. I would think most consumers would go for the variety."

Is this bright yellow-green color popular with nontoy items?

The use of ZnS is so widespread in its commercial applications that we take it for granted. Chances are that your sports watch or alarm clock is treated with zinc sulfide. Black-and-white televisions and computer monitors used ZnS as the active phosphor, and nostalgists fondly remember how they glowed green for a while after the TV was turned off.

All through now?

Yes.

Submitted by Tucker Cummings of Rumney, New Hampshire.

When the Sizes of the Holes Vary So Much, How Can the Marketers of Prepackaged Swiss Cheese Slices Know That Their Slices Are the Proper Weight?

Ever wonder what a disc jockey thinks about while records are spinning? In the case of "The Voice," WPEN-AM Philadelphia radio host Andy Hopkins, his mind focuses on holey Imponderables.

First, let's make sure you understand what bedevils Andy. Some cheese that you buy utilizes what the dairy industry calls "cut-weight" packaging. A price per pound is listed on the label, each package is weighed individually, and priced accordingly. For example, if Swiss cheese is unit priced at $5.00 per pound, and a given hunk is .80 pound, the price would be $4.00. Other packages alongside this one might contain slightly more or less cheese and cost commensurately more or less. Mass-produced sliced cheese utilizes what the industry calls "fixed-weight" packaging, and that's what we're discussing here.

Andy has in mind prepackaged, sliced Swiss cheese with preprinted labels specifying "8 oz." or "12 oz." A cursory inspection of these packages indicates that while the holes within any one package are usually uniform, presumably because the cheese was cut from the same block, the holes in different packages vary dramatically in both size and quantity. How can all the packages, usually with the same number of slices per package, hold exactly eight ounces?

To find out the answer, we contacted the two biggest producers of presliced natural Swiss cheese: Kraft and Beatrice Cheese. We regret to inform you that our old pal at Kraft, director of communications Patricia Shaeffer, who spoke to "two guys from the technology and manufacturing division," couldn't have been more charming or less specific about how Kraft deals with weight variation:

"Using technology and machinery, we can control the average weight."

We asked if the entire process was automated:

"Well, one can't really say anything is entirely automated."

Could she provide more details on the process they used?

"No, it's proprietary."

Any information about the cutting and wrapping production process?

"No, it's proprietary."

Etc, etc. Alas, Ms. Shaeffer knew more than she wanted to share and, with utter professionalism, resisted all our whimpering and annoying attempts to draw it out of her.

We called the Wisconsin Milk Marketing Board and spoke to its director of education, Regi Hise. Hise was not at all surprised that Kraft wasn't eager to share its operations strategies with us, but he was kind enough to confirm the information that follows. Hise informed us that contrary to what many consumers might think, prepackaged natural Swiss cheese is of the highest quality, partly because of the importance of the eyes:

"In the lower grades, the eyes often merge together. You can't really cut these into slices, because the eyes run together and the slices get 'mealy' and will tend to fall apart. The lowest grade, D, is generally made only on request. For Swiss, this grade usually means no holes, often called 'blind holes.'

"The eye development, in terms of the size of the holes and the number of holes, is what gives Swiss its flavor. In the highest grades, the eye development in any one region of the cheese is con-

sistent. So, when you make slices from high-quality Swiss, you don't tend to get much variation in slices cut near each other."

The savior of this Imponderable is Stan Ferguson, the plant manager for Beatrice Cheese, Inc., the second-largest distributor of natural Swiss slices. At Stan's plant in Mayville, Wisconsin, Beatrice produces cheese for several in-house brands, as well as many other brands, such as Dorman, County Line, Cheese Bar, Dorman-Roth, and Poly. Ferguson was extremely generous in detailing the exigencies of cheese production, and he confirms our theory that anyone who is both excited and knowledgeable about his or her job can provide a fascinating conversation. All the information and quotes below were provided by Ferguson.

Beatrice doesn't "make" any of the cheese it sells. Rather, big blocks of bulk cheese that are produced by other dairies are sent to the plant. These blocks can range from a typical weight of 40 pounds to as much as 180 pounds.

The first stage of the production process is cutting the cheese. Beatrice's equipment can vary the thickness of a slice to hundredths of an inch; most slices are cut approximately one-eighth of an inch thick and are either four inches by four inches or four inches (wide) by six inches (long) in dimension. So the big block is reduced to four-by-four or four-by-six size before it is sliced. These smaller blocks are called "loaves" (three-dimensional rectangles that are four-by-six-by-some-large-dimension).

These loaves are fed into a slicer. Depending upon the customer, the intent is usually to create slices that weigh one-half or three-quarters of an ounce. Then,

> *"after we do the slicing operation, the individual slices come down to a five-foot table—it's stainless steel and belt driven. There, the machine stacks the cheese slices nice and neat, real pretty. As the slices come out of the slicer, the machine stacks them right there at the slicer. They're stacked into prepackages, with each stack having the number of slices you want in each package. You can set the slicer to how many slices you want per stack."*

After a neat stack is formed, the cheese goes onto a belt that takes it to an "inline scale" that determines whether the stack is above or below the desired weight. The scale can take into account the weight of the thin "interleaf" paper that is placed between slices of some brands of Swiss cheese.

Each customer has his or her own parameters for how much overweight it will accept (Stan says the typical client will tolerate a package that is up to one-half ounce over the stated weight of the package; by law, of course, the contents can't be underweight). If a stack of cheese falls within these parameters, it continues down the production line to be wrapped. So far, this entire process has been automated.

But now we get to the crux of the problem. What happens if the inline scale determines that a stack of cheese is overweight? Or underweight? If so, the conveyor belt sends the offending stack to the side, to a "diverting table."

And what machine alleviates the problem? No machine, actually. The solution to the problem is, as Ferguson puts it: "Two gals."

> "We have two gals with manual scales, who weigh the whole unwrapped package. Then, they just manually add a slice or take a slice away to get the package into the desired weight range. Once the package has been adjusted, they simply put the stack back on the main conveyor belt. It's not really that difficult, fortunately. But each package is weighed out, and there are some manual operations involved in adding or taking away a slice."

What an amazing job: a cheese rectifier! Regi Hise confirms that in other plants he has visited, slices have to be added or subtracted manually, as well.

We asked Ferguson about what percentage of packages are "diverted":

> "It depends greatly on the cheese and how consistent it is. If the cheese is well aged, it's going to have more 'mechanical openings,'

so you're going to have a lot more variation in your weight. If it's a close-knit Swiss, with more consistent eye development, you hardly have any. It depends a lot on the bulkage you're cutting, not so much on your slices."

We asked if adjustments can be made if the one production run of cheese seems to be consistently overweight or underweight:

"Yes, you can adjust them a little bit. At some other facilities, they use a servo feedback unit, where the outgoing slices go across a scale, and the scale automatically feeds information back to the slicer to tell it to increase or lower the thickness. However, these automatic units don't tend to work well. They sound good in theory, but they don't work well in practice."

Occasionally, blocks of cheese will arrive with a high percentage of holes, threatening underweighting on the packages containing it. If so, the slicer can be adjusted manually to make the slice a little thicker. The attempt is not to vary the number of slices in a package if at all possible.

We asked Ferguson if the weight of cheese packages is monitored closely:

"Yes, everything is very much quality controlled. We have to keep weight charts for 'weights and measures.' We're inspected from time to time. Our scales have to get calibrated every three months. We have to keep the records on file for when the inspectors come by. We call it getting WDA'ed—the WDA stands for Wisconsin Dairy Association. They watch us real close."

And I hope, when they do spot checks, the WDA inspects the cheese rectifiers for heavy thumbs.

Submitted by Andy Hopkins of WPEN-AM, Philadelphia, Pennsylvania.

Why Does the Ice Found in Restaurants Often Have Holes in the Cubes? Why Do They Sometimes Have Dimples?

With few exceptions, restaurants can't charge for ice, yet many restaurants use hundreds or even thousands of pounds of the stuff per day. Cubes with holes cost less to manufacture because, as restaurant consultant Henry Verden points out, the majority of time and energy required to freeze an ice cube is spent freezing its center.

The commercial ice machines that create "holey" ice can make anywhere from 400 to 24,000 pounds in twenty-four hours. With the help of Verden and James S. Boardman, of the Packaged Ice Association, we'll provide a simplified explanation of how these machines work.

Inside a large metal cylinder with fittings along the top, bottom, and sides, lie many vertically inclined tubes that are open at the top and bottom. Water is pumped to the top of the cylinder and allowed to flow inside the tubes. At first, the water drops to the bottom, returning to an open tank only to be pumped up again.

But a refrigerant, usually freon or ammonia, is introduced so that the water forms as ice and sticks to the interior surfaces of the tube. The thickness of the ice can be adjusted by how long the water is allowed to run; on a timing cycle, the water pump and refrigerant are stopped, and the sides of the tube are heated sufficiently to cause the ice to drop out of the cubes. The portions of the tubes that were not filled become "the holes."

Occasionally, you will find finger-shaped cubes in restaurants. The machines that manufacture these cubes contain a grid of finger-shaped metal protrusions. These are lowered repeatedly into water-building layers of ice much as a hand-dipped candle is made. When sufficient ice has built up, heating elements in the protrusions warm, melting the ice closest to the metal, causing the ice to drop down and leaving the hole intact.

Dimpled ice cannot be manufactured as quickly or in as much quantity as ice with holes, so the dimples are there more for aesthetics than economy. Instead of water being sprayed into tubes, here it is placed on a plate that looks like an upside-down waffle iron. The liquid refrigerant is placed on the top while water is sprayed into the "pits," which are upside down. The water freezes to the sides and top of the small chambers. When heat is introduced into the chamber where the refrigerant was, the ice melts away, falls onto a screen, and is moved away from the water. The dimple is formed at the center and bottom because this is the place where the water is always flowing; thus, it will always be the last to freeze.

Submitted by Charles Myers of Ronkonkoma, New York. Thanks also to Karen Fraser of Merritt, British Columbia; and Michael Hamm of Brooklyn, New York.

Having a wonderful time! Wish it were WARM!

Fabulous Glacier Beach

If Hot Air Rises, Why Doesn't the Cool Air Drop to the Desert Rather Than Rise to the Mountains?

The sun is closer to the mountains than the desert below, right?

And even if the air starts out cooler in the mountains, warm air rises, right?

So why doesn't the cool air sink to the desert surface and the hot air ascend to the mountain peaks?

We live in the troposphere, the layer of the earth's atmosphere closest to the earth. The troposphere extends to approximately six miles above the earth's surface, comfortably encompassing human civilization, even the air surrounding the highest mountain peaks (the stratosphere is the level just above the troposphere). One characteristic of the troposphere, as opposed to most other zones, is that the temperature decreases with increased altitude. So why does the troposphere display this pattern?

1. *The earth's atmosphere is warmed not by the sun above, but the surface below.* The earth's air does a decent job of filtering out the dangerous rays radiating from the sun (e.g., ultraviolet, X rays), but it is far less efficient at absorbing the sun's heat. The heat from the sun radiates into the earth's surface, heating the ground. The warmed-up ground then sends heat into the air from below, through convection. This effect is even more noticeable in the desert, where there are less foliage and fewer other surface irregularities to interfere with the absorption of heat.

2. *As air near the surface of the earth heats, it expands and rises but loses heat by contacting the cooler, less dense air that it hits as it rises.*

3. *As the rising, warming air keeps expanding, the expansion generates a significant cooling effect when the rising air encounters cooler, less dense air.* Known as "adiabatic cooling," this causes the air to quickly lose density and integrate into the surrounding air. As densities and pressures equalize, the buoyancy force is nullified and the air stops rising.

In a sense, the cooler air is literally blocking the further rise of the warmer air coming toward it. Air higher up in the atmosphere literally rests upon the air closer to the ground (that's why the air lower in the atmosphere is at a higher pressure—it must support the higher air).

The cooler air in the mountains would "like" to drop down to displace the warming air that is rising. But the reverse of the process described above occurs: as the cool air tries to drop, the air is warmed by the lower air, and it encounters air at higher pressure, which causes the cooler air to contract and become more dense. This contraction causes the cool air to warm quickly and dramatically, keeping it from falling further. All of these forces conspire to make the troposphere remarkably stable, although try to convince someone who lives in the desert of Death Valley, California, of that.

Meteorologists have developed several rules of thumb to estimate the decrease in temperature as elevations rise. One textbook we consulted, Robert B. Gordon's *Physics of the Earth,* estimates that the rate of temperature decrease with altitude in the troposphere is approximately 3.5 degrees Fahrenheit per 1,000 feet. But Kenneth Kunkel, of the Midwestern Climate Center, wrote *Imponderables* that

> "*meteorologists long ago developed formulae for calculating the change in the temperature of air as it changes elevation—about 5 degrees Fahrenheit per 1,000 feet. For example, the average July high temperature at Flagstaff, Arizona, is 81 degrees Fahrenheit at an elevation of 7,000 feet. By contrast, the average temperature of Phoenix is 102 degrees F. at 1,100 feet.*
>
> "*Thus if we moved air at 81 degrees from Flagstaff to Phoenix, its elevation would decrease by nearly 6,000 feet and its temperature would increase nearly 30 degrees to 110 degrees F.!*"

Submitted by Robert Thimsen of Lake Havasu City, Arizona. Thanks also to Brian Hunter of Tulsa, Oklahoma; Laura Shaffer of Worthington, Ohio; Candace Martin of Fayetteville, North Carolina; and Donna Phillips of Catlin, Illinois.

When You Hear a Third Party While On a Telephone Conversation, Can the Third Party Hear You?

As New York City telecommunications consultant Harry Joseph put it, "If you say 'hello,' and they say 'hello' back, that means they can hear you."

But seriously, folks, the definitive answer to this Imponderable is: Yes. No. And maybe.

More than one explanation can account for what telecommunications types call "cross talk," and the nature of the problem dictates whether or not a third (or fourth) party can hear you when you hear them. Although there are other possible causes for experiencing cross talk, the three most common reasons include:

1. Physical Cross Talk. Defective wiring can initiate cross talk. Occasionally, two wires carrying two different calls can physically

David Feldman

contact each other, causing two separate conversations to merge. In this case, both parties can hear each other. Joseph told us that sometimes conductors carrying two separate conversations bend over the same sharp metal edge, which cuts through their insulation.

John Gilbert, a lead systems engineer at Motorola, adds that a wet or damaged cable can generate cross talk,

> *"when the magnetic fields created around the wires of one voice path interact with the magnetic fields of another, creating an unintentional connection. In this case, the voice usually goes both ways."*

2. **Electromagnetic Induction.** But the wiring need not be defective or out of place to create cross talk. Cable pairs carrying different calls are often physically adjacent to each other; when the electronic signal in one wire pair inducts itself to another pair, the result is a fainter copy of the signal from one call to the signal for another call. Induction is the primary cause of cross talk on the modern telephone, as Gary Becker, of AT&T, explains:

> *"Anytime you have a telephone conversation over analog equipment, you have a very small amount of electric current flowing through the wires . . . Anytime you have electric current flowing through wires, you have electromagnetic (radio) waves. Radio waves can travel through thin solid objects such as wire insulation, or, in the more familiar case of AM and FM radio, through the walls of houses.*
>
> *"In other words, the telephone wires are acting as mini-antennas. When one party can hear a third-party conversation, it means that one set of wires is acting as a broadcasting antenna and the other set is acting as a radio antenna. Depending on the arrangement of each set of wires, the ability to hear may or may not be mutual. Sometimes only one person in a conversation can hear the third-party conversation.*
>
> *"In general, this problem is minimized or eliminated by twist-*

ing the wires around each other in spirals. Wires with different rates of twist don't act as very good antennas toward each other, and the amount of cross talk between the two conversations is very small."

Matthew Landry, an Ann Arbor, Michigan, independent security consultant with "telco experience," points out that induction cross talk is usually the result of poor shielding on wires. If this is the cause, then chances are that the folks on the third-party conversation can hear *someone* else's conversation, but not necessarily yours.

3. Electronic Cross Talk. In the old days, when telephone companies used mechanical switching devices, it was not uncommon for a relay in a crossbar frame to stick and two paths would be connected, shorting the two lines together. The effect was to produce an instant party line, with all four callers hearing one another with equal volume.

With modern electronic equipment, this type of short is almost impossible. More likely, the electronic signals at the switching station are not aligned correctly. Today, bulk electronic lines carry many different signals, each one assigned to a particular "channel." When the fine tuning in the channel alignment is slightly off, you can sometimes hear the conversation on an adjacent channel. When this electronic misalignment is to blame, most often the third party can't hear your conversation.

We heard from Gil Stamper, a participant on one of the Internet's most impressive newsgroups, "comp.dcom.telecom." Stamper points out another way that fiber-optic and digital technology can go "out of synch" and solves the mystery of why third-party conversations often disappear quickly:

"Digital transmission makes use of time division multiplexing and packet switching, which allows many conversations to occupy the same physical path. The spaces between words, or the pauses in a conversation, are used to insert other calls. To make this work,

the two switches must be precisely timed together, so that when Switch A sends Packet A, Switch B receives it and not Packet B.

"The time slices are very small, so a mistiming of a few milliseconds will cause cross talk and the third party being connected to an ongoing conversation. Usually, with digital switches, the third party can't hear the ongoing conversation and can't join in. In a well-managed system, the switches retime themselves every few seconds, so the third party should disappear very quickly."

Matthew Landry adds that the genesis of cross talk on cordless phones is different from that on conventional phones: it is usually a matter of radio interference, not unlike when your car radio receives two commercial radio stations at the same (or adjacent) frequencies before you either cross the boundary between two market areas or fine-tune one of them into oblivion.

Can third parties hear your conversation when you are talking on a cordless phone? You bet your bippy, as Landry elucidates in scary detail:

"If it's critically important that something you say be secret, don't broadcast it on the radio. I'm amazed to learn that there are people who actually think that the radios in cordless phones are somehow different from the ones in Walkmen. The amount of security you get with an off-the-rack cordless phone is good enough to foil the merely voyeuristic, but if you believe someone could make money from your secrets, use hard-wired phones."

Submitted by Chris McCann and Don Cline, of New York, New York.

Why Is Oktoberfest Celebrated in September?

Oktoberfests spring up like hair balls in a barbershop. You find Oktoberfests sponsored by the biggest of cities and the smallest of minimalls. Somehow, they always strike us as little but an excuse to drink a lot of beer. But even if Oktoberfest is far from a sacred observance, can't it at least be held during the month for which it is named?

If we go back, though, and trace the roots of the first Oktoberfest, celebrated in Munich in 1810, we find that, wonder of wonders, the festivities did begin in October—October 17, to be exact. The first festival commemorated not the worship of beer but the marriage of Crown Prince Ludwig of Bavaria (later King Ludwig I) to Princess Therese von Sachsen-Hildburghausen. The prince, the personification of the cliché "a prince of a fellow," invited the citizens of Munich to attend, and an enormous party was held on the fields in front of the city gates. The event turned into a full-day party, capped by a horse race witnessed by forty thousand spectators.

The event was such a success that it was decided to repeat the horse race the next year, and the festival took on a life of its own. In 1811, an agricultural show was added, along with booths and exhibits that turned the festival into the equivalent of a Bavarian county fair. Slowly, amusements (originally a carousel and swings) were added. But the most popular diversion proved to be the beer stands.

On the twenty-fifth anniversary of the wedding, the festival was especially large and elaborate, and drew visitors from far and wide. But perhaps the key event in cementing the enduring popularity of the event occurred in 1896, when big beer tents replaced the more modest stands, and local breweries started sponsoring them. North Americans did not invent the idea of turning Oktoberfest into an excuse to consume massive quantities of beer—the Germans beat us to it!

Today, the Munich Oktoberfest is the largest folk festival in the world, with an estimated seven million visitors per year, who consume about five million liters of beer. More than three thousand separate Oktoberfests are held around the world, with Cincinnati, Ohio's, being the largest outside of Munich.

So what accounted for the movement of Oktoberfest? According to Don Heinrich Tolzmann, of the Society for German-American Studies, the answer lay in the inclement weather in October. Since the celebration was always held out in the Theresienwiese ("Theresa's fields," named in honor of the princess-bride), the organizers didn't want cold, damp weather to dampen the spirits of the revelers. In order to continue to honor the original purpose of Oktoberfest, the festival was moved back exactly one month, to the seventeenth of September, although as Tolzmann points out, in practice Oktoberfests outside of Munich can take place as early as late August and as late, as, well, October.

Submitted by Sherry Griffin of Dubuque, Iowa. Thanks also to Solomon Marmor of Portland, Oregon.

Why Don't Professional Golfers Wear Sunglasses When Playing?

*A*ctually, golfers *are,* more and more, starting to wear sunglasses, but reader Robert Allen is correct in observing that golfers, who are often out in the blazing sun for six to eight hours (including practice) a day, don't seem to have much protection from harmful ultraviolet rays.

We talked to Craig Steinberg, an ophthalmologist in Sherman Oaks, California, who was a former California State Champion golfer and, even now, boasts a two handicap. Steinberg told *Imponderables* that as recently as twenty years ago, no serious golfers were wearing sunglasses, for the dangers of prolonged exposure to UV were not understood:

> *"People would lie out in the sun all day. Sometimes they wore sunglasses, but this was just a response to their sun sensitivity. I tell my golfing patients to get sunglasses and to make sure they get something that covers their eyelids, both upper and lower—those are common locations for skin cancer."*

Now that research has proven that UV radiation is the main cause of cataracts and skin cancers around the eyes, golfers are progressively getting "scared straight" into making the move to sunglasses, and to applying sunblock before stepping onto the course.

Golfers have long worn hats or visors to block the sun, but these coverings have been used primarily to avoid eyestrain and squinting. Professional golfers objected to wearing sunglasses for several reasons:

1. Fashion. Scott Hansberger, national market manager for Ray-Ban Sunglasses, told *Imponderables:*

> *"In the past, sunglasses weren't considered an accepted fashion trend. For example, just recently hats have become the popular trend—before, it was visors.*
>
> *"Sunglasses were viewed in the past as being for movie stars— they hid your eyes. Golfers as a group are conservative, friendly, open, interacting type of people. The sunglasses were perceived as against this image. Consider the Bing Crosby 'Clam-Bake' Pro-Ams in years past. The celebrities were all wearing sunglasses— but the pros weren't."*

2. Fit. Says Hansberger:

> *"You don't want glasses slipping down your nose, moving while you're swinging, or to be seeing the glasses' frame while you're putting. When you wear glasses outside, and you sweat as you do when you're playing golf, your nose gets a little bit slippery, and the glasses start to move. Unconsciously, you start to push the glasses back up on your nose. People who wear prescription glasses certainly do this.*
>
> *"For any sport, you want equipment that you don't have to think about. In golf, you don't want to be fussing with your glasses. A lot of golfers who wear prescription glasses use contact lenses when they play golf, for this very reason."*

3. Color Distortion. Many decisions a golfer must make on the course are based on visual imagery. Conventional sunglasses were seen as blocking out light, and making it harder for golfers to, say, discriminate between the fairway and light rough, or to read the grain of the greens when putting.

4. Field of Vision. Many golfers felt that the frames of glasses blocked part of their visual access to the course.

5. Physical Annoyance. Traditional sunglasses were not designed for sports use. Steinberg recollects Professional Golf Association veteran Tom Kite, who has always worn prescription lenses,

> *"playing one tournament in the rain, and just going nuts having to stop under an umbrella constantly to wipe and clear his glasses."*

Sunglass manufacturers wanted to overcome the resistance of golfers to wearing shades, so recruiting professional golfers to wear them was a top priority. The first company to make sunglasses specifically for golfers was Bollé America, in 1993, and their products directly addressed some of the problems listed above. Their golf line, Eagle Vision, features wraparound lenses with thin bridges. As a result, golfers don't notice the frames when looking out at the course, and the frames don't slip while the golfer is moving. Bollé's lenses are manufactured to produce no color distortion. A Bollé customer-service representative, Mike Terry, told *Imponderables* that many pro golfers now use Eagle Vision sunglasses, although some take off the shades while putting.

Ray-Ban, the largest manufacturer of sunglasses, has only recently entered the golfing market (along with Bollé, their other major competitor is Oakley). Golf sunglasses feature lighter materials, such as nylon blends for the frames, that stay in place and aren't as cumbersome for the wearer as most conventional sunglasses. Ray-Ban's main selling point is its ACE

(Amethyst Color Enhancement) lens, which highlights certain golf colors. The lenses accentuate the contrast between some of the shades of green, for example, so that it is easier to detect the grain on a putting surface and therefore predict the trajectory of the ball.

Scott Hansberger estimates that somewhere between 15 to 30 percent of pro golfers each week are wearing sunglasses on the professional tours, whereas in 1993, only a few were. Two factors, besides the improvement in the equipment, have contributed to the newfound popularity of sunglasses. First, they are now considered to be "cool." Jim Frank, editor of *Golf* magazine, and other sources we contacted, indicate that whereas there was a perception ten or twenty years ago that sunglasses didn't project the proper image (golf has maintained its image as the last bastion of civility and good sportsmanship in big-money professional sports), they are now seen as fashionable, but not radical, statements.

Second, and perhaps more important, sunglass manufacturers are paying pro golfers to endorse their products. Bollé employs several sales reps that follow the tour. According to Terry,

"We have technical reps that sell products. They try to educate the golfers about the product. The idea is that if the pros start wearing them, the public will see it, and our sales will benefit."

Ray-Ban has been particularly aggressive about recruiting paid endorsers. Hansberger says:

"About seventy players are on endorsement. I'll drop some names: Paul Azinger, John Huston, Kenny Perry, Jane Geddes, Jay Sigal, and Bob Murphy on the senior tour. Big names. They agree to wear sunglasses during events, depending on the prevailing conditions, of course. We run ads in golfing magazines picturing the golfers we have under contract."

We spoke to Richard Gralitzer, an accountant and a player-manager who has several clients playing on the PGA, LPGA (female professional), seniors, and Nike (one rung below the PGA) tours:

> *"I have certain players that refuse to wear glasses. They say the glasses bother them. These players haven't worn them and they won't start now."*

An endorsement deal won't matter much (and for that matter, won't last long) if the golfer stops producing on the course. Few pros will sacrifice their comfort or their golf game if they feel that sunglasses aren't for them.

Submitted by Robert Allen of Santa Fe Springs, California.

Why Are the Potato Chips Always Placed Above the Candy and Gum in Vending Machines?

In this world, where Dennis Rodman's hair changes color on a daily basis, it's comforting to be able to depend on at least one thing: If you approach a snack food vending machine, the Doritos and pretzels are going to be placed above the Snickers and Doublemint gum. But why?

We spoke to Sheldon Silver, at the National Automatic Merchandising Association, who reminded us that the spirals that hold the salty snacks at the top of machines are wide and can thus hold products that are thicker, like chips and pretzels. The spirals on the bottom are narrower and more appropriate for less bulky items, like chocolate candy and gum. But he alluded to the fact that those spirals could be switched around. Silver suggested we speak to a vendor to find why no one ever does seem to vary from the traditional positions.

So we contacted Bob McDonald at Crane National Vendors in St. Louis, who confirmed that you could easily switch the spirals so that potato chips were on the bottom. But he didn't recommend it. Most importantly, the chips are the highest-profit product in the machine, so putting them at eye level helps generate even more sales. McDonald also claimed that bags of potato and corn chips tend to "flop forward" on the spirals, so placing them at eye level assures the vendor that the consumer will not miss them.

Before we researched this Imponderable, we assumed that the answer had to do with breakage. The snacks on top, once selected, perform a hair-raising death drop, accompanied by a dull thud. Wouldn't fragile chips be put in far more jeopardy than a tough chocolate bar? Jane Schultz, vice president of communications at the Snack Food Association, explains:

> *"Because heavier items fall straight down, vending machine snacks are designed so that cookies, candy, gum, and other heavy items fall the least distance to avoid breakage. Furthermore, the chips don't fall straight down but tend to hit the glass front of the machine, [breaking their fall], which further decreases speed."*

Although the fall could split a few potato chips, consumers do not expect to see a bagful of perfect rounds. The more brittle candy bar, though, could crack into little, unpleasing, shards.

Our other vending machine authorities weren't totally convinced by this explanation. Certainly, vending machines can be fitted so that breakage isn't such a problem. For example, Silver notes that Snapple has a vending machine that now releases a bottle from the top shelf without disaster, because there is such thick padding at the bottom that the glass container won't break.

Bob McDonald has obviously devoted great thought to this Imponderable, for he offered a final, and ingenious, explanation for the superiority of the "potato chip dominant" configuration:

> *"If you purchase chips and a candy bar at the same time, it is better that the candy drops first and the chips then fall on top of the*

candy. This is because the chips are less likely to break or damage the candy, whereas if the candy falls on the chips the bag could break."

Why do we think that the higher profit-margin on potato chips was more likely the original motivation for the placement of the snacks?

Submitted by Sheri Radford of Victoria, British Columbia.

Why Do Power Lines Hum?

In an attempt not to make your eyes glaze over, we won't begin this answer with a treatise on alternating current versus direct current.

Instead, we will attempt to make your eyes glaze over in the next few paragraphs (electrical engineers may skip to the sixth paragraph). Simply put, in direct current (DC), the electrons *continually flow through a circuit in one direction.* For example, if you use a dry-cell battery in a flashlight, the electrons flow from the negative end of the battery, through a wire to the bulb, and then through another wire to the positive end of the battery. At every point of the operation, the flow of electrons is in the same direction.

In alternating current (AC), the electrons flow in one direction and then switch directions. This alternation occurs several times a second. AC current is usually produced by a generator that converts mechanical energy (from a spinning coil) into electrical energy. By spinning a wire coil in a magnetic field, electric current is generated in the wire coil.

In order to understand what generates the hum, it's also necessary to understand that alternating current doesn't just change from maximum strength in one direction to maximum strength in the other direction. As the coil spins, the strength ebbs and flows. Once the current is going in one direction, it continues to spin in the same direction but loses some force. A quarter of the way through the cycle, the current stops flowing completely. But with the coil continuing to spin, the current starts flowing again, weakly, but this time in the opposite direction. It builds up until maximum force is reached at the halfway point in the revolution of the coil. The current wanes again until it reaches zero force at the three-quarter point, when it begins to flow again in the original direction.

In the United States, AC current has been standardized at a frequency of sixty cycles per second, often expressed as 60 Hz (Hertz), where 1 Hz equals one cycle per second. In other words, the generator coil spins at sixty revolutions per minute.

Now that we are *all* electrical engineers, we can better understand that the steady hum sound we are hearing is actually a physical vibration in the power wire, because some of the force driving the electrons is transferred to the wire itself. Depending upon the type of wire and how rigidly the wire is strung between poles, the wire vibrates, and the hum we hear is that sound, a hum with a frequency of 60 Hz. This hum turns out to be a low-pitched drone, close to the musical note A, three octaves below middle C.

The sound isn't unbearably loud. David Murray, power service engineer for the Nashville Electric Service, told *Imponderables* that this type of physical wire vibration produces "very faint" hums that "would be hard to hear with the human ear." The size of the power lines is a factor in the volume of the noise. Martin Gitten, of Con Edison in New York, tells us that the larger the power lines, the more likely they are to generate audible hums.

Allen Bradley, manager of Power-Use Engineering at Nashville Electric Service, notes an additional reason why the hum is so soft:

"Large AC power lines are not one big piece of wire surrounded by insulation. Rather, inside the insulation is a bundled

set of stranded conductors [wires]. That's because AC tends to flow around the perimeter of the wires, not so much in the interior of wires. So, to increase the surface area of the wires, we generally use several smaller wires bundled together rather than one large wire."

DC current has a more uniform flow throughout the wire, so one big wire is just as effective in transmitting power as the bundle of wires used in AC power. Because the AC cables are stranded together, one wire interferes with the others while each is "trying" to vibrate. They don't all vibrate at the same time, so as one cable tries to vibrate, the other wires near it are impeding the vibration. DC power lines, with a single bigger wire, generate louder hums than AC lines, if not the cacophony of heavy metal group AC/DC.

Speaking of cacophony, there is another sound that Bradley claims is far more common than the steady hum—a crackling sound that has scared us on occasion:

"The sound that I usually hear near power lines is not so much a hum, but rather a crackly noise. This is due to an undesirable phenomenon known as the 'corona effect.' It happens as air near the power lines becomes ionized in the vicinity of the power poles. The insulators on high-voltage lines (at the poles) sometimes break down a bit and a bit of current leaks onto the poles. The current is attracted to metal surfaces, especially the pointed protrusions on the poles. This ionizes the air around those points, producing a faint glow near the conductors. As the air particles become ionized, a crackly sound is created."

Any strong electrical current will produce a magnetic field in the vicinity of the current. With AC current, the magnetic field oscillates (contracts and expands) along with the current. Ionized atoms have either gained or lost electrons and are more common in stormy or humid weather. Indeed, Frank Young, senior vice president of Enertech Consultants in Campbell, California, notes that the crackling sound is most often heard after rainstorms that have caused a partial corona effect.

Lest you think that electrical engineering is dryly scientific, we must alert you to the wacky good times that must be had at engineers' conventions. For both Gitten and Murray had the exact same initial response when asked why power lines hum: "The reason they hum is because they don't know the words." [Rim shot]

Submitted by Kevin McCormick of Lisbon Falls, Maine. Thanks also to Louise Beveridge of Philipsburg, Pennsylvania.

Why Do Onions Make Us Cry?

Let's look at it from the point of view of the onion. An onion is perfectly polite to us until we start hacking at it with a knife. Alas, the act of cutting enlivens a gas, propanethiol S-oxide, which works in tandem with the enzymes in the onion to unleash a passive sulfur compound found within the onion. The result: As you cut, the gas moves upward and, combined with the water in your eyes, creates sulfuric acid.

Your eyes aren't happy, even if you are, and react in the way they know how when irritated by a foreign substance—they start tearing. Rubbing your eyes with your hands is about the worst way to alleviate the problem, since your hands are likely full of the tear-inducing agent, too.

We've heard all kinds of folk remedies for onion tears, ranging from rubbing the onion with lemon to wearing gloves as you cut to donning scuba masks while performing surgery. But we're of the old, masochistic school: no pain, no gain.

Submitted by Jonathan Greenberg of Cedarhurst, New York. Thanks also to Candice Ford of Stanton, California; Jason

Martin of Aiken, South Carolina; Megan Lavaty of Eden Prairie, Minnesota; Mindy Townsend of Aiken, South Carolina; Mike Wood of Sunset, Vermont; Greg Herr of Fremont, New Hampshire; Brian Dunne of Indianapolis, Indiana; Shira Ovidé of Dayton, Ohio; Andrew Bushard of Garretstown, South Dakota; and many others.

What's the Purpose of the Small Button Atop Baseball Caps?

According to Chris Kolanko, quality-control supervisor at Richmond, Virginia's, M&B Headwear Co., the esoteric, technical name for that thingie on the top of the cap is: a button. The button is made out of metal and is covered by the same fabric used on the rest of the cap.

All the cap makers we spoke to agreed that though the button supplies minimal reinforcement to the seams, the seams could easily survive without the button; indeed, some nonbaseball caps don't have buttons. Chris Kolanko, Rich Soergel, president of Pacific Sportswear and Emblem Co., and representatives of cap makers Town Talk (of Louisville, Kentucky), and M&B Headwear all agreed that the main purpose of the button is to camouflage the point where the seams of the cap meet. As Rich Soergel put it, the button lends the cap a more trim, finished look.

Submitted by Scott Kolbet of Tualatin, Oregon. Thanks also to John Edmonds of Stone Mountain, Georgia; Murad Hussain of Short Hills, New Jersey; Adam Light of Little Rock, Arkansas; Susan Bischof of Edmondton, Alberta; Stephen Johnson of Waco, Texas; and David Corona of San Antonio, Texas.

Why Are the Undersides of Baseball Cap Visors Usually Green?

Unlike the button on the top of the cap, the green underside actually does serve a practical function: It helps reduce light reflection that could interfere with ballplayers during daytime games and subject us civilians to the unpleasantness of glare as we gallivant through everyday life.

Baseball players and other athletes try all sorts of strategies to counteract unwanted reflections. In noncontact situations, sunglasses can be worn. In football, where sunglasses aren't practical, athletes apply grease around their eyes to give themselves that sexy raccoon look.

If the purpose of the green visor is to block out the sun, why not use a black underbill? According to Rich Soergel, president of the Pacific Sportswear and Emblem Company, a black bill would distract players because of the great contrast in color between it and the green grass. Compared to the grass (natural or artificial turf) and the blue sky, green is a neutral color.

Of course, civilians don't have to worry about dropping pop flies, and baseball caps have zoomed in popularity, so manufacturers have responded by introducing new color schemes. Chris Kolanko says that his company manufactures many caps with the same color visor on the top and the bottom. Kolanko thinks that the single-color style lends a slightly dressier effect to the cap, and these matched caps are much in demand by younger customers.

Pacific Sportswear manufactures caps with as many color combinations as Land's End's polo shirts. Maybe one day we'll see

Tommy Lasorda donning a Dodger Blue cap with a chartreuse underbill.

Submitted by Thomas Waggoner of Auburn, Alabama. Thanks also to Tia Anzelotti of Torrington, Connecticut; Amy Barber of Dearborn Heights, Michigan; and Adam Light of Little Rock, Arkansas.

Why Do Aquarium Fish Put Pebbles from the Bottom of the Tank in Their Mouths and Spit Them Out?

Humans should talk! We put some rather strange things in our mouths: our fingernails, chewing tobacco, grape-flavored bubble gum, and beef jerky.

But Geoff Rizzie asks about fish, not *homo sapiens*. Our aquatic experts offer three explanations:

1. *You want a cool chick? Better have a nice pad!* Biologist Glenda Kelley, of the International Game Fish Association, writes:

> "One reason aquarium fishes may go to the bottom of a tank and pick up rocks in their mouths and spit them out is to choose or clean the spawning substratum before enticing a female to spawn there. In some fish, availability and selection of nest-building material is most important in reproductive behavior. In the selection

*process, fish test the environment in various ways: mouthing po-
tential nest material; settling on the bottom to feel it; or making
preliminary digging or cleaning efforts."*

2. *Yum.* Hey, it's not that the fish doesn't appreciate that fish
food you drop from on high, but variety is the spice of life. In the
wild, with a rich and complicated plant life, pebbles can be festooned with all sorts of delicacies. According to Robert R. Rofen,
of the Aquatic Research Institute, many fish search for food

> *"by taking up sand, gravel, and pebbles into their tongues to
> remove food on their surfaces and then spitting out what is inedi-
> ble."*

It might seem strange to us, but then we can imagine a fish writing
a chapter about why humans put olives in their mouths and spit
the pits out.

3. *By all means necessary.* Let's face it, fish aren't equipped with
toothbrushes or dental floss. Doug Olander, of *Sport Fishing* magazine, told *Imponderables* that pebbles and gravel can be an im-
promptu substitute, a means to rid themselves of parasites that
gather in their mouths.

Submitted by Geoff Rizzie of Cypress, California.

Why Are There No Windows in Some Telephone Company Offices?

You'll be happy to know that the windowless telephone company buildings you see generally do not house unhappy employees but rather dutiful machinery. These offices are generally central offices, switching centers, and relay centers, which contain phone and cable wiring. The office buildings that contain administrative and technical personnel *do* have windows.

The windowless offices are of a particular vintage. Before World War II, most central offices did indeed have windows. As author and consultant John Levine puts it:

> "If you can find a central office that's old enough to predate automation, you'll find lots of windows. If you're ever in Cambridge, Massachusetts, the telco CO (telephone company central office) on Ware Street is quite attractive and was built fifty years ago to match the nearby Harvard buildings."

Most of the windowless central offices were built in the late 1940s and the 1950s. Bill Sohl, telecommunications consultant, put in time in a building that has the warmth of the monolith in *2001*:

> "I worked in one of the largest windowless CO's, at 811 10th Avenue in New York City, a twenty-one-story building with no windows. The building was almost totally devoted to electronic switching and transmission equipment, but I'd say there were probably 500 to 1,000 people that worked there. The building had a colored-light system to let you know what the weather was like outside:
>
> > red—inclement weather
> > yellow—cloudy, changeable
> > green—nice day"

So what prompted the telephone companies to eliminate windows? Clearly, machines don't demand a charming setting, but even in mechanical switching centers, some humans had to work there. The consensus among most of the telephone experts we spoke to was that two factors created the impetus for building windowless offices:

1. To Eliminate Sunlight. Much of the switching and relay equipment used by the telephone companies in the 1940s and 1950s was sensitive to both UV rays and heat. According to Jim Holmes, of General Telephone in Los Angeles, the cloth and plastic shielding used on phone wires became brittle, and ultimately cracked, when exposed to prolonged UV radiation. Originally, the telephone companies tried to paint over the windows with a dark color to block the UV penetration, but ultimately they decided it was preferable not to face having windows opened at all (see number 3, below).

2. Security. In the relatively peaceful 1990s, it's easy to forget that soon after World War II, we were waging a Cold War against the USSR. As one employee of a "Baby Bell" (who prefers to remain anonymous) told *Imponderables,*

> "*Central offices in the Bell System were almost all designed to be 'fallout' shelters, with all the cute psychological warfare tricks that went with them: few windows, large entrance doors, and brick construction.*"

Or as "Industrial Magician" Marty Brenneis puts it, "You can't toss a Molotov cocktail through a cement wall."

H. A. Kippenhan, Jr., of the National Accelerator Laboratory, points out that the U.S. telephone network was then considered to be part of the national defense infrastructure:

> "*If someone breaks into the switch room of a telco central office, that is a federal crime and such episodes are investigated by the FBI.*"

John Gilbert, lead systems engineer with Motorola, adds that a central office is potentially a prime target for terrorist attack:

> *"In addition to the havoc that would be caused to residence and business telephone users by a terrorist attack, many other types of 'special services' use the cable facilities that enter a telephone company's central office. Nine-one-one circuits, police and government private lines, radio transmitter control, power grid monitoring, and control and data circuits go through telco facilities. By not having windows, security against intrusion and bombing is increased."*

Now that the Cold War has ended, telephone companies are still concerned enough about security precautions that they've pulled a "double reverse" to try to fend off potential terrorists, as freelance security consultant Matthew Landry explains:

> *"Telcos are discovering that making the semisecret location of your most critical hardware look like a container for mission-critical hardware only makes it more attractive to saboteurs, and as a result, some are actually housing critical equipment in ordinary-looking, unmarked office buildings.*
>
> *"In a sense, this reflects a shift in the focus of their paranoia. Large institutions used to be afraid of destruction by random mob forces (like a riot). Their primary fear is now of deliberate destruction by enemies or anarchists through planned sabotage. The countermeasures are merely adapting to the new focus."*

Although shielding equipment from sunlight and security were the original inspirations for the creation of the windowless central office, several other advantages motivated the bizarre telco architecture:

3. Dust Reduction. Dust is the enemy of switching equipment (and it isn't exactly a close pal of today's computers, either). In the era of windowless buildings, the offices were not air-conditioned. Naturally, employees opened windows to increase ventila-

tion. Inevitably, dust infiltrated the contacts needed for the old mechanical switches, causing overheating and connection problems.

4. Equipment Climate Control. The sun, with access to a window, has a nasty habit of creating warmth in a room, which is potentially devastating to communication equipment. Now, central air-conditioning can alleviate the problem, but not in the "old days."

5. Saves Money. As we said before, telephone switching equipment doesn't care if it has a nice view, so the phone companies obviously saved money by erecting buildings without windows. Once they were built, windowless buildings continued to save money over the conventional windowed offices. David Lewis, of AT&T Communications Services Group, observes:

> *"Equipment in central offices generates a lot of heat. Cooling is a major expense. Add the heat generated by having sunlight streaming in through the windows, and the heat load increases significantly."*

6. Thwarts Vandalism. Although this issue might not occur to the layman, security expert Matthew Landry points out that

> *"a well-equipped telco central office contains more material wealth in easily stealable form than a small bank branch."*

In other parts of the world, vandalism is especially feared, as Kevin Jones, Canadian telecommunications specialist, explains:

> *"It's easier to go through a window than a brick wall. While this may seem silly in the U.S., where many new switches are going up, such as in South America, there is a large demand for metal of all kinds. Copper wire lines would be cut, dug up, and sold by criminals. This is why the wireless industry exploded in South America."*

7. Promotes Employee Efficiency. Many of our sources, particularly those who have worked for a large telephone company, mused about to what extent the windowless offices were a way to keep employees away from potential distractions that might have impaired efficiency. Randy Kendrick, senior manager of switched services for ICG Access Services, recounts his time spent paying windowless dues:

> *"About twelve years ago, when I worked for AT&T, we had a training center in Cincinnati. AT&T owned the Terrace Hilton downtown, which had the lobby on the fifth floor. The lower floors were the AT&T National Training Center and it was entirely windowless.*
>
> *While working at Southwestern Bell prior to divestiture, I worked during a labor strike, filling in for the directory assistance operators. The building was not a central office but still was without windows. Maybe it keeps the operators from being distracted by things outside, since they are measured by computer on how many calls they handle and how fast they get off the line. Raises, promotions, and continued employment are granted or denied based upon what the computer report says."*

8. Freeing Wall Space. Mark Fletcher, an advanced systems technician at Bell Atlantic Meridian Systems, notes an obvious attribute of a windowless office: If you don't have windows, you don't have to worry about covering them up. Fifty years ago, the mechanical switching equipment was far bulkier than it is today. Allowing racks of equipment to be stacked along the entire surface of the wall provided "desperately needed space."

When I posted this Imponderable to the marvelous Internet newsgroup comp.dcom.telecom, a participant, Ron Bean, pointed out that libraries often have windows on only one side of the building (or have very narrow windows) for the same reason.

9. Protection Against Natural Disasters. New York consultant Harry Joseph points out that windowless offices are more earthquake resistant and fireproof than their glass-laden cousins.

As telephone switching equipment has been progressively and dramatically downsized, all sorts of dislocations have been visited upon these old central offices. Even though most of these buildings were designed primarily to house equipment, John Gilbert reminds us that a considerable staff was needed to clean and maintain the relays in the large electromagnetic switches. The easiest way to see the difference in employment needs is take a look in the bathrooms:

> "There are enough stalls to support a very large staff . . . Today the place is like a ghost town, with only a few technicians on duty during the day and the place monitored remotely during the night."

Our favorite story, though, about a telco white elephant of a CO, was proffered by telecommunications expert Ron Natalie:

> "The AT&T longlines facility in Finksburg, Maryland, is underground. It has two football-field-sized floors, as when it was built it was designed for a tenfold increase in capacity. It had three turbine generators and a whole lot of fuel to keep the place in operation through an extended power failure.
>
> "What they didn't plan for was the fact that the size of the equipment got smaller faster than the capacity growth. Only about a quarter of one floor is occupied. Engineers in slack time have been known to go to the unoccupied lower level and practice tennis."

Submitted by Judith Dahlman of New York, New York. Special thanks to Pat Townson, editor and publisher of the *Telecom Digest*.

What Is the Significance of the "Canada" in Canada Dry Ginger Ale?

Even though there might be no more evidence of the fact other than the name on the label, Canada Dry was indeed born in Canada (Toronto, Ontario, to be exact). Like Dr Pepper, the soft drink was created by a pharmacist (and chemist), John J. McLaughlin, who originally opened a small plant to manufacture soda water. He sold the water to drugstores in siphons for use as a mixer for fruit juices and flavored extracts.

McLaughlin worked for more than a decade to develop a "dry" ginger ale, and in 1904, he introduced "McLaughlin's Pale Dry Ginger Ale." But by 1907, he had changed the name to Canada Dry Pale Dry Ginger Ale (not much catchier, in our opinion). In 1919, McLaughlin started shipping carloads of the soft drink to New York City, and the weird folks to the south lapped it up. To keep up with U.S. demand, in two years a manufacturing plant was opened in New York. The first foreign license was awarded to a bottler in Lima, Peru, in 1936, and ever since, Canada Dry has been sold throughout the world.

McLaughlin sold the company, in 1923, to P. D. Saylor and J. M. Mathes for the unprincely sum of $1 million. Canada Dry has undergone so many changes of ownership that the Canadian roots of the corporation have been long shrouded, as this time line indicates:

1958: The company is renamed the Canada Dry Corporation.

1968: Canada Dry merges with Hunt Foods and Industries and the McCall Corporation to form Norton-Simon, Inc.

1982: Canada Dry is sold to the Dr Pepper Company for $175 million (we're betting that McLaughlin was slamming his forehead up in heaven for having sold his business so cheaply).

David Feldman

1984: RJR/Nabisco's Del Monte unit buys Canada Dry, combining it in a unit with Sunkist and Hawaiian Punch.

1986: Canada Dry and Sunkist are sold to Cadbury Schweppes, PLC, for $230 million.

The purchase by Cadbury Schweppes is not without irony. Cadbury Schweppes is an English company, so once again Canada Dry is a subject of British colonization! And most interestingly, Canada Dry Ginger Ale is now owned by the parent company of its biggest competitor, Schweppes Ginger Ale.

Submitted by Erik Reichmann of Howell, New Jersey.

Why Is a Dead Octopus Thrown on the Ice During Detroit Red Wings Play-off Games?

Would you expect them to throw a *live* octopus?

This bizarre ritual originated during the 1952 Stanley Cup play-offs. Back then, there were only six teams in the National Hockey League, and the play-offs consisted of four of those teams participating in semifinal matches to end up with a final showdown with two teams. In 1952, the Red Wings faced Toronto in the semifinals and Montréal in the finals, and swept both series. Not only did they win all eight games, but the Red Wings' goalie, Terry Sawchuck, did not allow either opponent a single goal against him on Detroit's home ice.

On April 15, 1952, the Red Wings clinched the series at their own Olympia Stadium. Pete and Jerry Cusimano, who owned a local fish store/restaurant, decided to commemorate the eight wins. How could they best memorialize the eight straight victories? They must have quickly decided that throwing an eight ball on the ice might not be a brilliant idea. Why not toss an octopus instead? Pete and Jerry smuggled a boiled octopus into the stadium, and after the win, threw it on the ice. The eight tentacles symbolized the eight Detroit victories.

The Cusimanos meant their ritual to be a one-shot event, but it became the start of a grand (?) tradition that survives to this day, especially during play-off games. In some years, the octopi appear after regular-season victories, sometimes even after Red Wings' goals and, rarely, during play. An octopus was thrown onto the ice to christen the first night's play of the Red Wings in their current stadium, Joe Louis Arena, in 1979.

We spoke to a public-relations representative of the Red Wings (who prefers to remain anonymous), who recounted some wonderful octopus lore. Sadly, Jerry Cusimano died in 1953, but Pete has been outspoken about the proper form for octopus hurling. Boiling the creature, according to the originator of the practice, is the "proper way." Increasingly, fans have been throwing raw octopi, and the mollusks tend to break apart when they hit the ice, whereas well-cooked octopi maintain their structural integrity. The raw ones squish all over the ice and create a slimy mess.

One Red Wings fan, Matt Anderson, reports that the proper way to prepare an octopus for its moment of glory is to "half cook" it:

> *"This imparts firmness to its slimy body, gives it a proper reddish hue, and makes the tentacles point upward to symbolize the eight victories formerly required to hoist the cup. It also keeps the beastie from leaving a slimy spot on the ice."*

Presumably, league officials are not trained in the specialized field of octopus removal. Red Wing fans expect attendants to remove the octopus with their hands—this rates a cheer; when a shovel is used, the octopi removers get booed.

We asked the P.R. representative if the Red Wings or Joe Louis Arena has any stated policy prohibiting the throwing of octopi. As you might expect, you can't find a "No Octopus Throwing" sign anywhere:

> *"There isn't any stated policy. There aren't any signs around the arena about throwing them. No announcement is made if and when it happens. Certainly, we don't encourage the throwing of them during games. You know, you could say that the octopus has become the Red Wings' mascot."*

We doubt if any other school or team would deny the Red Wings' exclusive right to use the "Dead Octopus" as their mascot.

Our P.R. source indicated that to her knowledge, no one has been hurt from the throwing of an octopus, although one Red Wings fan told us that although the people who toss them are usually seated close to the ice,

> *"More than one fan has been the recipient of an octopus in the back of the head. They are not very aerodynamic creatures."*

Another obvious mystery is how these octopi are smuggled into the arena in the first place. Our fan sources report that die-hard octopus throwers have been known to stuff them down the front of their pants ("Is that an octopus in your pants, or are you just excited about the game?") or browbeat their girlfriends into stuffing them in purses (Why do we assume no female would throw an octopus on ice?). Pedestrian octopus carriers also include duffel bags or baggy coats. Many of the octopi are small enough to fit in a purse; most weigh less than ten pounds. But during the 1994 play-offs, a thirty-five-pound monster was thrown on the ice.

As the octopi are symbols of victory, they are disposed of with the proper dignity, as a fan describes:

> *"If you are wondering what happens to all those octopi, they are tossed into the Detroit River (only a hundred yards or so from the rink) to provide a source of food for the river's inhabitants. No studies have been done on whether or not fish flock to the river's edge at play-off time!"*

Although fish in the Detroit River might root for octopi to be thrown on the ice, the Red Wings' opponents aren't as sanguine about the prospect. The P.R. representative told us a wonderful story about what happened during the Western Conference finals during the 1994–95 season:

> *"In Chicago, they didn't want Red Wings fans throwing octopi on their ice. If you were caught throwing one, you would be arrested. The state of Illinois was so concerned, they actually had merchants in Illinois ID anyone if they tried to purchase an octopus during the play-offs. If you had a Michigan driver's license, you weren't allowed to purchase an octopus in the state of Illinois by law. I think one or two people were actually arrested."*

Submitted by James C. Crivellaro of Easton, Pennsylvania.

Why Does the Red Light (Designating "Use Correct Change") Flash After Putting Money in Soft-Drink Vending Machines?

Larry Eils, director of health, safety, and technical standards for the National Automatic Merchandising Association, takes issue with the premise of this Imponderable. He rightly points out that the "Use Correct Change" is meant to alert consumers *before* they insert money that they may not receive their money back if more than the cost of the amount of the drink is plunked into the machine:

> *"This would not be a good customer-relations move on our part. Since the machine could not make correct change, it would not accept [a dollar] bill either, which would be another frustrating event for our customer. Thus, when you walk up to a machine, 'Use Correct Change' should already be lit."*

David Feldman

The operative word is *should,* for eagle-eyed *Imponderables* readers have noticed the same thing that has always confounded us— many machines *do* quickly, but clearly, flash this warning, even when they do proceed to give us our correct change.

Not until we heard from Melissa Packwood, of Coca-Cola's consumer affairs department, did we finally receive a logical explanation for this inexplicable pattern. Packwood stresses that most modern electronically controlled vending machines should not flash, but a few machines produced today, and most of the vending machines produced prior to 1991, will flash. Here's why:

> *"The coin changer within the machine stores money to repay appropriate change. This change is stored in tubes that have switches in the bottom called the 'change tube switches.' These switches are used to determine if there is adequate change stored within the coin changer, and they control both the correct-change lamp and a series of blocking arms within the changer that prevent the acceptance of coins that are not 'correct change.'*
>
> *"Once enough money is inserted to purchase a soft drink, control of the blocking arms is switched from the 'change tube switch' to a device called the 'credit relay' to prohibit the acceptance of any money during the dispensing cycle. This momentarily turns on the correct change lamp, but the credit relay also opens a switch that breaks the circuit between the credit relay and the correct change lamp and switches the correct change lamp back to the control of the change tube switches.*
>
> *"For a brief instant, the correct change lamp is powered by the credit relay circuit regardless of the true ability of the machine to accept correct change. The lamp can turn on faster than the relay can switch it back to the control of the change tube switch. All of this happens in less than 0.05 seconds and most people don't notice the lamp flicker."*

Alas, thirsty *Imponderables* readers notice just about everything.

So the flicker of lights isn't meant for our consumption. Chris Jones, of Pepsi, puts it this way: The vending machine has two modes, "standby" and "vend." Once the money is inserted, the machine is in the vend mode and isn't capable of accepting coins or bills. So the "indicator lights" aren't really indicating anything to *us,* but merely resetting to snare the money of the next customer. They love us for buying their soft drinks, but heck, it's the *next* customer who's doing something for them lately.

Submitted by Christine Thomas of Toledo, Ohio. Thanks also to G. J. Hollis, Jr., of Tacoma, Washington; Michael DeVore of Montgomery, Alabama; and L. Gualtieri of Brampton, Ontario.

Why Are There Ridges on Stick Licorice? How Do Manufacturers Make the Ridges Without Distorting the Shape of the Candy?

The first part of this Imponderable is easy: There are ridges on many companies' stick (or "rope") licorice because consumers like the looks of them. An additional benefit of the ridges, as Allen R. Allured, assistant secretary of the American Association of Candy Technologists, points out, is that the ridges aid in handling the candy. Some rope licorice is ridgeless and has a smooth texture that can slip out of your fingers more quickly than a politician's handshake.

How are the ridges put in place? Robert J. Zedik, director of technical services at the National Confectioners Association, explained the process. Stick licorice is extruded through a die, under heat and pressure, in one continuous rope. The rope is a cylindrical shape with ridges along the perimeter, the cross section of which would look like a star.

As the rope is extruded, it is slowly twisted into a spiral shape and cut into individual pieces. According to Zedik,

"The twisting motion is mild enough to avoid collapsing the center of the rope but enough to give the unique spiral design to the

ridges. The crimped ends of each piece are due to the cutting knives, which separate and seal each piece of licorice from the main rope coming off the extruder."

Submitted by Patty Sturm of Lake Havasu City, Arizona. Thanks also to Kirk Bobst of LeRoy, Illinois.

Why Do Things Fade? Why Does One Poster on a Tree Fade, While the Poster Adjacent to It Does Not?

Buddy Holly, the Rolling Stones, and the Grateful Dead might agree that "Love is love and not fade away," but colors on a poster are always going to fade, because two of the sworn enemies of bright colors are substances that we've grown fond of here on earth: sunlight and oxygen.

Donald Beaty, professor emeritus of physics at the College of San Mateo, wrote *Imponderables* about what happens when things fade:

> *"As everyone who sunburns easily has discovered, sunlight includes a much larger span of the electromagnetic spectrum than the eye sees as visible light. Those wavelengths in sunlight that are too short to be seen, ultraviolet light, are very energetic compared to the light that we can see. The energy of any color of light is carried by photons and those photons pack enough energy to break chemical bonds."*

All the other types of radiation in the electromagnetic spectrum (X rays, ultraviolet, infrared, radio waves, etc.) are all around us—each occupying a unique wavelength range that we are incapable of seeing. But we are able to discern different colors, each of which also has a unique wavelength, within the "visible light" spectrum. When we say "That dress is orange," a physicist might put it differently and say "That dress has absorbed all the other colors of the visible light spectrum and reflected the light of the orange wavelength back to our eyes."

Chris Ballas, Vanderbilt University physicist and a member of the American Association for the Advancement of Science, explains further how ultraviolet rays from the sun actually work to degrade colors:

> "*Light has (actually is) energy and UV is particularly energetic compared to electromagnetic radiation in other wavelength ranges. The chemicals/dyes that give objects their colors, when exposed to sunlight, will absorb some of the energy from the sunlight (mostly the UV 'light'). When they absorb this energy, the electrons in the chemicals and dyes become excited.*
>
> "*When electrons are excited, they have a greater chance of getting involved in a chemical reaction. If they do get involved in a chemical reaction, the very nature of the chemical or dye is changed, because the altered substance will reflect different wavelengths of light than the original chemical or dye.*
>
> "*The usual chemical reaction that takes place when electrons are excited by sunlight involves a combination with oxygen. Most substances lose their color when oxidized.*"

Many substances besides chemicals and dyes oxidize. We are most familiar, perhaps, with what happens when iron oxidizes to form iron oxide, a fancy technical term for what we usually call "rust." Although the oxidation of dyes is not as dramatic as what happens in the formation of rust, the chemical change is just as real: and the reaction of most dyes is to fade when oxidized.

But not all dyes are alike, and the different chemical compositions of dyes will usually explain why one poster might fade while the adjacent one remains pristine (assuming the two posters are exposed to the same amount of sun/UV light). As Beaty puts it:

> *"Some dye molecules are more stable, and colors produced by these more resistant molecules are able to resist the fading effects of ultraviolet light. A color photograph or a poster may start with a balanced palette of hues before the UV photons do their damage, but the picture may soon lose almost every color but blue as a result of the photons' action on the dye chemistry."*

The oxidation that causes fading tends to be quite slow (some types of oxidation occur quickly). But there is a "steamrolling" effect once oxidation does start to occur. One poster might have been put on the tree months before the other, or perhaps one did get more exposure to the sun. Rest assured, though, identical posters given identical exposure to UV light will both eventually fade in the same way and at the same pace.

Physicist Harold Blake, of Zephyrhills, Florida, told *Imponderables* that dyes can be made out of aniline (a poisonous liquid, derivative of benzene), minerals, chemicals, or other natural substances. The natural dyes tend to fade less than the chemical ones:

> *"More stable colors are the natural minerals, like the siennas, ochers, and inorganic oxides and sulfides. The color of the old country barn is stable because of the cheap iron ore, hematite, that is used. It gives southern clay its red color, which carries over into bricks. Another name for hematite is 'rust.'*
>
> *"The old painters used many colors of paint, but those that tended to endure best were earthen colors, like burnt and raw sienna and the ochers. Some bright crimsons come from the dried carcasses of the female cochineal insect. I do not believe this color is as stable as the mineral and earthen colors, but cochineal is stable enough to be used in women's lipsticks [Aggggh]."*

Blake recounts a personal story about the hardiness of the color of his army uniform:

"The most unstable dyes are the organic ones. Green is a hard color to make stable. Most greens tend to fade. The green camouflage colors in our Army's uniforms, if made from an azo or aniline dye, would fade rapidly in a chlorine gas assault.

"So a mineral green was used during World War II. I believe the mineral was chromium. I poured concentrated chlorine bleach on my fatigues when I washed them, just to kill the stench [chlorine, when combined with water, will usually bleach out colors of most fabrics] and the green was just as bright as ever."

Fading is an important issue in the clothing and photographic industries, too. Up until very recently, users would assume that color prints would fade in a few years, but recent advances in photographic-dye chemistry have improved the stability of print colors dramatically. Unfortunately, Beaty points out an irony: If you keep your photos in the closet, they won't fade much; but every time you take them out to look at them, you are exposing the prints to the UV light and oxygen that will potentially fade them. Each viewing causes some deterioration.

That's why art museums often ban the use of flash cameras—not because the practice annoys other viewers (like us!) but because the ultraviolet photons from electronic flash units can promote fading. Even more precautions are taken to protect our most precious documents, as Beaty explains:

"The National Archives in Washington, D.C., has a strictly enforced rule preventing the use of flash units by anyone attempting to photograph the Declaration of Independence. Additionally, this national treasure is protected by a yellow filter that blocks the shorter wavelengths of light, thus, it is hoped, preserving the appearance of the Declaration of Independence for centuries to come. If viewed in normal room light, the writing on this document would soon fade."

Submitted by Rick Kot of New York, New York. Thanks also to Christopher Drake of Lawndale, California; Lori Tomlinson of Newmarket, Ontario; Alan Funk of Everett, Washington; Virginia Hay of Harrisburg, Pennsylvania; John Kominek of Waterloo, Ontario; Douglas Watkins, Jr., of Hayward, California; Sandi Montour of Honolulu, Hawaii; David Coppersmith of Mishawaka, Indiana; and Judy Hinchcliffe of Houston, Texas; and many others.

David Feldman

How Do Groundskeepers Rebuild the Pitcher's Mounds in Multipurpose Stadiums?

Even though a baseball pitching mound might look like little but a hunk of dirt surrounded by grass, in reality it is constructed with great care and more than a little difficulty. Major League Baseball mandates the exact specifications of a pitching mound. In the past, a home team with a dominating pitcher would try to raise the mound to gain further advantage (or lower it in advance of an overpowering fastball pitcher on an opponent's team taking the mound), or would construct warmup mounds in the visitors' bullpen that didn't match the dimensions of the real mound.

To forestall such petty larceny, an inspector from Major League Baseball visits every ballpark at least twice a year (including once during preseason) and checks the pitcher's mound and all bullpen mounds for such specifications as: height of the mound (it must be exactly ten inches higher than home plate); slope of the mound (the area six inches in front of the pitcher's rubber must be flat, and then, slope down at a constant pitch of one inch per foot toward home plate—this six feet constitutes the area onto which the pitcher's lead foot will land during the follow-through); size of the pitcher's circle (the large dirt area onto which the mound is built must be exactly eighteen feet in diameter); flatness of the pitcher's rubber; flatness of the area on which the pitcher's rubber is laid; and other equally exacting criteria.

Beyond these objective criteria, pitchers tend to grow fond of and accustomed to the mounds in their home parks; they notice and are made uncomfortable by any changes in their usual environment. Even if pitchers weren't so finicky, it takes so much manpower to build and maintain a mound that there is no question of rebuilding it from scratch every week after a football game or if an occasional rock concert necessitates temporarily dismantling the mound. Although pitcher's mounds have to be groomed every day, with luck they can last for several years.

So how do they move and rebuild them? We spoke to Steve Wightman, head groundskeeper at San Diego's Jack Murphy Stadium, who has faced the problem working in a park that plays home to both the Padres and the Chargers. Jack Murphy's solution to the problem is common among other multipurpose stadiums: the mound is built onto a circular steel plate; a giant forklift is then used to move the plate (with the mound on it); and then the same forklift moves the plate back in place.

Sounds easy, doesn't it? Think again. The steel plate with the mound weighs close to a ton (and remember the pitcher's circle is eighteen feet in diameter; the steel plate is thirteen feet in diameter). In order to prepare the mound to be carried off, the groundskeepers have to dig around the edge of the plate to expose the metal (and the channels with which the prongs on the forklift will pick up the mound). Just getting the forklift to the pitcher's circle is a project, because a temporary plywood roadway must be laid down anywhere the forklift travels on the field. Once the plate is picked up, the groundskeepers add some dirt and clay to the area where the plate was and even it out, which takes about one hour. In essence, the groundskeepers become grave diggers.

When the mound has to be restored, the opposite process takes place, although rebuilding takes longer, for it is essential

David Feldman

that the steel plate be completely covered and that a seamless mound be crafted. It takes the groundskeepers at Jack Murphy between two and three hours to rebuild the mound after the plate has been put in place.

Wightman says that even when the park is used exclusively for baseball, each year, before the season starts, the mound must be regroomed by hand to restore the exact slope, and a new rubber is installed every year. When they do destroy a mound, it takes about three hours to tear it down and about six hours to rebuild it approximating the proper specifications.

One park, Anaheim Stadium, which is now home to the Angels and various concerts and events but once was also the St. Louis Rams' stadium, built a hydraulic system to take care of the portability problem. They dug a circular well under the pitcher's mound, and the hydraulic system raises or lowers the mound, as needed. We spoke to Phil Larcus, operations manager of the "Big A," about how his crew takes down and reconstructs the pitcher's mound.

The mound sits on a metal plate, and the well is the same diameter as the plate, so that the plate fits snugly into the well. The well's hydraulic system can pump water into and out of the well. When the groundskeepers need to put in the mound, they pump water into the well and the plate rises with the water. The plate contains indentations that lock into matching spots on the well. The plate is then turned to engage the indentations and locked in place. As with Jack Murphy Stadium, the groundskeepers groom the edge of the plate to cover the exposed metal to hide any traces of seams.

When events necessitate eliminating the mound at the Big A, the groundskeepers dig around the perimeter of the plate at the edges, and then unlock the plate by turning it the opposite direction. The water in the well is pumped out and the plate automatically sinks. On the bottom of the well, another set of matching indentations in the side of the well locks the plate in place again.

Obviously, the well at Anaheim Stadium is far deeper than the hole dug at Jack Murphy; if the groundskeepers attempted to fill the well with dirt every time they unlocked the plate, they'd never have time to tend to anything else. Instead, a "mound cap," a flat metal disk with a flat plywood top, is brought out (from underneath the stands) to cover the exposed opening. The plywood is covered with artificial turf. Artificial turf is used in order to blend as well as possible with the natural grass used in the stadium (and to provide a surface that gives sufficient traction for athletes to run on). The whole process of conversion from baseball to football, or vice versa, would take the crew about three hours.

Submitted by Tom Emig of St. Charles, Missouri. Thanks also to John Ryan of Portsmouth, Rhode Island.

David Feldman

Why Do We See "Snow" on Television Stations When a Channel Stops Broadcasting for the Night?

According to Dick Glass, president of the Professional Electronics Technicians Association, the power of a signal is measured in millionths of a volt at the input terminals of a TV set, so when the station shuts off the transmitter power for the night,

> *"the screen will show random 'snow' and the sound will usually 'hiss.' This is similar to the 'hiss' you hear on a radio, in between stations."*

What causes the "gray" in snow and the irregular noise? Surprisingly, often *we* do. Jim Tanenbaum, a production mixer at Sound Recording Services in Los Angeles, explains:

> *"Most TV sets will indeed show gray 'snow' in the absence of a signal, but not all. Some sets have 'squelch blanking,' which blacks out the screen when no signal is present. Snow results from the ac-*

tion of the amplifiers in the tuner that receives the TV signal from the antenna or cable. Because the level of this signal can vary, the amplifiers have an 'Automatic Gain Control' (AGC), which increases the amplifiers' gain for weak signals and lowers it for strong ones.

"In the absence of any signal at all, the gain goes to maximum. In this condition, the tuner picks up 'static' signals generated by other devices like car ignitions, vacuum cleaners, lightning, computers, fluorescent lights, etc.

"Also, the circuits in the TV tuner itself have a certain amount of inherent noise that is discernible at maximum gain. The video and audio circuits in the TV set interpret the static as legitimate video and audio signals and pass them along to the picture tube and loudspeaker."

When the transmitter is not sending signals, the picture "should" be white. If it weren't for the random electrical blips, most stations would be as white as the driven, as opposed to electrical, snow. On some sets, a vacant channel will be black, with no snow whatsoever. These monitors come equipped with a feature called "squelch blanking," which blacks out the screen when the tuner receives no signal. It is unclear just who the consumer is who cares about such a feature, let alone who would be willing to pay extra to reduce the snow on an empty station, but then we always were coupon clippers.

Submitted by Sean Roy of Hollywood, California.

Why Do Auctioneers Talk Funny? And Why Do Auctioneers Often Speak Unintelligibly?

Auctioneering dates back to Anglo-Saxon times, when all sorts of merchandise and commodities were sold in open markets. Bernard Hart, executive secretary of the National Auto Auction Association, wrote *Imponderables*:

> "The reason for the funny talk by auctioneers is that before the advent of public-address systems, especially the portable type, an auctioneer had not only to be in good voice but to talk in a method that was pleasing rather than irritating to the ears of his audience of prospective buyers."

The modus operandi of the auctioneer has not changed much since its origins, as Peter Lukasiak, executive director of the National Auto Auction Association, explains:

"A typical auctioneer describes the products offered for sale; chants to find the lowest (or floor) price for the items being sold; acknowledges each bid received; and attempts to move bidders to the highest bid level possible. This results in a rolling, sonorous tone that actually builds competition among bidders and secures the highest market price for sale goods and the seller."

Although the "chant" might sound funny to the uninitiated, it's an essential element in the strategy of the auctioneer. The auctioneer usually must try to sell as much merchandise as possible in the shortest amount of time (not only so that more goods can be sold but also so that buyers uninterested in the particular item on sale won't leave the premises before they have a chance to bid on later items). As Joseph Keefhaver, executive vice president of the National Auctioneers Association put it,

"Rhythm is as important as speed in developing an effective chant. Auctioneers will adjust their speed, depending on the bidding experience level of their crowd, and the numbers of a good chant will be readily understood."

Lukasiak indicates that some auctioneers have personal preferences for slow or fast paces, but conditions often dictate the chant speed. A wholesale tobacco buyer does not want a leisurely pace at an auction; and an auctioneer trying to sell a multimillion-dollar Monet at Sotheby's had better not carry off the bidding at a breakneck pace, as Keefhaver amplifies:

"The purpose of an auction is to sell items at a rapid and steady pace. Unlike other types of sales, an auction is a one-time event where all the customers are present at the same time. Thus, the auctioneer is responsible for selling all the items within a few hours, and his or her use of the chant helps keep the items moving.

"Since auctioneers have a limited amount of time to sell many items, they need to move at a rapid pace. At an average household estate auction, the auctioneer's chant uses speed and rhythm to sell an average of 60 items per hour. Certain types of auctions go even

*faster; wholesale automobile auctioneers frequently sell 125 to 175
cars per hour and tobacco auctioneers may sell 500 to 600 lots per
hour."*

Obviously, it is far more difficult for the uninitiated to understand
what is going on at a tobacco auction. Many auctioneers pepper
their chants with regional speech patterns or terms understood
only by the cognoscenti within the field.

O.K. We've established that the form of the auctioneer's chant
makes some sense, but why can't you understand them? When
we've gone to auctions, a typical chant might sound to bidders
something like this:

> *"Hey, budda budda budda twenty-five, hey wonka wonka
> wonka thirty, got twenty-five, thirty, budda budda, twenty-five,
> thirty, hey thirty, budda budda budda, do I have a thirty? Budda
> budda."*

Of course, that's not what the auctioneer is actually *saying*. More
likely, he is using "real words." Joseph Keefhaver provides a classic,
basic chant:

> *"One-dollar bid, now two, now two, will you give me two?"*
> *"Two-dollar bid, now three, now three, will ya give me three?"*

The culprits in misunderstanding the chants, in the previous example the "budda's" and "wonka's," are called "filler words" (or
simply, "filler") by auctioneers. The purpose of filler is to give bidders a chance to think about bidding while keeping the momen-
tum of the chant (and with luck, a frenzy of interest in the item)
alive. Bernard Hart told *Imponderables* that a good auctioneer develops several different filler words and alternates them throughout an auction, to avoid the monotony of "budda budda budda":

> *"In one of the auction schools where I worked, they trained the
> students to base their fillers on words that would encourage an in-
> crease in the bids such as 'make,' 'bid,' and 'go.' For example, 'I*

have twenty-five, will you make it thirty?' This is a five-word filler and only a select few are able to handle that many words. It can be shortened in several ways such as 'twenty-five go thirty,' 'twenty-five bid thirty,' and so on."

We were shocked when every single one of the auctioneers we consulted insisted that the bidder should be able to understand every single word of the auctioneer, even the fillers. The comments of John J. McBride, director of information at the Livestock Marketing Association, were typical:

> *"Actually, if you can't understand what an auctioneer is saying, he or she is not doing their job, and we should know, because we sponsor the granddaddy of all auctioneer contests, the World Livestock Auctioneer Championship.*
>
> *"I direct your attention to the judging criteria for this year's contest. Under the section 'Advancing to World Finals,' you can see that 'clarity of chant' is a major judging criterion. [Indeed, it is the first criterion mentioned, along with 'voice quality,' 'bid-catching ability,' 'conduct of the sale,' and 'Would the judge hire this auctioneer?']*
>
> *"Granted, it may take awhile for you as an auction observer to 'pick up' on the auctioneer's particular chant. And the auctioneer may sometimes use patter or fill words that are not crystal clear. But to sell, you have to be understood—and that's true whether you're auctioning off cattle or fine crystal, ranch land or Rembrandts."*

Submitted by Morgan Dallman of Martin, South Dakota. Thanks also to Valerie Grollman of Kendall Park, New Jersey; and Myron Meyer of Sioux Falls, South Dakota.

Why Are Clean Things Squeaky? Why Do Drinking Glasses Sometimes Squeak and Other Times Remain Squeakless When You Rub Them?

When you rub two substances together, all sorts of interesting things happen. Just ask the birds and the bees, or your local biochemist. Our local biochemist happens to be Dr. Donald Graham, of Langara College in Vancouver, British Columbia, who told us that when you hear a good, clean squeak, the glass has overcome the "coefficient of friction."

Say what? The coefficient of friction is simply a forbidding term to describe the force necessary to overcome the friction between two objects. When the coefficient is high, it means greater force is necessary to overcome the friction; when the coefficient is low, there is little friction between the two objects.

When an object, say a drinking glass, is full of dirt or the residue of a beverage, or your fingers are greasy or oily, these impurities act as a lubricant, and your fingers can glide along the surface of the glass. But if the object is free of impurities, it generates *more* friction between it and your fingers when you rub, because the two surfaces come into full contact with each other; the rubbing material keeps sticking for a moment before the force moving it overcomes the friction. It then releases, only to get caught again, ad infinitum.

The force of the friction, and the accompanying catching and releasing, causes the squeaking object to move, or to vibrate (in some cases, both objects vibrate, although not all materials are capable of vibrating); if the vibrations occur at frequencies that correspond to audible sounds, we hear those vibrations as squeaks. Of course, the force of the rubbing surfaces against each other and the kind of motion used during the rub will affect the volume and tempo of the sound.

With some surfaces, very little force is needed to generate a squeak, and glass just happens to be one of them. Another scientist pal, Harold Blake, of Zephyrhills, Florida, is so committed to research pursuits that he even works in restaurants, astounding and, we'd guess, occasionally annoying his friends:

> *"Often, even in a fancy restaurant, I take my beverage goblet, if it's thin and on a stem, and when the liquid is nearly gone, I moisten my finger and slowly glide it along the rim. When I achieve the necessary 'drag' on my finger to the glass, my finger sort of jumps rapidly, scuffing along the glass, and the goblet begins to sing. It is usually a high-pitched tone, melodious and penetrating.*
>
> *"In one restaurant, no one knew where the sound was coming from. Other patrons started looking around. Even the people at my table refused to believe my finger was making that loud a whine.*
>
> *"What happened, of course, is that friction causes the finger to push against the glass rim, and then added force releases the finger on the rim as it advances to a new spot. This sets up a natural vibration in the glass. It is the same frequency you hear if you 'tink' the glass with your finger.*
>
> *"You can do this with dinner china, windowpanes, and chalkboards [uh-oh,* bad *vibrations]. You just need to have the right amount of friction to create the series of scuffs and releases. The reason for some squeak-failures is the lack of the right amount of friction, or surface tension, or stickiness."*

You might think that both our hands and the glass have smooth surfaces, but you'd be wrong. As Blake puts it:

> *"The epithelial cells on a finger, or edge of a fingernail, the cotton fibers on a towel, the cells in the hairs of a horse's tail, all, under a microscope, look like furrows in a plowed field, or the cobblestones in the roughest street in London. Rough!"*

Blake reminded us that as far back as the Middle Ages, Europeans enjoyed "musical" or "tuned" glasses, which eventually were used as concert instruments. Rims of different glasses of different sizes, tuned in different keys by the amount of water put in the vessel, were played by squeakmaestros, presumably with impeccably clean hands.

The principles of friction and vibration explain the sound generated by all stringed instruments. You can take a violin bow, drag it along a Stradivarius, and achieve a resonant, mellifluous vibration. Drag the same bow along a carpenter's saw, and you'll hear a penetrating vibration that only a dog could love. And not a very smart dog, either.

Submitted by Scott Goldman of Calabasas, California.

How Do Astronauts Scratch an Itch When They Have Space Suits On?

Most of the time, an itch presents no problem for an astronaut in space. If an itch is pesky, the astronaut reaches to the offending nerve endings and scratches. If the itch is in an "unfortunate" place, perhaps the astronaut will look around the cabin, make sure no one else is looking, and then scratch. Still, no problem.

That's because most of the time when an astronaut is in space, he, and increasingly, she, is in street clothes—typically comfortable trousers or shorts and a polo shirt. There are only three times when the space suit conspires to foil an itch: upon launch, during reentry, and during "extravehicular activity" in space, such as a space walk.

During launch and reentry, astronauts wear an "LES" (launch-and-entry suit), the bright orange garb we see the astronauts wear when boarding the shuttle. These are "partial pressure" suits, designed to pressurize in case the cabin has a sudden loss of pressure

David Feldman

during launch or entry and are not unlike the suits worn by jet fighter pilots. Of course, a helmet is an essential component of the LES.

The "EVA" (extravehicular activity) suit is far bulkier and designed to withstand the rigors of outer space. This is the "big white uniform" that we associate with astronauts and with space walks, and that dominated the imagery in the movie *Apollo 13*. But even back in the Apollo days, astronauts rid themselves of the bulky suits once they were in orbit. Today, space shuttle astronauts wear EVAs while doing repair work on satellites or the Hubble telescope.

While EVAs are more flexible than the old Apollo suits, they are hardly a model of comfort. An astronaut first dons a bodysuit, akin to long johns, made of thin fabric. Over this go many layers of insulation and life-support equipment, including many tubes carrying liquid and gas. Then the "HUT" (hard upper torso), a stiff upper suit, is placed over all these other layers. The suit proper ends at the neck, with a hard metal locking ring, which clamps onto the helmet. Once the suit is pressurized, it puffs up, making it difficult to move freely within the EVA.

The helmet is locked rigidly at the neck clamp. If an astronaut swivels her head to the left, the helmet doesn't turn with her. So if she wants to see something at "three o'clock," she had better move her whole body in that direction.

In the Apollo days, suits were individually constructed for each astronaut. Now, they come "off the rack." No, there is no Gap for Astronauts, but they are sized "small, medium, and large," with allowances for long and short limbs.

By all accounts, the LES suits are more comfortable than the EVA suits. Astronauts are ordinarily in these suits, before takeoff, for at least one and one-half hours before launch. With delays, they can be stuck, unable to move freely, for up to four or five hours: plenty of time to contemplate itchiness, and what they are going to do about it. But once the launch takes place, the shuttle is in orbit within eight and one-half minutes; at that point, they can put on street clothes and scratch to their heart's (or other body part's) content.

So, is itchiness a burning issue among astronauts? Have they come up with solutions to this intractable problem? To find out, we assembled a group of five experts:

1. Wendy Lawrence, a former naval aviator and current astronaut, who flew on shuttle flight STS-67, an historic sixteen-day mission, which was the second flight of the ASTRO observatory.
2. G. David Low, who retired in 1996 after a ten-year career as an astronaut. Dave has flown on three shuttle missions and performed a six-hour space walk. He currently works at Orbital Sciences Corporation.
3. Mike Lounge, a former astronaut who trained for space walks but never did one. He currently works for Space Habitat.
4. James Hartsfield, NASA public affairs director.
5. Glen Lutz, a NASA "subsystem manager," whose specialty is the design of space suits.

We asked the three astronauts if itching bothered them, particularly when wearing the stiff EVA suits. They all agreed that the biggest problem was with facial itches, particularly on the nose. Luckily for them, that is one of the few parts of the anatomy that the space suit is equipped to help—but not because NASA was concerned about itching!

Built into the side of an EVA helmet is a V-shaped object called a "Valsalva device," which is designed to relieve earaches created by pressure changes in the cabin. To execute the "Valsalva maneuver," you hold your nose shut and blow through your nose to equalize pressure in the middle ear and clear the Eustachian tubes. Obviously, an astronaut can't "hold his nose" (there's that nasty little problem of the helmet being in the way), so instead the astronauts rest their heads on the "V" of the Valsalva device and blow. The Valsalva device is built into the side of the helmet, so astronauts can simply turn their heads and place their proboscises right on it.

Ingenious astronauts discovered that they seldom needed the device for ear problems; they more frequently could use it for itch problems! In his funny and informative book, *How Do You Go to the*

Ｄａｖｉｄ Ｆｅｌｄｍａｎ

Bathroom in Space?, ex-astronaut William R. Pogue addresses this issue directly:

> "*Not only did my nose itch occasionally, but also my ears. Because a scratch is almost an involuntary reaction, I frequently reached up to scratch my nose and hit my helmet—which can make you feel really dumb. I scratched my nose by rubbing it on a little nose pincher device we used to clear our ears [the Valsalva device].*
> . . . "*If our ears itched, we just had to tolerate it. I usually tried rubbing the side of my head against the inside of the helmet, but it didn't help much. The best thing to do was to think of something else.*"

Some of our astronauts had their own workarounds:

> LAWRENCE: "*On an EVA you don't have direct access to your face. Hopefully you can wiggle your nose to satisfy it. You just try to move your nose around, maybe see if you can get your nose down to the base of the mounting ring on the inside—you see if that'll work.*"

> LOUNGE: "*The Valsalva device can help you with your nose. If you get an itch [elsewhere] on your face, you kind of move your head around and find something inside the helmet to rub against it.*"

Astronaut David Low had a hate relationship with the Valsalva device that turned into love:

> "*I had hundreds of hours in EVA training. I'd probably used that Valsalva device only a few times on a couple of different training runs. It always got in my way. In fact, a lot of times when just moving my head around, I'd bump into it and it became somewhat of a pain to me. I found I could always clear my ears by just moving my jaw around.*
> "*In training, I never used it for what it was intended for. I was considering asking them to remove it from my helmet for the mission. But for some reason, about two weeks before flight, I was sit-*

ting in my office one day and I thought, 'What if I have to use the Valsalva device on my real space walk?' I called up our support guy and asked if they could make sure that there was a Valsalva device on my helmet.

"It turns out that I had the worst ear block I've ever had in my life when I was coming back in from my space walk and repressurizing. If you've ever had one of those, they're very uncomfortable and you can have a lot of pain. Nothing you can do about it. You can't get your hands in there to blow your nose. I was so happy that I had that Valsalva device."

Included on every EVA helmet is a straw, leading to a water pouch, and a food bar. Dehydration is a problem during space walks, so astronauts are encouraged to drink. Although it is possible to try to satisfy itches with these two devices, James Hartsfield indicates it isn't wise:

"The water straw is within reach of your mouth. You can get a drink by just bending your head down to get your lips onto the straw. There's also a food bar. But you don't want to use them to scratch facial itches. If you jiggle them around, they might come loose."

LUTZ: *"On an EVA, it's possible to scratch a facial itch with the water straw and/or the food bar. But because both those things are going to be ingested, you probably want to avoid as much body contact with them as you can. Most of the guys eat that food bar before they get outside or quickly thereafter, because the EVA is usually pretty task-intensive and they don't want to be messing around eating things."*

The prognosis for nasty facial itches in the LES suit is much more favorable, because the visor is flexible:

LOW: *"You can raise the visor on the helmet of an LES suit. For most of the ride uphill and downhill, we leave the visor open. We close them for the first two minutes of each launch, until solid* rocket booster separation occurs. After that, we raise the visor. So when the visor is open, you can easily scratch a face itch. But if the orbiter lost pressurization, you'd have to leave the visor down."

What about body itches? In some cases, the space suit is as unforgiving as the helmet. It's difficult to work in an EVA suit; David Low compared it to being inside the Pillsbury Doughboy:

> "It's hard to move in the things. They are pressurized and they balloon up. It wants to stay in the same, blown-up state. Anytime you bend it, it pops back to that original state."

Our other experts had slight disagreements about how easy it was to scratch an itch in the EVA suits:

LOUNGE: "The EVA suits are pressurized enough that you can't feel sensation if you try to scratch from the outside. It's not like a soft garment; it's like a hard shell. The tips of the gloves are rubber. You can move your fingers, but you don't have a good tactile sense."

LUTZ: "When the suit's not fully pressurized, that is, before you go out the door us you're getting ready for the space walk, if you get an itch on the soft part of the suit, like your arms, for instance, you can sort of compress it a little bit. You do that by squeezing with your arms from the outside of the suit.

"However, once it's pressurized and you're on the space walk, the suit makes a pretty rigid balloon. It's feasible to rub your body against the inside of the suit. We're trying to make the suits as close as we can to a snug fit, but there is enough free volume that you can move around some. You can often get enough friction to scratch a bit."

LOW: "It depends where the itch is. You can feel certain skin parts from the inside. The space suit is fairly tight. It looks bulky, but there are enough layers on the inside that you're almost touching something everywhere. You can just bend your leg or elbow [if you had an itch there]. You also typically have a little bit of room inside the chest cavity. If your shoulder itched, you could just contort yourself around there and scratch it the best you can.

"If you get a muscle cramp or charley horse, you're out of luck. You can't rub muscles from the outside at all. You can try to bend joints and flex them. You can try to rub from the inside, but basically you just have to grin and bear it."

HARTSFIELD: "I've asked the suit technicians about this. The best you can do is try to rub against some part of the suit that might be close by. If you can't do that, you're out of luck. You just grin and bear it." [Where did we hear that line before?]

"If your leg itched, you couldn't scratch it. That is, you wouldn't feel it through the suit at all if you reached there with your hand. Externally, you can't scratch through the outside of the suit. The pressure in the suit is such that, for instance, if you work with your hands and you have to make a grip, it's like trying to squeeze a balloon. If you push your leg, the pressure would go somewhere else. There are just too many layers to go through. In fact, once you're in the suit, you wouldn't even try—it's obvious that it isn't going to work.

"If you were lucky enough to have an itch somewhere close by some part of the suit you could feel on the skin, you could try to scratch it up and down but that would still be hard to do because you're wearing a liquid cooling vent garment, like a pair of long underwear. You'd have to try to scratch through that by rubbing your leg against some part of the suit."

LES space suits, much to the relief of the astronauts, are much more forgiving. Barring an emergency, they are not inflated, so they are not as stiff as EVA suits:

LUTZ: "It is a soft suit, so you can kind of press in and get to whatever scratch you have."

LAWRENCE: "For the most part, the suits are comfortable. What makes it uncomfortable is if there's a launch delay—you're lying *on your back for maybe four hours, strapped to a seat. That's the uncomfortable part. If you had an itch, however, you could scratch it through the outside of the suit."*

This is a substantial improvement from the earlier Apollo days. In his book *Liftoff,* astronaut Michael Collins talks about the exigencies of itches and other physical discomforts during the Gemini era:

> *"Inside the suit were other odds and ends, such as biomedical sensors taped to the chest with wires running to electronic amplifiers placed in pockets in the underwear. Finally, there was a 'motorman's friend,' a triangular urine bag with a condomlike device into which the astronaut inserted his penis before donning the suit. Once you're locked inside the suit, none of this gear could be adjusted, nor could an eye be rubbed, a nose blown, or an itch scratched. Some of the most fundamental amenities that we take for granted on Earth are difficult or impossible for an extravehicular astronaut."*

To be honest, we were surprised that itching wasn't more of an object of complaint or concern. But look at it this way: When the astronauts are performing a space walk or about to launch, they might actually have *other things* on their minds. Hartsfield, who has worked with so many astronauts, comments:

> *"Most astronauts, when they do a space walk, are so enthralled by the experience that their mind doesn't wander to small things like this. But perhaps we will confront this when we get into the construction of the station and we do space walks regularly— essentially construction work in orbit.*
>
> *"It might get to the point where an itch here or there would be something the astronauts actually talk about. Today, I think it doesn't even enter their minds with the six hours they've got on a typical space walk.*
>
> *"Also, they've trained in these suits for hundreds of hours. They are very comfortable with the suits already. If they're comfort-*

able on the ground, they're going to be really comfortable out in the weightlessness of space."

And it's not as if astronauts lean toward the wimpy or whiny. Many astronauts have a military background, and even those that don't tend to share the stiff-upper-lip demeanor depicted in *The Right Stuff* and *Apollo 13*. Perhaps astronaut Wendy Lawrence put it best:

> *"You just deal with it. My background is that of a Navy pilot. If you get an itch when you are in military formation and standing in ranks, you just can't scratch it. You do what you can to alleviate the discomfort, but at the same time you realize that you have to stay at attention. You come up with ways to work around the problem and try to alleviate it, but you can't get out of your main responsibility.*
>
> *"But let me tell you. When the engines are on, and you're on solid rocket boosters, it's a nit! I was so wrapped up in what was going on with the launch, and all my responsibilities with the launch, I didn't even notice any of that stuff."*

Submitted by Dallas Brozik of Huntington, West Virginia.

Imponderables X Contest

Because our tenth volume of *Imponderables* will be a milestone, of sorts, for one time only, we are going to forgo a new set of Frustables and use that space to run a few special features that we think you'll enjoy—one of which will be the results of our first-ever contest. In fact, we have three separate contests. The winners of *each* will receive a complimentary copy of our next book, a first-edition copy of the Imponderables Game, and a special surprise. Enter one or all three contests.

Contest 1:

MY IMPONDERABLES STORY

Do you have a personal story concerning anything regarding *Imponderables?* Some ideas: What's your favorite Imponderable? What's your strangest personal experience with Imponderability? How have Imponderables changed your life? What's the weirdest place you've ever read an *Imponderables* book? Has Imponderables ever had any practical benefit in your life? Has any Imponderable question or answer made you angry, made you laugh? Have you ever met another *Imponderables* reader? We'll share some of the best entries.

Contest 2:

CALL OUR BLUFF

The Imponderables (board) Game is a game of bluffing and deception. In many cases, the *real* answers to our mysteries are more unbelievable than anything we could make up. Here's your chance to see if you can shine at the gentle art of BS. The following are five Imponderables that we plan to include in *Imponderables X*. Your job is not to try to provide the *actual* answer but to come up with funny, unbelievable, bizarrely convincing, witty, or grotesquely stupid alternatives to the real answer.

1. Why is he called the "Lone Ranger" when he always travels with Tonto?

2. Why do many singers raise their eyebrows when they sing?

3. Why do passengers always seem to duck when exiting helicopters?

4. What accounts for the warm spots we sometimes encounter when swimming in the ocean?

5. Why don't dogs get cavities?

Remember, you are not trying to provide the actual answer (we'll do that) but a great bluff.

⊙⊚

Contest 3:
FIND THE MISTAKE

Eagle-eyed veteran readers will notice that one of the Imponderables in this book has been asked before in another *Imponderables* volume. What was the question, and in what other book did it appear? (The winner of this contest will be chosen at random from readers who submit the correct answer.)

As always, you can reach us at:

IMPONDERABLES
P.O. BOX 24815
LOS ANGELES, CALIFORNIA 90024

INTERNET: feldman@imponderables.com
Prodigy: imponderables@prodigy.com

The winners of contests #1 and #2 will be at our whim.

Good luck!

Frustables

Frustables Update

Our Readers Respond to the Frustables First Posed in *What Are Hyenas Laughing At, Anyway?*

Frustable 1: Why do we bite our fingernails?

When in doubt about the solution to a Frustable, why not posit a theory that nobody can disprove? And nothing is more disprovable than an anthropological answer. Reader Kwan Yeoh traces the origins of nail biting back to the Flintstones:

> *"Imagine a caveman going out to hunt with fingernails the length of his arm—not too easy to grip and throw that spear. Biting fingernails let him keep them short enough for hunting purposes."*

Presumably, cavemen didn't have the luxury of nail clippers, but we'd imagine that the vicissitudes of hunting, chopping down trees, fashioning tools, and fulfilling other chores might have provided our ancestors with a natural manicure.

Still, the notion that biting fingernails is an instinctual behavior persisted among readers, most eloquently argued by Michael J. Colvin of Lawrence, Kansas:

> *"Human pride compels us to defend the premise that instinct is only for the lower animals, but most would be surprised by how much of our behavior is still genetic and unconscious. The big drives are obvious: hunger, thirst, sex, sleep, alertness, sex, self-preservation, sex, and so on.*
>
> *"These drives are so important that they usually mask the smaller, less important drives, such as grooming. Grooming is*

something that we can do anytime, so thank goodness it is suppressed if we are being chased by a lion or if that someone special is receptive. However, if two major drives come into conflict, they may 'cancel' each other out, and smaller drives can then be expressed.

"For example, imagine you're in a job interview. You know that you must make a good impression. Your sympathetic nervous system, part of the autonomic nervous system, and sometimes known as 'fight or flight,' is preparing you to run or at least club the head of personnel over the head. These two drives compete and cancel each other out, allowing another drive to surface. You start grooming. You play with or smooth your hair, brush your already clean clothes with your hand, straighten your coat or, yes, you may start biting your nails.

"Civilization has created an artificial lifestyle that is often in conflict with what nature intended. We're put in cars and then told we can't attack someone who cuts us off in traffic. Our jobs put us under inordinate amounts of stress, but if we turn and flee we could get fired. Any situation that makes us frightened, maddened, confused, unsettled, or nervous, and which we are forced by social mores to endure, can lead to this grooming drive being expressed."

Freud lives. The most popular single argument among readers is that nail biting is a reflection of *another* instinct, the need to suckle. Is nail biting an attempt to satiate an oral fixation? Yes, argues Marvin Skudin of Merrick, New York:

"Human beings are very predictable. When in danger, whether real or imagined, a human being reverts to prenatal comfort and safety, hence the fetal position. Next best to the fetal position, which may be inconvenient during a meeting or a confrontation, is sucking your good old thumb . . .

"But thumb sucking is a no-no, and we know it. So we get our hand close to the mouth and nibble on our nails. Oral satisfaction! If adult pacifiers were put out on the market with some intelligence, there'd be no nail biters.

"Have you ever seen a nail-biting cigar 'sucker?' Cigar and

pipe suckers are really nail biters who hide behind those hideous substitutes. Chain-smokers are closet thumb suckers and nail biters."

Some of you feel that psychology is more pivotal than instinct. Reader Jana Salvatori's theory is typical:

> *"I know three people who bite their fingernails consistently and constantly. The one psychological characteristic that these three people share is a tendency to worry about everything! From college classes to work problems, these people fret about little things and torment themselves about almost anything that could possibly go wrong.*
>
> *"These three usually bite their fingernails when they have idle time—watching television, driving/riding in the car, reading a book, waiting for sleep to overtake them. This idle time allows them to think about what is worrying them and to blow things out of proportion."*

We heard from a reformed nail biter who, along with several other readers, argues that nail biting has a biological basis:

> *"Nail biting might be just a nervous habit, but from personal experience, I believe it is due to a calcium deficiency. A few years ago, a friend suggested I take a calcium supplement because my hair was in poor condition. Soon after I started, I lost all desire to bite my nails."*

"Hold it!" some readers argue: "What's wrong with biting your nails?" Rob Levandowski's response was typical:

> *"When I bite my nails, it usually seems to be because I've been noticing that my fingernails are digging into my hand, particularly if I've been clenching my fist due to stress. If the proper equipment and environment for a proper manicure aren't available, and I'm starting to lacerate myself, well . . ."*

Frank D'Agostino of Hillside, New Jersey, sent us a résumé of his nail-biting experience. He remembers, as a child, seeing his aunt trying to cure her own habit by applying nail-polish remover and iodine on her nails in an attempt to cure her compulsive nail biting. Frank admits to being a selective nail biter:

> "I put my fingernails between my teeth while pondering (including Imponderables and Frustables). For my personal life, I would prefer having well-groomed long nails, an incentive not to bite. I leave long nails alone as long as they are well rounded and not cracked. I wouldn't bite a perfectly shaped nail but have no problem biting a short, ragged one (they are already short, so no one will notice).
>
> "For my work (as a computer word processor), I need trimmed nails so I don't strike the wrong keys on the keyboard. I trim them at work. But in the absence of an emery board or scissors, away from my desk, if I feel a cracked nail I might bite it into shape. And a hanging cuticle hangs no more."

We would think that persnickety folks would be the last to bite their nails, but a few readers echoed the sentiments of Kate Stutzel of Alexandria, Virginia:

> "I bite them because I am a perfectionist. If they don't look right, I bite them to make them look better. When they don't, I bite them some more. Soon I have no nails left."

Perfectionist, heal thyself!

Some readers are convinced that the drive to bite one's nails is so strong, foul play must be involved. We received the following e-mail from Matthew Smith, at Clemson University:

> "As a lifetime nail biter, I have come to the conclusion that we bite our nails because keratin is a narcotic substance! This is obviously the reason—keratin is more addictive than heroin.
>
> "Think about it: You see nail biters everywhere. You see smok-

ers and drug addicts, too, but nail biting is much more prevalent, even in highbrow society. It seems that we can't go ten minutes without taking a whack at those sad little stubs on the ends of our fingers.

"In some cases, the urge to nibble gets so bad that people will chew on the skin at the base of the nail, in a pathetic attempt to actually make their own fingers shorter so as to allow for more room to gnaw away at the nail.

"I think it's about time our government starts funding research into the addictive powers of keratin. Maybe, just maybe there is a 'Nail-Anon' waiting to be discovered that will finally put an end to this terrible scourge."

While you're at it, better set up a "Feline-anon" branch. Kathy Howe, of San Lorenzo, California, reports:

"When my son bit his nails, our cat bit her nails to keep him company."

Of course, there's a danger to forming such groups—people will *get ideas*. Bill Gerk, who is to Frustables what a hungry Doberman is to a hot dog, has moved from northern California to Tucson, Arizona (no doubt to be in a better position to work on Frustables twelve months a year in a sunny clime), and has an idiosyncratic take on why we bite our nails:

"To bite our fingernails is our personal responsibility. We cannot reasonably expect other humans to bite our fingernails for us. After all, who knows where someone else's hand has been in the last ten years—or even as late as yesterday.

"Dave, how many times in your lifetime have you or any of your thousands of readers had the urge to bite another's fingernails? Case closed."

We're beginning to think that closing this case is a *very* good idea.

Original Imponderable submitted by Anthony D. Townsend of Advance Mills, Virginia. Thanks also to Richard Morrow of Warrendale, South Carolina; Michelle and Mitchell Szczepancyzk of Grand Rapids, Michigan; Zina Bennion of Spring City, Utah; Connie DePew of Boulder, Colorado; Etan Goldman of North Hollywood, California; Lacey Callow of St. Joseph, Missouri; Thomas Hilleary of Chesterfield, Missouri; Richard Galya of Spotswood, New Jersey; and many others.

A complimentary book goes to Michael J. Colvin of Lawrence, Kansas.

Frustable 2: Why do people feel the urge to urinate when they hear running water?

....

Occasionally, a reader will ask: "What does it mean when at the end of the list of Imponderable submitters, it says 'and many others' after the last name?" Our policy is to list the first ten readers who ask a question and to include the "many others" if more than three other readers pose the same Imponderable. In this case, the tenth reader, Michael Rusak, wrote us about this question in 1993. More than ten readers have asked the same question since Michael.

We've been trying to track down the answer to this mystery for ten years. And we've come to one sure conclusion, after consulting scores of urologists: Urologists don't know. We got sick of asking urologists this question and receiving a collective shoulder shrug. Would *Imponderables* readers do any better? We think they have.

Urologists were fond of citing "Pavlov" and "conditioning" and "involuntary reflex," without offering any particular context.

Some readers echoed the physicians' sentiment, but with a little more panache. Typical was the University of Virginia's Will Shaw:

> *"It's simple conditioning. As people urinate their whole lives, they are conditioned to associate the sound of running water with urination. To condition and frequently reinforce the association of water noise with urination, in our bathrooms we hear running water from sink, baths, and showers—right there in the room with the commode.*
>
> *"In [public] rest rooms, [private] bathrooms, and outhouses, what do we generally hear when we urinate? Running water, right? It would be surprising were people* not *to eventually be conditioned to associate the action with the sound. Even Pavlov's dog could figure this one out."*

Is it quite so simple? Not according to New York City's Ronni Bennett, who puts the "blame" on Mom:

> *"I think it's because it is an age-old custom of mothers to toilet train us by sitting us on the toilet (even little boys when they are that young—Dad teaches them to stand later) and leaving the water running in the basin until we get the idea. It usually takes several weeks until a kid 'gets' it, and by then the die is cast for life."*

Ex–early-childhood teacher Nadine Lada of Salem, Massachusetts, subscribes to Bennett's theory and can't resist adding a gratuitous parting shot:

> *"Urologists were the wrong group of experts to ask. Next time, try Mother first."*

Bennett added that regardless of when she last visited the bathroom, a prolonged bout of dishwashing will soon require another trip to the john. The power of association is so strong that even verbal references can induce torture. David Lieberman of

Decorah, Iowa, pleads guilty to conducting some questionable "field research" of his own:

> *"My friends and I play horribly cruel jokes on each other, usually when we're in the middle of nowhere, miles from a bathroom. If someone mentions the need to go to the rest room, we start teasing him or her about running water and that overwhelming feeling of relief when you finally, actually, urinate. I don't play that trick anymore ever since Kris missed urinating in my truck by about two seconds on the way to Winnipeg."*

A few readers insisted there were deeper, anthropological explanations for the association between hearing running water and the urge to urinate. Rockford, Illinois's, Chris Beach notes an article he read about sloths in the Amazon rain forests that he felt cast some light on this subject:

> *"In studying the sloths, the researchers noticed a curious pattern. The sloths would typically not defecate or urinate for days at a time. However, when the rains came, these sloths would simply let loose. To prove it wasn't just a coincidence, researchers duplicated the phenomenon with a captured sloth and a garden hose.*
>
> *"Was this an odd curiosity or was there an evolutionary advantage to it? Researchers concluded that it was indeed related to survival.*
>
> *"Sloths, because they are so slow, are very susceptible to predators. In fact, many times Amazon hunters just cut the limb from which the sloth is hanging and carry it back to camp, hanging sloth and all. So the key to the sloth's survival is being undetected. In a quiet jungle, sloth droppings from ten feet above would be a giveaway. Even if the sound isn't heard, the evidence on the forest floor would still be a problem. So the sloth evolved to evacuate whenever the Amazon rain falls.*
>
> *"So how could this relate to humans? The article didn't say, but the parallels are very clear. Humans were both hunters and hunted (sometimes by other humans). In both cases, stealth is the*

key. Having an involuntary urge to urinate when the sound is masked would be an advantage."

If the sound of a human urinating could attract unwanted predators, what about the smell? Ketan Gangatirkar, of Essex Junction, Vermont, provides us with a fascinating theory that he warns us is "backed up by absolutely *no* scientific data or reasoning but that can masquerade as a product of such." Sounds good to us!

> *"Urine has a scent. Back in pretool times (when we were the hunted and not the hunters), we had to be careful about being smelled. A dry-land sprinkle deposit could more or less trace our path through the untamed wilds of the African savanna.*
>
> *"By urinating in running water, we not only dilute the scent greatly but we disguise where it comes from, as well. Thus, when running water is heard, our subconscious says, 'Go do your business.'"*

We were astonished to receive this biological explanation from retired science teacher Marvin H. Skudin of Merrick, New York.

> *"Urination is an involuntary reflex when the sound of water is heard. Running water emits a sound whose frequency not only runs in the audible range but also has an inaudible harmonic. This harmonic causes a vibration similar to the vibration of a glass when the soprano hits a high note and cracks the glass.*
>
> *"This harmonic tone causes a tiny ossicle in the inner ear to vibrate gently. The ossicle transmits a signal to the brain . . . which in turn sends a coded message to the bladder controller. Once the bladder controller descrambles the message and you get the 'go,' you had better hurry up because you can't stop it.*
>
> *"Once the bladder is cleared, the ossicle's signal can no longer affect the brain's bladder-control center. Therefore, the urge is gone."*

David Feldman

Skudin claims that as we age, the brain starts receiving many "false positive" signals. He concludes:

> *"Doctors, especially urologists, blame incontinence on the prostate gland, but now you know the truth. Forget about prostate medicines; get a pair of earplugs."*

Actually, we already have the earplugs. But we were using them to solve the next-door-neighbor playing AC/DC CD's problem.

Finally, after appearing on Derek McGinty's talk show in Washington, D.C., listener J. R. Myers e-mailed us with some observations about this Frustable. As an active outdoorsmen for more than twenty-five years, Myers notes that many men seem to be "pee shy," unable to urinate either in silence or when in the presence of other men. He speculates that although such men are often thought to be modest or sensitive about urinating in front of others, many of them are exhibiting the behavior that many women have written to us questioning about: Why many men flush the toilet *while* urinating:

> *"They will flush once or many times before or during the time when they urinate, regardless of whether the urinal was flushed or not after its previous use. They need to hear the water flowing to get going! As a guy, I can't know but would be very fascinated to know the experiences of women regarding this."*

We haven't met a female multiflusher, but we'll bet there are some out there, J.R. Most of the urologists we contacted mentioned that they often run the sink in their offices to induce a patient to "start his urinary stream," but they seem to be referring only to males.

Submitted by Scott Geller of New York, New York. Thanks also to Karen Maynard of Snohomish, Washington; Alena Smith of Millbrook, New York; Ruth Egan of Thompson Falls, Montana; Robert Matlock of Houston, Texas; Mary Kay Smith of Piqua, Ohio; Peter Geran of Bethesda, Maryland; Mark La

Chance of Pleasanton, California; Jason Roeller of Bristol, Tennessee; Michael Rusak of Sun Valley, California; and many others.

A complimentary book goes to Chris Beach of Rockford, Illinois.

Frustable 3: Why do many children refuse to say "thank-you" for gifts received, especially if their parents pressure them to express appreciation?

Most of the child psychologists we consulted about this Frustable noted the prevalence of the phenomenon but were less articulate about trying to explain it than were our readers. We had hoped that maybe we'd receive some confessions from minors. We get many letters from kids, but none would own up to being an ungrateful wretch, let alone explain why. So we'll have to be content with adults theorizing about the behavior of kids, and in some cases, remembering how they felt when they refused to say "thank-you" when they were younger.

By far the most common explanation for the "no-thank-you" behavior, especially from parents, was some variation of this statement by Foster City, California's, Randy Delucchi:

> *"As a parent of two, I can tell you that this one is easy. They refuse to say thank-you for the same reason children do other things 180 degrees differently than parents just asked—to assert authority. Kids beginning to realize they can influence the world like to test it out. So if Dad says, 'Move your glass away from the edge of the table, you're going to spill,' they don't. If Mom says, 'Sit on the chair,' they don't."*

Once a parent asks a child to do something, the issue of control inevitably rears its ugly head. As many of you, such as Erik Hanson, of Richmond, Virginia, argue, kids do not respond well to pressure:

"Children tend to refuse to do anything *their parents pressure them to do. I used to get so upset when my parents told me to do something that I knew I should do or that I was planning on doing, I would often then not perform that activity, just because I felt that I was being controlled . . ."*

And as Erik Reichmann, of Howell, New Jersey, points out, giving thanks for a present is hardly an exciting or fulfilling behavior for a kid:

"Kids hate being forced to comply with stuffy old manners, because they take all the fun and spontaneity out of life."

Several readers wanted to put the blame solely in the laps of the parents. Kathy Czopek, of St. Louis, Missouri, was vehement:

"Parents should be able to discipline well enough that their child cannot refuse to do anything. If their parents let them get away with it, it's the parents' fault."

Likewise, Bill Gerk sees it as the parents' job to teach their children not only proper manners but also to *feel* appreciation for the little blessings of life:

"In fact, those children will extend their thankfulness through their teenage years and into their adult life, so their children won't be surprised, as Mark Twain was, "at how smart my father became between the time I was eighteen and twenty-one years of age."

But a strong minority of you were far more sympathetic with the plight of children in these circumstances. Sandra Hildreth, of Burleson, Texas, wrote:

"Some children have not learned to lie and cannot show gratitude for gifts they either don't like or don't want."

And Erik Reichmann shows sympathy for the kids' point of view:

> "Children resent hypocrisy, especially if they've witnessed it themselves in adults. That's why kids can be unrelentingly cruel to their less popular peers—they lack the skill of empathizing with others, and they cannot understand that a certain amount of hypocrisy is necessary to be socially accepted.
>
> "Think back to your childhood: When you received a gift that you couldn't stand or had absolutely no interest in, did you really want to thank the grandparent or aunt or cousin who gave it to you? More likely, you were upset that you were stuck with these ugly clothes or boring books and angry that the giver didn't bother to find out what you wanted.
>
> "Compounding this was the indignity of composing a thank-you note in which you had to describe the pleasure you derived from the gift, plus the impending horror that your benefactor would expect you to wear the hideous outfit the next time he or she saw you, or would ask if you enjoyed the present. Even as an adult, it's difficult to muster phony gratitude for an underwhelming gift, but at least you know you can take it back to the store whence it came and exchange it for something better.
>
> "This same aversion to hypocrisy explains why children refuse to apologize when compelled to. After all, if you're not sorry about kicking sand in some other kid's face, or calling the fattest kid in the class a 'tub o' guts,' why should you humiliate yourself by saying you are?"

Is it humiliating for a child to say thank-you or to be instructed to say thank-you? Several of you argued that it was. Jenny Litz, of State College, Pennsylvania, wrote:

> "For my son and from what I remember about being a kid, it's belittling and embarrassing to be controlled in this way. How would you feel if someone told you what to say to a person who is much larger and scarier than you, especially if you were shy? It doesn't stop me from asking my son to say these things (I want

him to learn manners), but I know that it's really difficult for him."

Finally, some of you noted the enormity of the importance that children assign to gifts. Often, silence interpreted as rudeness is actually an inability to express appreciation. Kwan Yeoh, of Eastwood, Australia, observes:

"Maybe kids are embarrassed at the kindness bestowed upon them by the giver of the gift. Being young, they cannot properly vocalize their embarrassment (especially if they've just damaged that person's backyard flower bed), so they don't say 'thank-you.' "

New York City's Ronni Bennett remembers the embarrassment of being reprimanded publicly for the failure to issue an immediate thank-you and feeling the very sentiments Kwan Yeoh theorized about:

"Two simple words did not seem to be sufficient in response—particularly to family members—who went out of their way to do something nice for me. It's also the reason it's hard to get kids to write thank-you notes—nothing they can say in a note is comparable to the bulk of a gift to a kid, so they feel inadequate to the task and believe they will fail . . ."

In conclusion, after musing about his bouts of ingratitude, Erik Hanson offers an alternative, and rather simple, reason why he and many kids often don't offer up a "thank-you":

"The gifts usually sucked."

A complimentary book goes to Erik Reichmann of Howell, New Jersey.

Frustable 4: Why do people tend to reposition their plates when served?

We'll admit it. This Frustable has become an obsession with us. We've observed thousands of restaurant and banquet diners over the past few years and found that plate repositioners come in all ages, shapes, and sizes, and they live all over North America. Much to our surprise, *Imponderables* readers have also mulled over the significance of this ritual; we received an outpouring of mail on this Frustable.

Many of you objected to our observation (in *What Are Hyenas Laughing At, Anyway?*) that most plate repositioning is probably unconscious. On the contrary, asserted the majority of readers— most people are quite conscious of feeling uncomfortable when confronted with a new plate of food. David Sampson, who works for KCAL-TV in Los Angeles, put it this way:

> *"Try letting someone else put your hat on your head. Guaranteed, it won't feel right until you adjust it. I think the same is true for plates. It doesn't 'fit' until we adjust the plate just right."*

Another Los Angeleno, Craig Miller, notes that in fancy restaurants, waiters take care in positioning the plate, noting the food's distance from the diner, as well as where the food lies on the plate. According to Miller, even the position of a humble piece of pie can raise hackles:

> *"In the United States, most diners will turn a wedge of pie so that it points to them. In Europe, they'll generally leave the pie facing whatever way the waiter puts it down."*

Lest we think that this is an American fixation, Steven Hanov, of Hamilton, Ontario, insists:

"Everyone has an exact place in front of them where they are used to eating from plates. When a waiter or waitress places the plate in front of a customer, it is unlikely that it will be in this exact position, so before eating, everyone will adjust their plate so that it will be in the right position."

Everyone? Judging from the vociferousness of readers, Steven might be right. But not everyone has the same priorities when readjusting the plates. Readers shared many different positioning strategies:

First Things First. (Dave Hanlon, Manassas, Virginia)

"Each of us has a personal preference as to how far away we want our plate to be. Sometimes, this preference extends to what we want to eat first. Maybe you want to eat the peas before the meat, or at the very least, get the broccoli as far away from you as possible.

"Now, how likely is it that a server is going to put your plate exactly where you want it? Not very. The server is probably more concerned about getting the right plate to the right person without spilling anything on the table."

The Knife's the Thing. (Edward Suranyi, Fremont, California)

"Hold a knife and fork in the usual way and pretend you're cutting some food on a plate in front of you. There will be one most natural place for the cutting action to take place . . .

"I always move my plate so that the first action I take on the main item of food on my plate (which is usually a piece of meat) is the most comfortable. Often that means not only moving the plate as a whole to the best position but turning it as well, so that the angle of the first cut I want to make matches that 'natural' angle.

"For most food items that require cutting, the shape of the item makes one cutting direction preferable. For example, a long, thin piece of meat practically demands to be cut across its width."

The Fork's the Thing. (Mary Zimmerman, via Prodigy e-mail)

"I adjust my plate so that the food is at the most comfortable and accessible angle for my fork. When someone else sets the plate down, it is awkward to reach the food and bring it to my mouth without dropping some. I suspect we each have a comfortable fork range of our own."

The Main Course Is the Thing. (David Crowder, Miami, Florida)

"I like to have the main course nearest to me and the side dishes some reach away. I would definitely turn a plate around so as not to have to reach over the fries to get at the hamburger. Keeps your sleeves out of the ketchup, too."

Proximity Makes the Stomach Grow Fonder. (Rob Levandowski, Rochester, New York)

"This Frustable seems simple enough: the purpose is to get the portion of food you want to eat close to you! Perhaps you wanted to start with the side-dish item that was positioned away from you. Humans are 'into' minimal effort, and it takes less effort to turn the plate once than to reach over it several times.

"Besides, if one goes the extra distance, there may be other things in the way (like heaping mounds of mashed potatoes, one of my favorite navigational hazards), increasing the difficulty of getting to the desired food, and increasing the likelihood of an embarrassing social gaffe through slippage."

Aesthetics, Baby, Aesthetics. (Ashley Roach, Arlington, Virginia)

"It seems to me that when I adjust my plate, it is so that it looks correct, balanced and 'pretty'—visually aesthetic."

So many readers insisted on these issues of positional preferences that we feel wretched mentioning a four-letter word: *soup*. If all these readers were right, diners wouldn't have any need to

𝕯avid 𝕱eldman

reposition bowls of soup or, for that matter, bowls of pasta. But they do. So while we're not disputing their preferences, other factors must be at work as well.

Andy Pforzheimer of Wilton, Connecticut, notes that many folks touch the plate to see if it's hot. Indeed, many servers we have spoken to about this Frustable have told us that a warning about the hotness of a plate seems to be interpreted as a command to touch it anyway. Not enough folks have taken the advice of reader Grant Porter:

> *"They haven't been to enough Mexican restaurants where the temperature of the plate is about five hundred degrees Fahrenheit. A few trips to one of these places and you'll start leaving your food where they put it."*

Funny that we consider a child who puts his hand on a stove as reckless and immature, yet we seem to have an instinctive need to test our food for hotness.

Two readers indicated that many folks feel tense in restaurants when food is first served. Reader David Hopkins e-mailed us:

> *"Nobody wants to be the first to start chowing down at a table full of people, so moving the plate is a simple way to 'stall' and put the pressure on others."*

Others found different reasons for the tenseness at the table. Cyberspace correspondent Norman Shosid thinks that we reposition our plates for "the same reason dogs guard their food dishes"—to mark our territory. If your friends are like ours, a restaurant meal can be a competitive sport. As Bill Gerk puts it, repositioning the plate gives the diner

> *"a feeling of personal control in a social situation and a physical staking out of their territorial claim."*

Could this strange ritual be explained as an anthropological throwback? Do we unconsciously look at our tablemates as competitors for our grub? And are we made uncomfortable by the close proximity of the waiter or waitress when delivering our food? Ketan Gangatirkar of Essex Junction, Vermont, who argued for a prehistorical explanation two Frustables back, makes a similarly compelling case here:

> *"Repositioning plates is a way of asserting control. In prehistory, competition for food must have been fierce. Thus, touching one's food (or more broadly, throwing in a little unnecessary command or laying a hand on a mate's shoulder) could be just a way of asserting control, indicating that 'This is mine. Don't touch or you'll have to deal with me.' "*

Watch most animals before they eat food and you'll notice rituals surrounding the enterprise. We're convinced that the repositioning is far from a strictly rational act. Since we've been doing field research on this Imponderable, we've noticed some folks who move their plates mere centimeters in one direction or the other. The need to make food "our own" seems to supplant even our insatiable need to devour it.

Submitted by Jim Vibber of Tustin, California.

A complimentary book goes to Ketan Gangatirkar of Essex Junction, Vermont.

David Feldman

Frustable 5: Why do so many public buildings keep the internal temperatures so warm in the winter and so cold in the summer, particularly because this policy increases fuel bills during all seasons?

This question didn't attract the passionate arguments that some of the other Frustables did, but as usual, disagreement reigned. Most of you believe that businesses are trying to lure customers by offering superior comfort during the two most uncomfortable seasons. As University of Oregon architecture student Mike Wheeler puts it:

> *"In the summer, it feels refreshing to enter a cool space when you've been out in the hot weather; vice versa for the winter. This temperature difference will supposedly make the customer think the place cares a lot about their comfort and will spend a lot to provide it."*

Or as Howard Wilson II of Mustang, Oklahoma, sees it,

> *". . . the reason is they want you inside. What do you want in the summer? You want one thing: to cool off. You start dreamily thinking of the movie theater, wonderfully cold . . ."*

So, a cold movie theater in summer or a warm, toasty department store in winter may be a refuge for some. But it doesn't explain this phenomenon. On a ninety-degree day, a walk into a seventy-two-degree room will feel wonderful—there's no need to make the room simulate Arctic conditions. Furthermore, the comfort reaction ceases quickly, as humans rapidly adjust to changes in the ambient temperature. The eighty-degree office that seemed so wonderful when you started work at 9:00 A.M. on a winter's morning will make you drowsy and lethargic within a half hour. Most businesses would prefer to keep their interiors on the cool side all year long: workers are more efficient and consumers more active in cooler temperatures.

Besides, it's hard to believe that businesses would want to spend the extra money for overcooling or overheating their physical plants. Reader Greg Zywicki notes that with some heating and air-conditioning systems, it can be cheaper to

> *"just cool or heat the heck out of the place on a set schedule than to try to deal with the constant fluctuations that would have to be dealt with when trying to actually maintain a more reasonable temperature."*

Several readers blamed the annoyance on outmoded or improperly designed HVAC (Heating-Ventilation-Air-Conditioning) systems, and many of you recounted stories about your futile efforts to maintain a comfortable temperature in your own apartments and houses. Dallas Brozik, a professor at Marshall University in Huntington, West Virginia, wrote to us while temporarily living in Boston:

> *"The crux of the problem has to do with positioning of the temperature sensor and the ventilation ducts. If a large building has a single thermostat in the middle of the building and the ducts are along the outer walls, it takes time for the hot or cold air from the ducts to reach the thermostat. Along the way, this air must heat or cool everything in its path, so the temperature gradient from the outer edge of the building to the core could be pretty steep by the time the thermostat senses the proper temperature and shuts down the system. Of course, by this time, the edges of the building are uncomfortably high or low, but the radiation of heat from the windows (either in or out) begins to reverse the gradient. It takes time for this new temperature to reach the thermostat, and the whole process starts all over again.*
>
> *"Actually, in large buildings, there is a complex system of multiple sensors and air ducts, but there is often only one central heating or cooling unit. The distribution of the conditioned air is a real trick, and when the outdoor temperature is significantly dif-*

ferent from the indoor temperature, there are bound to be imbalances. In the winter, these imbalances involve heated air, so you feel hot. In the summer, the air is cooled, so you feel chilled. You could probably have a system designed that would keep every room a perfect temperature, but it would surely be quite pricey and require a lot of maintenance.

"You probably have seen this effect in your apartment. There is a central heating plant, but you control the heat locally through an individual thermostat or the knob on your radiator. In our Boston apartment, the whole building is so warm that we sometimes have to open the windows to get the rooms down to a decent temperature [this letter was dated January 3]. If every office had its own radiator and window air conditioner, everyone would be happy. In our house in Huntington, the thermostat is upstairs near the center of the house. The bedrooms have outer walls, and the temperature in each room is the result of its location relative to the thermostat, the configuration of the air registers, and air leakage around the windows. Aren't you glad you're not a HVAC engineer?"

Yep.

With thermostats unable to keep pace with the temperature changes inside a room, let alone an entire building, the problems of factoring in the heat generated by humans can cause an amazing amount of havoc. Last New Year's Eve, reader Greg Zywicki "roasted" at a packed movie house:

"It turned out that the theater didn't even have the heat on. It was just body heat, probably made worse by everyone taking off their nice warm coats and releasing that layer of warm air."

At first we questioned the veracity of the following story, but consultation with HVAC engineers indicates that what reader Patrick Couzens, a construction worker, recently encountered is a growing trend—heatless hot offices:

"As far as the heat in most office buildings today is concerned—there is none. We recently finished construction on a *twenty-story structure here in Kansas City, Missouri, and the only heaters in the place were very small ones aimed at the windows to keep them from misting over.*

"The technician from Honeywell said that all the bodies, lighting, and computers provide more than enough heat to keep the place warm, and the only way to mitigate the heat is to fire up the air conditioning. This also explains why office buildings are so cold after a long weekend and why they take so long to heat up."

One reader, Raymond Fischer of Campbell, California, insists that much of this temperature discrepancy consists of end user perception. He makes three interesting observations:

1. "People notice the temperature most when it changes. In the summer, when they come into a cool(er) building, the building at first seems cold. Similarly, in the winter, the building seems warm when coming in from a cold day."

2. "People are dressed for the outdoors when they enter a building. They are bundled up in winter and lightly dressed in the summer. Of course, a building seems warm when you're wearing a coat, or cool when you're lightly dressed."

3. "I suspect that people's bodies adapt to ambient temperature. You sweat when it's warm; skin capillaries open or constrict to radiate or retain heat. When one first enters a building, the body is trying to maintain temperature for the outside, and when inside, it often provides the wrong response. The building's temperature seems more extreme because of that.

"As an example, put one hand in a glass of ice water and another in a glass of hot water. After a minute or so, put both in a lukewarm tub. That hand that was in the cold water will feel warm, and the hand that was in the hot water will feel cool, even though both were in the same tub."

Fair enough, although we'd guess that after a minute or two, both would feel lukewarm!

We don't think this perception is all in our heads. You can call us paranoid if you wish. But at least we're not as paranoid as Guinevere Knight, of Fallon, Nevada, who offers a "unique" solution to this Frustable:

> *"It is a government plot to make this country into a superrace of people. It is well known that repeated exposure to extreme temperature changes causes people to get illnesses, such as pneumonia. The majority of the population would survive such an illness, but slowly all of the weaker people would die off, leaving only the strong people alive to procreate.*
>
> *"If they raise the thermostat a few degrees higher every winter and lower it a few degrees every summer, eventually they will kill off everyone but the extremely fit people and will have a superrace."*

Original Imponderable submitted by Karole Rathouz of Mehlville, Missouri. Thanks also to Daniel Springer of Allentown, Pennsylvania.

A complimentary book goes to Dallas Brozik of Huntington, West Virginia.

Frustable 6: Why do bands in nightclubs always start performing late?

....

When we posed this Frustable originally, we mused:

> *"Is this a deliberate policy of club owners? Are bands in the dressing room ingesting controlled substances? Or tuning their instruments? Or combing their hair? Or dirtying their hair? Are customers invariably tardy and the clubs bowing to reality?"*

After being flooded with responses, mostly by musicians, we have come to the conclusion that the answers to these questions are: Yes. Yes. Yes. Yes. No (at least they won't admit to it). Yes.

The reasons why bands never seem to start on time are legion, but we've classified them into five general categories:

1. Inadvertent Fumbling. Erik Reichmann of Howell, New Jersey, innocently suggests:

> *"I should think that bands in nightclubs start performing late for the same reason that weddings always start late—there's just so much to do!"*

Patrick Plaskett, a Tampa Bay, Florida, area guitarist who has played in bands for more than twenty-five years, elaborates:

> *"There are countless points of preparation for a performance, and a performer is never acutely aware of them until the moment that it's time to go on: The microphone cord that you intended to fix is acting up again. Or the sax player's reed isn't quite pliable enough. Or the G-string on the guitar just started slipping.*
>
> *"If everyone isn't ready, the band isn't ready. Many musicians show up early to take care of any preperformance difficulties, but many feel like most Americans that if they show up at the job site on time, they're doing their job."*

2. **Band Preferences.** A few readers interpreted this Frustable to mean "Why aren't set times at nightclubs *earlier?*" rather than the intended "Why don't bands start at the scheduled time?" Karen Miller, of San Jose, California, posed the former question to the owner of J.J.'s Blues Lounge in San Jose and was told that it is hard to book bands any earlier than 9:00 P.M. because musicians have day jobs or other professional work: producing records or videos, personal appearances, and, in the case of semipro bands, nine-to-five jobs.

But the exigencies of employment and other obligations are often a reason for tardiness, too. Musician Mayhap Ben Yeast of Lebanon Junction, Kentucky, told *Imponderables* that traffic jams and running low on gas have been reasons for late gigs in his experience.

You wouldn't think of it by looking at them, but musicians are athletes of sorts. Bopping around onstage with instruments is not unlike doing aerobics while carrying weights. Reader Ted Janowski, bass player for the band Take It and Go, reports that his gigs often are scheduled to run from 8:00 P.M. until 2:00 A.M.:

"If we start on time, I know that I get very tired. Playing in a band is like a gym workout. The average guitar or bass weighs twelve to eighteen pounds. Try dancing around with twenty sacks of flour around your neck for four hours."

So is that why bass players are always so skinny? We think we'd prefer to be drummers, so we could sit down on the job.

3. Band Psychology. Larry Reckner, who hails from Saratoga Springs, New York, is a member of an "alternative" band called Synergy and admits to preshow jitters that can cause delays:

"Just before you go on, you tend to get very nervous. You don't want to go out and play in front of 300-plus people when you are nervous. That tends to make things go very bad (I know this from experience). You want everyone in the band to be ready and semi-calm before you go out and play."

New York City musician Matthew Sharlot sees the tardiness as a chicken-egg phenomenon, with plenty of the responsibility squarely on the shoulders of the audience:

"It is a vicious circle to some degree. Nowadays, everybody assumes a band will go on at least thirty minutes late, so people go to the clubs later and later.

"But I'll admit from my own personal experience that for the sake of one's ego, it feels a lot 'safer' to go on after people have loosened up with a couple of drinks. After waiting around, the crowd is much more receptive to the band taking the stage. Of course, when you're the unknown opening act and have to get up in front of a crowd that has just realized the act they're paying to see won't be on for well over an hour, the response isn't always so 'welcoming.'"

The musicians we heard from all seemed to prefer the second set to the first. Typical was Patrick Plaskett's response:

"The early crowd is in no great rush. In fact, they're rather laid-back. The band doesn't wish to keep the audience waiting, but they know that the first set will be a warm-up, with more people coming in later on. The later crowd will be looser and more fun to play to, so at the beginning of the evening, there is not the same level of motivation [for the band].

"In the final analysis, most musicians would like to start on time, but if it doesn't happen, they feel that getting upset about it will do nothing to enhance the quality of the performance."

A few readers felt there were elements of "power trip" in the tardiness of bands. As Frank Gilbuena, of Rosemont, Pennsylvania, put it:

"Some bands like to start late to build the audience's anticipation, and some are just plain rude, and sometimes there's a fine line in between. A group that's full of itself will take an 'audience be damned' attitude . . ."

Musician Kwan Yeoh asserts that the same kind of psychology persists in Australia:

"Waiting for the performance to start increases the frustration of the audience. As any good businessperson knows, this gives the party that is late more perceived power and more control over the situation. The audience is then more hyped and will respond better to the band."

4. Nightclub Preferences. What's in it for the nightclub to have bands start late? *Imponderables* readers found several. As orchestra leader of his eponymous big band, Mike Sloan writes:

"We start late so that once the performance starts, there is an absolute minimum of disruption and distraction. You delay the start a few minutes so you give the audience a chance to get settled into their seats."

By waiting, the club also maximizes the size of the audience, especially in clubs that have only one set per night.

But the most popular theory among readers to explain the club's equity in tardy bands was simple: the later a set starts, the longer patrons have to hang around. Ergo, the club can sell more drinks before the music begins. Some readers felt that this was the *only* reason for late bands and let us know in no uncertain terms that only a twelve-year-old would think this was a Frustable. Come to think of it, we did hear from a twelve-year-old, Adam Moses of Oak Park, Illinois:

> *"I'm only twelve years old, so I don't have much experience, but my parents do, so that's okay. If a band is scheduled to start at ten o'clock, and they do, then an average person might arrive on schedule and buy just a couple of drinks. (All right, a few more.)*
>
> *"But if they start an hour late, a person will buy that many drinks and more before the show begins! It's a plot to get people to buy more drinks and spend more money. I would suggest that maybe it isn't the band's fault but the fault of the nightclub's owners. Now remember, I'm only twelve, so don't sue me if I'm wrong, huh?"*

Don't try to get away with that ageist defense, Adam. But many of your more venerable peers agree with you, such as Grant Porter of Norcross, Georgia:

> *"If a customer were to arrive late and hear the band (and didn't like it) before he was settled with a beer, he might not come in. Once a customer has a beer, he is committed."*

And the way some bands sound, he is ready to *be* committed.

Our pal Ted Janowski reminds us that there are rarely any clocks on display in nightclubs. Owners want us to forget time, just as the casinos in Las Vegas do. One of the reasons why clubs keep music until closing time is to distract the majority of the patrons from the realization that they have to go to school or work the following morning.

Richard Chisak of Kingston, Pennsylvania, offers an ingenious reason why club managers would want their bar bands to start late every set:

> *"Most bar bands in Pennsylvania (with its 2:00 A.M. closing time) perform from 10:00 P.M. until 2:00 A.M. Dividing this time into four one-hour sets, this means that a band usually performs for forty minutes followed by a twenty-minute break.*
>
> *"Thus, if a band started 'on time' at exactly 10:00 P.M. and took its break at forty minutes past, its final set of the evening would begin at 1:00 A.M. and end at 1:40 A.M.—twenty minutes before the bar's closing time.*
>
> *"What bar owner wants his paid entertainment to conclude a rollicking performance—and a crowd of customers to leave—a full twenty minutes before closing time?"*

Of course, customers who remain at the bar until the bitter end tend to be hard-core drinkers, the bar owner's greatest friend.

5. Controlled Substances. We'd be remiss if we didn't add that an occasional musician has been known to partake of certain illicit substances, and said abuse has led to tardiness (and far worse things). Most of the musicians we heard from indicated that most performers are smart enough not to abuse drugs or alcohol before a gig (if drug taking does occur, it would be far more likely after the show).

Still, we did hear from a few club owners and music promoters who indicated that drugs have been the reason for lateness at shows in nightclubs and bigger venues, as well. As long as there are nightclubs and musicians, there will be illicit substances, which makes us happy to report that there are no hot spots in Earlville, New York, for we would otherwise fear for reader Ariel Godwin's future:

> *"I live in a two-thousand-population town, without anything approaching a nightclub. But if I were in one of those bands, yeah,*

I'd probably be in the dressing room ingesting controlled substances."

A complimentary book goes to Adam Moses of Oak Park, Illinois.

Frustable 7: Why is advanced math required in high school and college, when many think that, say, geometry and calculus are irrelevant to their lives?

As we said in *Hyenas,*

> *"In an age of calculators and computers, many readers have posed this question as an Imponderable, wondering why anyone but aspiring mathematicians and scientists should be required to learn advanced math."*

We were inundated with responses to this Frustable, and as you might expect, more than a few of our correspondents were mathematicians, who argued persuasively for the inclusion of higher mathematics in school curricula. But there were a few cynics, who saw the persistence of math in schools as a vestige of the liberal-arts tradition. Harlan Sexton, of Menlo Park, California, writes:

> *"My first reason is inertia. Training in Greek and Latin (in order to read the classics) has pretty much died out, but a lot of collateral subjects (such as mythology and Euclidian geometry) are still in the curriculum.*
> *"My second is the 'liberal arts' model of education. You are supposed to be exposed to a little bit about a lot of topics, because that will make you better able to hold your own at a cocktail party, or something."*

David Crowder, the son of a college president ("I thought everybody's last name was Ph.D."), observes:

"These academicians are incredibly hidebound traditionalists. Once something gets started, it becomes enshrined. For example, pharmacists, according to my old Latin teacher, need about two pages of Latin to do their jobs but are required (or at least were some years ago) to take two years of the language to qualify as an RPh.

". . . So the reason that you have to take courses in subjects that are of no use whatsoever to you is: because they are there. Besides, what are you going to do with a math professor who has tenure if you don't have him teach?"

Sure, some high schools may include advanced math only so that their brighter students can more easily get accepted to better liberal-arts colleges (where a well-rounded academic background is prized) or technical schools where math training is essential. But the irony is that the "outdated" curriculum has never been more useful than it is today, as our ex-cynic, Harlan Sexton, forcefully argues:

"The problem is not that people take too much mathematics but that they take too little, and what they take is very poorly integrated with other topics. Technology, in its many forms, is certainly the most important force in modern history, but it is impossible to have any appreciation for engineering or science without some understanding of these disciplines. In fact, a great deal of the progress in engineering in the last thirty years is the result of using much more sophisticated mathematical modeling, made possible by the development of digital computers.

"I believe that the most important cultural achievement of the twentieth century is the development of quantum mechanics. Most people laugh when I say this. Certainly modern electronics, such as the transistor and integrated circuit, would be impossible without it. Yet trying to explain quantum mechanics to someone who is mathematically illiterate is much harder than trying to explain Shakespeare to someone who can't read."

Stephen Brick, a math professor at the University of South Alabama, echoes the above arguments:

> *"What we need is more education, not less. It is what will help change the society for the better. And basic science should be part of that education. And of course,* math is the language of science.
> *"And don't forget, an educated populace will be more likely to buy your books, Dave."*

Bring on the math classes, then!

One of the country's foremost math historians, Judith Grabiner of Pitzer College, feels that high schools have an obligation to train students in math for purely practical reasons:

> *"Many careers—in social work and business as well as in medicine and science—are closed to students who can't handle algebra, calculus, graphs, and statistics. Students in high school who drop math are often unwittingly shutting themselves out of a large section of the economy."*

Reader Edward Suranyi makes the same argument, adding that most nonscience students do not decide they are interested in a career that requires math until it is too late.

And Suranyi and Brick argue that "innumeracy," which is to mathematical skills what "illiteracy" is to reading skills, is dangerous on the job or off. In her book, *Tainted Truth,* Cynthia Crossen enumerates the many ways in which research has been misused by everyone from big business to the federal government to the mass media. Such abuses would not be possible if we were numerate. Several readers mentioned that anyone who reads John Allen Paulos's (wonderful) book, *Innumeracy,* would have little trouble answering this Frustable.

Our favorite responses didn't focus on the practical applications of a math background. Over and over again, readers with extensive math training told us that the particular subjects they studied didn't necessarily help them directly with their future work, yet they didn't regret the effort necessary in their study. We heard from a longtime reader, Jeff Chavez of El Segundo, California:

> "It's true that a lot of the stuff I learned in school never comes up now. In fact, I have a Bachelor's and Master's degree in electrical engineering, and I've worked as a software engineer for the past eight years. And I have realized for quite some time that very little of what I learned in college has come up in my work. Not even much of the electrical engineering material I learned comes up.
>
> "My theory is that the stuff we learn in college is intended to get your mind into shape and prepare you to be able to learn new things in the future, and to prove to employers that you are able to learn new things.
>
> "In other words, college is intended to make you a trained monkey! It's not about acquiring knowledge—it's more about acquiring abilities to learn. The real learning starts on the job (and, hey—so does the money)."

Kathy Czopek probably wouldn't buy the monkey analogy, but she makes a similar argument:

> "How did you do in math? [We take the Fifth Amendment.] Most who did well now have a greater understanding of basic principles of life. They're smarter.
>
> "They may never have to use a cosine formula, but they understand why some things work the way they do because they've studied calculus. And like learning a foreign language, or [memorizing] all the territories of Canada, etc., it teaches you how to learn, which is more important than the learning itself.
>
> "Learning math sets a pattern in your brain—and not all people do it in the same way—of how to learn, remember, process, and understand information. It develops more common sense."

Dallas Brozik, an undergraduate math major, who now teaches business at Marshall University, argues:

"The purpose of math education is not to teach numbers; it is to teach thinking. The sheer mechanical manipulation of numbers is important for the running of the society, but that is a job that can be left to machines or unimaginative types.

"There are many ways to teach creativity and self-expression, but mathematics is the only area that requires logic to be applied to the process. While the ability to draw a pretty picture is nice, the skill is not readily transferable to other types of activity, especially those that are rewarded by the society in the form of a paycheck. Mathematics teaches logical thought processes, and the ability to use logic to figure things out is a survival skill in today's world.

"I recall sitting in a calculus class toward the end of my freshman year, when suddenly the realization came to me that what I was studying had nothing at all to do with numbers. Though not quite an epiphany, it did change my approach to the topic, and what had been pleasant before was now a lot of fun."

Erik Hanson of Richmond, Virginia, makes one of the strongest arguments we've ever encountered not only for learning math but also for learning a wide range of disciplines:

"You never know what you'll need to know.

"Let's pretend that I love reading poetry. All through high school, I read poetry and take English classes and shy away from math classes. Then I get to college and take lots of English and no math or science, except the basic stuff that the school requires.

"At the end of my sophomore year, I buy a computer to write poetry on and discover that I love playing with the computer. The next semester, I find out that I am no good at writing poetry, and I'm getting sick of reading it, but I love my computer and I start learning how to write computer programs.

"I change my major to computer science, but now I'm stuck at school for a billion more years because I have to take this 'ad-

---

　　　　　　　　　Ｄavid Ｆeldman

vanced math' just to get where the other computer science majors were when they were fifteen years old.

"Plus, don't you always wonder what the length of the arc that makes up the crust of your two slices of pizza is, given that the angle between the two outermost sides of the still-connected slices is 47.4 degrees? And don't you want to express that as a complete answer and list the theorems you used on your napkin?"

Agggh. Get us back to poetry classes!

Ultimately, the most popular answer to this Frustable is that math provides students with the ability to solve problems, and not just math problems. As Burleson, Texas, reader Sandra Hildreth claims:

> *"Math is the greatest teacher of learning how to solve problems, and this desperately needed ability spills over to all aspects of life."*

Ken Braly, who heard us on the Ronn Owens show on KGO in San Francisco, e-mailed us:

> *"I studied astrophysics in college—lots of advanced math, of course. Today, I don't use a bit of it.*
>
> *"But I think advanced math is useful because it teaches how to analyze problems, figure out what is being asked, determine an approach, and solve the problem logically. Those skills are useful even if the problem isn't mathematical in nature.*
>
> *"I suppose if we had a curriculum that taught these skills by solving nonmathematical problems, we might not need to teach the math to those who aren't going to need it in later life. But I think your worldview is different when math isn't a mystery, and in this ignorant age, that's reason enough to teach it, in my view."*

The executive director of the Mathematical Association of America, Alfred Willcox, also argues for the ability of math to provide problem-solving skills and, ultimately, much more:

"Although it is not always evident to the individual, society attempts to be logical and achieve order out of chaos, our world. Thus it is with the mathematician, who attempts to identify patterns in our observations of real-world phenomena, then works with these patterns using any available mathematics, and finally achieves a deeper understanding of the processes of the real work— to bring order out of chaos."

And lest the noninclined think that math must have a direct, practical application to be of value, we heard a vociferous objection from mathematics professor Cyndi Crumb:

"Not all that we learn in any area has direct application. Shall we stop studying music because we are not all going to be concert musicians? Shall we stop studying biology unless we plan to become involved in a field of biology? Why should math be of lesser value than, say, the study of literature, mythology, geography, etc.?"

We were surprised at the passion and articulateness with which "math types" made their argument. Indeed, it is safe to say that the practitioners of math are far better able to communicate with "verbal types" in their language, words, than most verbal types are with numbers. Reader Gordon Clow argues for the importance of math in "enforcing a discipline of logical thought processes that can be applied to solving real-life problems," but we think he spoke for many of the mathematicians who wrote to us when he concluded with:

"There is a purity and beauty that exists in mathematical problems that you just don't find in many other places, except perhaps in nature."

It's that beauty, we're afraid, that too many math teachers have a hard time demonstrating and that "verbal types" have a hard time appreciating.

David Feldman

Submitted by Aleta Moorhouse of Mesa, Arizona. Thanks also to Dianna Gregory of Sandusky, Ohio; David Campbell of Columbia, Maryland; Mary Rose Taylor of Charlotte, North Carolina; and Katy Stratigos of Flossmoor, Illinois.

A complimentary book goes to Gordon Clow of Alexandria, Virginia.

Frustable 8: Why do people put plastic deer ornaments on their front lawns?

One of the highlights of our publicity tour every year is an annual visit with the terrific folks at the *Morning Exchange* in Cleveland. And ever since our first appearance on the television show, we've been accosted by executive producer Terry Moir Cheplowitz, who begs us to answer the bizarre predilection, especially among midwesterners, for displaying plastic deer on their lawns. She, like us, wondered whether a deer on the front lawn meant that the owner liked deer, liked to hunt deer, or liked to pretend that the hunk of plastic was a real deer.

Most, but not all the mail on this subject (which, to be honest, didn't exactly set a record for volume) did come from Midwesterners. Readers from other parts of the country wondered whether there was anything special at all about deer. Virginian Gordon Clow, for example, assumed that just like any other outdoor ornament, the deer was a way of saying "Hey, look at me."

Kathy Czopek, of St. Louis, Missouri, argues that displayers of plastic deer do so because they think they're pretty:

> *"They think real deer would look nice in their yard, but that's impractical. And as with suction-cup Garfields in car windows, they saw someone else do it and they want to keep up with the Joneses.*
>
> *"P.S.: They're often plaster, not plastic—that way, they don't blow over!"*

As you might guess, the majority of responses to this Frustable consisted of cheap shots. And we are not above publishing a few of the good ones.

> *1. "Plastic animals don't require feeding or pooper-scoopers."* (Sandra Hildreth, Burleson, Texas)
>
> *2. "The same reason people buy cars with fake wood on the sides: either massive head trauma or too much crack."* (Erik Hanson, Richmond, Virginia)
>
> *3. "Because they have to save room in the back for their Big Wheel mudder trucks and life-size statues of Elvis!"* (James Vaught, "somewhere in north Florida.")

Tucson, Arizona's, Bill Gerk anticipated our objection to most of the responses to this Frustable: readers tended to focus on the "plastic" rather than the "deer."

> *"To suggest that people display them for ornamentation is to evade answering the specific reference to deer. I believe that people put plastic deer on their lawns to show that they think highly of deer and wish to affirm this preference in their public display. Such people identify with the grace that deer show as they glide through the air, even at high running speeds.*
>
> *"Also, ordinarily deer are not ferocious or threatening. Disney World has a big, artificial swan by one hotel and a huge dolphin by another. They chose each animal for its nonviolent symbolism. In like manner, the person or persons living in the house chose the*

deer because they have identified with what they think are positive characteristics of live deer. Consider the book Bambi, *by Felix Salten, and the Disney movie extolling the admirable characteristics of that forest deer."*

One intrepid reader, Dave Lieberman, of Decorah, Iowa, conducted his own field research on this Frustable. He lives not far from the epicenter of plastic deerdom, and he files this report from the front:

> *"Lord Almighty, how I* hate *those plastic deer. However, I asked a farmer's wife on North Winn Road, outside of town about ten miles, why she had those blasted deer on the lawn, and she gave me three reasons:*
>
> *"1. To get cars to slow down. When you see a deer-shaped object on the ditch of a straight road, what's your first impulse? Right. The brake. I must say, it works admirably.*
>
> *"2. To get real deer to come closer to the house. She said she likes to look at deer and they'll never come close enough to the house. So if they see stiff, unmoving deer, supposedly in their dinky deer minds, they say, 'Hey, there's a stiff, unmoving deer there. Let's get closer.'*
>
> *"3. It makes a more natural landscape. I think she's certifiable."*

Can we get some plastic deer owners to come out of the closet (or the house, perhaps) and speak for themselves?

Original Imponderable submitted by Terry Moir Cheplowitz of Cleveland, Ohio.

Complimentary copies go to Bill Gerk of Tucson, Arizona, and Dave Lieberman of Decorah, Iowa.

Frustable 9: Why do construction workers soap the windows of retail stores when they are working inside?

Of these ten Frustables, this achieved the closest to a consensus. We heard from enough folks in the construction industry to feel confident that the main reason why windows are soaped is to "mark" the window. Before windows are installed, construction workers become accustomed to walking in and out of the window frame with impunity and throwing tools through the "window-to-be." Once the plate glass is installed, all sorts of heck can break out:

> *"Plate glass, especially if new and clean, can be difficult to see, as is often evidenced by birds and other animals repeatedly flying or running into windows. At construction sites, where people walk around with ladders, pipes, and other awkward objects, it can be difficult to distinguish between empty door/window frames and those that have glass in them.*
>
> *"To avoid the cost and safety problems associated with breaking windows, the glass is visibly marked with soap, colored tape, or stickers, so that it is easily seen by the construction crews." (Alan Benheim, Fairfax, Virginia)*

Several readers mentioned that masking tape has supplanted the usual soap (traditionally a paste made from Bon Ami detergent) for a practical reason, as Walt Gesell of Bridgeview, Illinois, explains:

> *"Masking tape has the added advantage that if a window should be broken, the shards of glass will be held in place by the tape and not fly all over the area—or injure someone."*

Ian Lindsay of Framingham, Massachusetts, who has experience in the construction trade, speaks for several readers who

---

noted that another purpose of soaping windows was to provide security for valuable goodies inside the site:

> "Many of the tools used in building renovation are expensive and should not be left out in the open, just as we would not leave jewelry or cash where a passerby could see them. The soaped windows cover up whatever tools or materials may be stored within the construction site."

One correspondent, Andy Pforzheimer, was opening a restaurant as he wrote to us and noted:

> "As soon as the phones are installed, we're soaping the windows so nobody knows it. You'd be amazed what people will rob a place for."

What are construction workers doing behind those soaped-up windows? Many passersby would like to know, which is another reason why construction workers *do* soap up windows. John Karamazin, a plumbing and heating contractor in Edison, New Jersey, writes:

> "Yes, they are trying to keep you from looking in, and no, they are not trying to keep the workers from looking out. It's not pleasant to work with a bunch of old guys and kids staring at your every move, which is often what happens at such a site. As you work, you know very well that the old guys staring at you are criticizing everything you do and telling each other how much better they would have done the same job back in 1954."

Or as Peter Naughton of Rome, New York, phrases it:

> "Would you want people coming up and watching you all day? It's a construction site, not a zoo."

And distractions can be dangerous, too, as reader Rob Levandowski argues:

"When working with heavy equipment, distractions can be fatal. After all, people do some pretty dumb things. It wouldn't surprise me if some bozo tried taking flash photography of a poor guy using a saber saw at just the wrong instant . . ."

And Sandra Hildreth, of Burleson, Texas, has a slightly more cynical take on the subject:

"The soap is not to keep people from seeing them while they work—it's to keep people from seeing them as they don't work."

And apropos of the following Frustable, some of you agree with Peter Naughton that "it's all a publicity gimmick":

"When a Kmart opened last year in Rome, New York, they had cardboard (even more secretive than soap) on the windows until opening day. I think it's because they want people to wonder 'What's the inside of the new store going to look like?' Then these same people are there opening day, looking and (most importantly) buying."

Rob Holzel of Burlington, Massachusetts, agrees, arguing that

"the sense of awe is heightened when the transformation is taken in all at once rather than a little at a time."

Original Imponderable submitted by Robert Baumann of Fort Lee, New Jersey.

A complimentary book goes to Alan Benheim of Fairfax, Virginia.

Frustable 10: Why do construction companies care so much if advertisements are posted outside their commercial construction sites? And why is the name of the architect and construction company usually listed, but not the name of the future tenant?

We admit that the perimeter of a construction site festooned with hastily plastered posters is not a thing of beauty, but neither is a wooden fence dotted with hundreds of "Post No Bills" warnings. Why do construction companies care if the ugly wooden fence is covered up by ugly posters?

Some of you argued that the vehemence of construction companies is motivated mainly by aesthetics. As Julie Prince of Corvalis, Oregon, sees it,

> *"If you leave a surface out in public that people can drive nails or staples into, they will."*

Chances are, today's posters will be tomorrow's trash; in fact, as Erik Reichmann of Howell, New Jersey, points out, some communities prohibit the posting of handbills on construction sites:

> *"Even though the construction barriers themselves hardly enhance the landscape, they are even more unsightly when covered with flyers, especially when papers fall off (or get torn down) and blow into the gutter or down the sidewalk. To minimize disturbances in the neighborhood, construction crews are expected to keep the surrounding area as clean as possible."*

Construction companies also have to worry about the content of the flyers on their property. Kathy Czopek points out:

> *"If you let one person put up a poster, it's discrimination if you don't let another do the same. And do you want Ku Klux Klan flyers in your neighborhood?"*

But more readers felt that builders were far more worried about other kinds of content, namely advertisements for other businesses, particularly competitors. As Julie Prince put it,

> *"The construction companies don't want to plaster free advertising all over their barriers."*

Bill Gerk adds:

> *"The architect and construction company don't want signs from any other competitors or even signs of companies that are not in their fields. They want those who drive or walk by to remember only their two names . . ."*

Architect Matthew Smith of Clemson, South Carolina, confirms the disdain the contractors and architects hold for other ads on their sites, and the importance of the signs in generating new business:

> *"It is only natural that the builders get antsy about advertisements on their property. It is their property, after all, while they're working on it. Construction companies and architects don't get much advertising other than the projects they work on, and many times, after a building is built, the architect and contractor are forgotten. At least, if potential customers see the signs on the road, they can watch the construction, see the final product, and decide if perhaps they like the construction work or think the architect did a good job.*
>
> *"Furthermore, advertisements for the tenant often appear in local newspapers during the construction phase, so it's only fair, in that odd protocol that the construction industry magically adheres to, that the tenant get out of the way and let the contractors do their work. Part of that work involves finding more work, and on-site advertising is considered the best way to do so."*

Several readers mentioned that signs with the name of the tenant are posted (e.g., "Future Home of Imponderables Central") on the site. Some businesses might find it to their advantage to hide their debut from competitors until the last possible moment. In other cases, a leasing agent might erect a building before a major tenant has signed a lease.

And then a few of you insisted that just like the soapy windows in the Frustable above, the lack of a sign for the tenant is all a master strategy to lull passersby, ever so slowly, into an ever-deepening obsession with the identity of the soon-to-be-revealed occupant. We have our doubts, but we have grudging admiration for readers trying to kill two Frustables with one theory.

Submitted by Carol Rostad of New York, New York. Thanks also to Scott Russ of Knoxville, Tennessee.

A complimentary book goes to Matthew Smith of Clemson, South Carolina.

David Feldman

The Frustables
That Will Not Die

Relentless. That's the only word that can describe the tenacity of *Imponderables* readers. The more frustrating the Frustable, the more you want to nail down the solution to these knotty mysteries. Here are some of the more interesting observations about old Frustables that we've received in the five months since the hardbound release of *What* Are *Hyenas Laughing At, Anyway?*

Please remember that we do not have space to review all the theories advanced in the original write-ups; this section is meant as a supplement, not a replacement for the discussions in previous books.

Frustable First Posed in *Why Do Clocks Run Clockwise?* **and First Discussed in** *When Do Fish Sleep?*

Frustable 1: Why do you so often see one shoe lying on the side of the road?

....

We frequently receive the question "Why do I see shoes [usually athletic shoes] hanging from power lines?" We haven't answered it because we've seen this issue discussed in other places. Sometimes, the shoes' location may be the results of children's pranks; in other cases, they can be markers of gang territories.

But have you ever seen a *single* shoe hanging on a telephone wire? Maybe you should visit your local Marine base for another take on the etiology of Single Shoe Syndrome. We heard from Sgt. Thomas Brown at the Department of State:

> *"As a U.S. Marine, having traveled all over the world, I have come across many strange traditions. One of the strangest is the*

Marines' tradition of hanging a single shoe or boot when someone is departing from a unit.

"I have seen them hung on power lines, light posts, flagpoles—you name it, they'll hang 'em there. What happens to the other shoe? Maybe they are thrown on the side of the road on the way to or from the gate."

Frustable First Posed in *When Do Fish Sleep?* **and First Answered in** *Why Do Dogs Have Wet Noses?*

Frustable 8: Why do kids tend to like meat well-done (and then prefer it rarer and rarer as they get older)?

Several readers protest that the preference for well-done meat has nothing to do with age but rather with sophistication of taste. We have already observed that most gourmets insist that discriminating palates prefer meat rare, to better savor the intense flavors. It's ironic, then, that in the Midwest, where much of our cattle is raised, folks seem to prefer their beef cooked more well-done than the folks on either coast. We especially enjoyed this letter from David Lieberman of Decorah, Iowa:

> *"Here in the upper Midwest, meat is almost always served well-done. Let's face it: Midwestern food is bland. I'm originally from New Jersey, and I like my meat rare because it tastes better.*

"I once went into a restaurant in Rochester, Minnesota, and ordered a steak. My eyes lit up when the waitress asked, 'How do you want that, sir?' I replied, 'Medium-rare.' She looked perplexed and said, 'I meant, did you want rice, potatoes, or a salad?' "

Frustables First Posed in *Why Do Dogs Have Wet Noses?* **and First Answered in** *Do Penguins Have Knees?*

Frustable 1: Does anyone really like fruitcake?

*L*est you think midwestern Americans are the only folks on the North American continent that have peculiar culinary predilections, we need go no farther than our northern neighbor, Canada. If we are to believe Melva Rae Graham, of Toronto, Ontario, fruitcake is as beloved in Canada as hockey, curling, SCTV, and leaving headlights on while driving in the daytime.

In the spirit of full disclosure, Melva admits that she was born in the United States. Her story concerns an event so aberrant that we must remain skeptical. Still, we feel it is our obligation to share Melva's story:

> *"My biggest surprise [after she was married and moved to Canada] was the popularity of fruitcake in Canada. My mother-in-law and almost everyone else we knew who still did their own Christmas baking made fruitcake in late November.*
>
> *"I didn't try it out right away, having only had American fruitcake that deserved its reputation. But when I ate a dark fruitcake that was actually so moist it was gooey, I was truly converted. People here not only make their own, they age them in brandy or rum for at least a month [as the cliché almost goes, 'Bad food takes time'?].*
>
> *"At my wedding in Baltimore, Maryland, in 1972, we had two cakes: an American yellow cake made there and a traditional Canadian wedding cake—dark fruitcake made by my new mother-in-law. It is traditional here to save the topmost small layer to have*

on your anniversary or after the birth of your first child. Since we didn't expect many of our American guests and family to want fruitcake, we didn't even bring the top layer to the wedding.

"We regretted our decision, because the fruitcake was so popular that evening, we ran out. And we had a lot of yellow cake left over."

Perhaps this wedding party was a fit of mass hysteria? No, Melva insists: *It's a Canadian thing!* And lest we disbelieve, she continues:

"A story about fruitcake made the national news here last December 1995. The province of Prince Edward Island is at the end of the truck routes and sometimes has trouble with supplies. Ski wax, for example, only comes in once a year, and when it is gone, you have to wait until next winter for more, no matter how much snow falls.

"This year, the supplies of the large raisins that Maritimers use in their fruitcakes (which they call 'sticky raisins') were very low. At the end of November, word got out that there wasn't enough, and stores began receiving hundreds of calls each day from people who wanted raisins for their Christmas cakes (i.e., fruitcakes). They said it just wouldn't be Christmas without their traditional cakes!"

We imagine that such physical isolation might lead us to strange behavior. But fruitcake obsession? No thanks.

Although many of you continue to claim that you or someone you know actually likes fruitcake, few provided the historical context of Moorestown, New Jersey's, Christine Faulkner ("My mother likes fruitcake and orders some at Christmas, although the rest of us don't really care for it. We sometimes tease her about this."), whose grandmother conducted some research about this very Frustable:

"Recently, my grandparents have been cleaning out their attic, and they came across some letters Granddad wrote when he was in

World War II. In many of these letters, he mentioned fruitcake. He asked his family to send him a fruitcake, and in later letters, when it had still not come, he asked if the fruitcake had been sent yet.

"He mentioned that there had been some trouble with people stealing objects from the mail, and no one had ever heard of anyone stealing a fruitcake. The fruitcake arrived months later, in good condition."

Please note, readers, that you could hardly find more stressful events than weddings or wars. In our humble opinion, folks cannot be held responsible for fantasizing about fruitcakes in such anxiety-producing states.

Frustable 9: Why does the heart depicted in illustrations look totally different from a real heart?

In our initial discussion of this Frustable in *Do Penguins Have Knees?*, we mentioned that anthropologist Desmond Morris speculated that the form of the symbolic heart might have been based on the shape of the female buttocks. Reader Dennis Kingsley, of Goodrich, Michigan, found a similar citation in Carl G. Liungman's *Dictionary of Symbols*. Liungman notes that in Sweden, the heart shape is

> *"strongly associated with the behind and defecation, and it is the sign used to denote a toilet for both sexes."*

Kingsley adds:

> *"Kinda gives a whole new meaning to 'I ♥ NY,' doesn't it?"*

Frustables First Posed in *When Did Wild Poodles Roam the Earth?* **and First Answered in** *How Does Aspirin Find a Headache?*

Frustable 1: Why do women go to the rest room together? And what are they doing in there for so long?

Is this purely a Western phenomenon? Not exactly, posits Joel Becktell, of Austin, Texas, who notes that women *and* men dally in the "rest room" in at least one place he has visited:

> *"When I lived briefly in southern India, I had several opportunities to go to isolated villages with teams that were providing health care to the people. The members of these teams were constantly frustrated by the fact that the main threats to the health of many of the people were things they considered entirely controllable. Chief among the preventable causes of disease was poor sanitation.*
>
> *"However, the doctors and nurses had precious little success in convincing rural Indians to use toilets. There were two main reasons noted for this reluctance on the part of the Indians. First, the people thought it would be* less *sanitary, not more, to all use the same facilities time and again, and second, and most pertinent to our topic, the morning toilet ritual was an enjoyed social occasion for all.*
>
> *"Each morning in small, remote villages, all of the women would proceed to one field and the men to another. There, they would relieve themselves and wash while enjoying each other's company. This was the principal social time of a day otherwise filled with too many tasks to allow for idle time. Perhaps this is reflected in the restroom habits of Western women, who just want to enjoy each other's company apart from the hustle and bustle."*

With the gangs of women crowding into rest rooms in public places, we're not so sure they are as free of hustle and bustle as a south Indian field, but the notion is a fascinating one—rest room as refuge.

Frustable 3: Why do some women kick up their legs when kissing?

Susan R. Cronk of Maryville, Missouri, noted a point we missed when discussing this Frustable:

> *"Why don't men do it? Come on, Dave! You haven't been watching your share of Groucho Marx or Three Stooges films. Groucho and Harpo Marx repeatedly raised one leg, especially when kissed by some overzealous she-male."*

Good observation, although we think it makes our point. The patented Marx kick takes all the sexuality and romance out of the kiss. The very act that connotes passion when performed by a woman is interpreted as silliness when done by a man.

Frustable 10: Why do so many policemen wear mustaches?

Although we doubt that even reader Nathan Trask of Carterville, Illinois, would argue that this accounts for the profusion of police mustaches, he notes that he read a book, *Cops: Their Lives in Their Words,* which noted that before women were common in police forces, men were often asked to pose as women in order to snare criminals.

By growing mustaches, crafty cops were able to evade the cross-dressing detail. Captains occasionally forced some of the men to lop off mustaches in order to pass themselves off as women.

David Feldman

Frustable First Posed in *How Does Aspirin Find a Headache?* **and First Answered in** *What* Are *Hyenas Laughing At, Anyway?*

Most of you had no quibbles at all with our discussion in *Hyenas*. In fact, only one Frustable generated any heat:

*F*rustable 3: Why do the clasps of necklaces and bracelets tend to migrate from the back toward the front?

....

*T*he arguments still fall within the two camps we outlined—those who believe the relative weight of the clasp is not determinative, and those who believe that the weight is crucial to determining the movement of the clasp. The most passionate advocate in the first camp was Michael Marcoccio of North Attleboro, Massachusetts:

> *"Having studied the creation and design of jewelry in high school, I can safely say that it is not the weight of the clasp but the shape and design of the clasp. The normal wear of a necklace leads to the chain twisting and sliding, presenting less surface area to adhere to the neck, while the loops and catch of the average C-clasp are less likely to slip when the head turns and the neck subsequently moves.*
>
> *"Since most chains these days are designed to be flat, the rolling as it moves up requires it to be straight to be comfortable. This causes the chain to have a grain similar to that on wooden beads and speeds up the drifting of the clasp.*
>
> *"The weight of the chain also causes the chain to move up on the back of the neck, forcing the wearer to straighten it out by hooking it with his or her fingers and sliding it between them to straighten the links and lower it. Since one hand is usually stronger, the chain is more likely to slip through the fingers of the*

weaker hand and thus the clasp is 'pulled' toward the stronger hand."

Elisabeth Groeneveld of Lery, Quebec, cannot claim a background in jewelry design, but she's the only reader who has conducted empirical research to back up her claims. Elisabeth, a college student, decided to test the migration of six different bracelet clasps and reported her results in five single-spaced typed pages. A summary of her conclusions:

"Six bracelets were tested a total of 96 times to determine in which direction the clasps migrated when the arm was shaken for 30 seconds. The clasps were started at various positions around the wrist, and the final position was determined with the palm of the hand facedown.

"In 48 trials, the clasps that were lighter than the rest of the bracelet (in terms of linear density) migrated upward 17 times (35.4 percent), downward 16 times (33.3 percent), and didn't migrate at all 15 times (31.3 percent).

"In 32 trials, the clasps that were heavier than the rest of the bracelet migrated upward 2 times (6.25 percent), downward 22 times (68.75 percent), and didn't migrate at all 8 times (25 percent).

"One of the bracelets tested was made to fit with the clasp sideways, and in 16 trials the clasp ended up as such 12 times (75 percent).

"What all of this means is that clasps tend to move upward if they are lighter than the rest of the chain and downward if they are heavier. If the bracelet has been made to fit in a certain way, then the clasp won't migrate as much. I believe that the same results would also apply to necklaces.

"I would like to suggest that where the clasp is heavier, the equation

$$F = ma$$

(where F = force, m = mass, a = acceleration, in this case due to gravity) applies.

"Without going into too much detail, the clasp tends to migrate

downward because its mass per unit length is greater than that of the rest of the chain, and therefore it has a greater force pulling it downward. This would also explain why the pendant on a necklace tends to stay put at the front of your neck.

"In plain English, the clasp moves down because it's heavier."

Ahhhh. Plain English.

Letters

*Y*ou let us off relatively easy this year! Readers had only a few major beefs with the material in the last book, What *Are* Hyenas Laughing At, Anyway? However, you seemed more than eager to revisit controversies from previous volumes. As always, this space is reserved not for your bouquets but for your brickbats. We'll continue to publish your brickbats, as long as you'll let us duck and cover.

Space allows us to print only a fraction of the letters of comment we receive. Many other suggestions and criticisms have led to revisions in subsequent printings of prior books (we wouldn't, for example, include a letter pointing out a typo here, but we appreciate any such "catches")—this space is reserved for letters that we think will entertain and amplify the discussions in our books. So if anything in Astronauts makes you itchy, please let us know.

Many readers wrote to let us know about news developments that have rendered some of our answers obsolete. Literally within days of each other, Gina Catalano-Pieri of Nassau, Bahamas, Tony Mohr of Ames, Iowa, and Andrea deRoode of Tucson, Arizona, all sent us letters confirming the news that will warm the hearts of Flintstones fans. In When Did Wild Poodles Roam the Earth?, we chronicled the sad story of how Betty Rubble had been left out of Flintstones Vitamins. Mohr writes:

> "I thought it was amazingly coincidental that only a day after reading about the Flintstone vitamins in *When Did Wild Poodles Roam the Earth?*, the enclosed photograph was in the *Des Moines Register* on January 16, 1996. Probably, someone in your intelligentsia network has already alerted you of this change."

Don't you understand, Tony? You are part of the intelligentsia network! The photo showed an assembly line laden with the new packaging for the vitamins, along with a caption that said, in part:

How Do *A*stronauts Scratch an *Itch?*

"Rectifying a 25-year omission, Bayer made Betty a vitamin in response to a nationwide vote. She'll join Fred, Barney, Wilma, Pebbles, Bamm-Bamm, and Dino, replacing the Flintmobile."

Andrew and Gina both sent coupon circulars featuring the image of a fetching Betty, standing atop a vitamin bottle, adjacent to the headline, "Now, Betty is in Flintstones Vitamins." Even the package itself, reads: "Betty Vitamin Inside!" We hope to have played a small part in putting Betty in the bottle next to her husband and best pal, Wilma, where she belongs.

Michael McLaughlin of Santa Barbara, California, was the first among many readers to draw our attention to a far more publicized event—the introduction of blue M&M's, the first realignment of colors in M&M's in many years. We wrote extensively about the color mix found in an M&M's package in Why Do Clocks Run Clockwise?*. Here are the old and new ratios:*

	PLAIN		*PEANUT*	
Color	Old %	New %	Old %	New %
Brown	30	30	30	20
Yellow	20	20	20	20
Red	20	20	20	20
Orange	10	10	10	10
Green	10	10	20	10
Tan	10	0	0	0
Blue	0	10	0	20

And before you ask, the color ratio for M&M's Almond Chocolate and Peanut Butter Chocolate Candies is 20 percent each of browns, yellows, reds, greens, and blues. As Bayer did, M&M / Mars conducted a public vote to choose the fate of its color mix. Blue crushed pink and purple in popularity in the plebiscite, as well as easily beating the option of not changing the color mix.

Alas, orange is absent from the almond and peanut-butter candies, and the venerable tan color has now exited the M&M family completely. Perhaps, in sympathy, Betty Rubble should sport a tan.

And our last piece of breaking news comes from Barbara-Anne Eddy of Vancouver, British Columbia. In Do Penguins Have Knees?, *we discussed why the middle digits of area codes start with a 0 or 1 and indicated that the phone companies would be forced to use other numbers for middle digits "in the next century":*

> "It has already happened. In western Washington, just south of my home, all numbers used area code 206. As of last year, the use of 206 has been restricted to the Seattle-Tacoma-Olympia region, and the rest of the area, including cities such as Bellingham, Mount Vernon, and the 'other' Vancouver, now uses area code 360."

Yep. We are running out of area codes, as faxes, cell phones, and modems have created explosive demand for new phone lines. So although the prediction was correct, phone sources were too conservative in estimating exactly when the change would take place.

Industry experts weren't conservative enough in one of their predictions, as Etan Goldman of North Hollywood, California, was more than eager to point out:

> "I've finally purchased all of your books and have just read your first book, *Imponderables*. At the end of your discussion about why there aren't national brands of milk and meat, the last paragraph quotes a meat expert as predicting that by 1990, we'll see branded beef in supermarkets.
>
> "Well, it's 1996."

Yes, it is later than we thought. Hormel, Wilson, and other brands have *tried to market fresh meat, but with relatively little success. Companies are facing the same problems in 1996 that they did in 1986: consumer resistance to even slightly higher prices, and the suspicion that nationally branded meat isn't as "fresh" as the meat provided by grocery store butchers. So far, the poultry industry has found far more success branding fresh products.*

It isn't so easy to find branded nectarines either, as we discussed in Why Do Dogs Have Wet Noses? *Far less popular fruits are canned. But*

Dianne Miller of Victoria, British Columbia, proudly sent us a label from a can of Royal City sliced nectarines in light syrup (or as they say in Montréal, "brugnons en tranches"). So at least our neighbor to the north has domesticated and branded the neglected nectarine.

Speaking of food, the most vehement objection to an answer in Hyenas *came from a contributor to that book, Angela Stockton, who evidently was so furious with our discussion about the origins of the name of the candy Baby Ruth that she has moved from Mississippi to Clermont, Florida. Angela did not accept the story provided by Nestlé, that the confection was named after President Cleveland's daughter, and cited the work of writer Tom Burnam, and his entry about the origins of Baby Ruth in his book* More Misinformation. *Stockton writes:*

> "Burnam concluded that the candy bar was named not after Ruth Cleveland, but after the granddaughter of Mr. and Mrs. George Williamson, candy makers who developed the formula for the original Baby Ruth and sold it to Curtiss.
>
> "Ponder it, Dave: To believe that Baby Ruth was named after Ruth Cleveland, one would have to believe that a candy company chose to name their product after the long-dead child of a long-dead ex-president [Ruth Cleveland died at the age of thirteen]. This even though many candy buyers are children and the name of Ruth Cleveland, dead since 1908, would mean nothing to a 1920s child."

Of course, the name of a grandchild of an obscure candy maker would mean nothing, either, but we'll let Angela complete her point:

> "To put it in a modern context, Dave: If you were the CEO of a candy company and were marketing a new candy bar, would you announce that you were naming it Baby Patrick after the son of John F. Kennedy? Would you have launched Baby Patrick in say, 1990, while Jackie was still alive? If so, you'd be a very unusual candy maker—one who goes out of his way to associate bad taste with his product!
>
> ". . . As implausible as the Ruth Cleveland yarn appears under closer scrutiny, you yourself heard Nestlé's PR depart-

ment spin it. Why? Why indeed—they're in the PR business, and 'Baby Ruth was the daughter of President Grover Cleveland' simply has more sizzle than 'Baby Ruth was the no-name granddaughter of a no-name candy maker.' "

We have to admit that Stockton's argument rings true, especially because, according to Burnam, a longtime friend of the Williamsons wrote syndicated columnist L. M. Boyd, confirming the "Ruth Williamson theory."

But you had more than food on your mind. Like, uh, drink. Randolph C. Nolen of St. Louis, Missouri, had tequila on his cranium:

> "I would like to respond to your answer in *How Does Aspirin Find a Headache?* to the question about the worm in the tequila bottle. I have spent most of my life in West Texas, where they drink a lot of tequila, and I have always heard it was included as a quality control. A firm, intact worm meant that there was enough alcohol in the mescal to preserve the worm. A mushy or fragmented worm in the bottle meant that it was under-proof.
>
> "It was also said that when you were drunk enough to eat the worm, you knew you'd had enough."

Even totally sober folks have trouble with some liquid containers. Francis H. Baker of Arlington, Texas, wasn't satisfied with our discussion (in Do Penguins Have Knees?*) about why paper and plastic drinking cups are usually wider at the top than at the bottom:*

> "If the sides were straight [as in a glass container], they would slip through your fingers and because of their thin construction, would collapse under the additional pressure required to hold them. The sides of the cups used for snow cones are sloped for the same reason, but they have a more radical slope to the sides because the contents are heavier."

We've crushed a few plastic drinking cups in our time. But no container irritates us as much as the humble milk carton, which is difficult to open and nearly impossible to close so that it is airtight. We whined about this sorry state in Imponderables, *but William Larson of Nyon, Switzerland, reminds us of the veracity of the cliché "The grass is always greener on the other side":*

> "In Switzerland, milk packages are almost impossible to open without spilling some milk. You must tear off a corner. They do not even make a pretense of being reclosable. So don't complain."

Consider us chastised.

Speaking of chastised, Terri A. Zeh Jacobson of Plymouth, Minnesota, writes:

> "I think there may be some correction needed on your piece "How Did Kodak Get Its Name?" in *Do Penguins Have Knees?*
>
> "I was a tour guide in the early 1980s at the Cass County Historical Society . . . A gentleman by the name of David Henderson Houston, who lived in the Red River Valley area of North Dakota, invented the roll film process. If my memory holds correct, this process was originally named after North Dakota. 'No. Dak.' was a commonly used abbreviation for North Dakota at the time."

Jacobson doesn't speculate about how "Nodak" was turned into "Kodak," nor about why George Eastman might want to call attention to the little-known Houston's hometown.

The other quarrel about technological matters came from Lee Radtke of Gatlinburg, Tennessee, who disagreed with the "experts" regarding why carpenters' pencils are square (which we discussed in How Does Aspirin Find a Headache?*):*

> "Anyone who has tried to draw a thin, straight line on wood that is anything but smooth sanded has found that the fine point of a round 'lead' will break and/or wear down before two or three inches of line production. Someone discovered that a chisel-shaped point will not break as easily and will produce a much longer line before

wearing to the point of making the line too thick for accurate work.

"Additionally, this chisel point is easier to refurbish with a pocket knife or sandpaper. Both of these are commonly handy to woodworkers. The (not square but) oblong outer pencil shape is helpful in orienting the chisel point for use."

While we are on the subject of points, Amy Vollmer of Eldorado, Wisconsin, thinks that we missed the point (in Why Do Dogs Have Wet Noses?*) when we claimed that the only purpose of the white dot on the frog of a violin bow (the frog is the screw that secures the hair of the bow and keeps it away from the stick at the point where the player holds the bow) was its ostensible function. Amy writes:*

"I'm eighteen years old and have played the violin for half my life, starting when I was nine. There is a specific bow hold that violinists are supposed to have. Some players, including myself, use the dot as a reference point. It tells us where the ring finger on our right hand is supposed to be pointing when we're playing. Some violin bow frogs don't have the little white dot. Those who own or use bows like that are making life a whole lot more difficult for themselves."

But not as difficult as several folks who took another reader to task for his letter, in Hyenas, *about the reasons for the obtuse rules defining when U.S. presidential elections should take place (at the time, there was an existing law mandating that the electors meet on the first Wednesday in December and within thirty-four days after they were chosen by the voters). Several readers made the same point as Don Woods, who e-mailed us:*

"J. Bradley King commented on how there are more than thirty-four days between the earliest possible election day (November 2) and the latest 'first Wednesday in December' (December 7), and that therefore Congress had to do something to ensure that the thirty-four-day limit between election day and the electors' meeting would never be exceeded.

"But that's not so, because Wednesday, December 7, and Tuesday, November 2, can never fall in the same year. I suspect Congress repealed the thirty-four-day deadline, not because it was already being exceeded, but because they wanted to change the electors' meeting to occur later and doing so would exceed the deadline. I have no idea why they wanted to move back the electors' meeting."

A couple of comments about the color purple in When Did Wild Poodles Roam the Earth? *made readers see red. In a discussion of why purple is associated with royalty, we started with an offhand remark, "Although pagans once believed that purple dye was the creation of Satan . . ." Several readers who embrace pre-Christian beliefs took us literally and took us to task. Typical was Tasha Feather of Chapel Hill, North Carolina:*

"Pagans did not once believe in purple dye as a creation of Satan. Pagans, or Wiccans, if you prefer, believed in neither 'bad' nor 'Satan' because in the matriarchal beliefs of an Earth-based religion, there were no deities of the Christian sort. [The word] *pagan* comes from the Latin word *paganus,* which means simply 'country-dweller,' *not* 'heathen,' as our dictionaries commonly say now.

"If there are other pagan references, please use them correctly if you would; some of us take our beliefs seriously."

We apologize if we inadvertently gave offense. Of course, nowhere in the original write-up did we indicate that pagans believed that there was anything specifically evil about purple dye, *but rather about the color itself. Nor did we mean to imply that pagans believe in the existence of the Christian Satan. Unfortunately, we have a problem with the definition of the term* pagan. *Actually, every dictionary we consulted does indeed trace the etymology of the word to the Latin word for "country dweller." The problem is lack of agreement about the denotation of the word. Both "pagan" and "heathen" are sometimes defined as anyone who is not a Jew, Christian, or Moslem, and could theoretically refer as accurately to a Buddhist as to an atheist or Wiccan. Unfortunately pagan and heathen, in particular, tend to be used with negative connotations. There is much evidence that* the "pagans" of ancient Rome, for example, who were polytheists, believed that colors had intrinsic qualities. And purple wasn't their favorite.

Our other purple Poodles problem? We wrote about why you don't see purple Christmas lights. We quoted an official from General Electric who reminded us of the old mnemonic, ROY G BIV [red, orange, yellow, green, blue, indigo, and violet], that was used to identify the order of length of wavelengths. David Moeser of Cincinnati, Ohio, isn't happy with the current scientific merger between indigo and violet:

"Today's physicists say there's no such color as indigo in the spectrum. They say Newton thought he saw it but he was wrong. (Musta been due to the mood he was in, huh?) That leaves only six spectral colors. I guess today's schoolkids have to remember ROY G.B.V. (Sorta sounds like a brand of underwear.)

"Your GE correspondent seems to use the terms *violet* and *purple* interchangeably. Many people confuse these colors, but some sticklers (stamp collectors, for example) differentiate between them. Purple is darker and bluish; violet is more reddish and brighter. One can't just open a box of crayons anymore to get the answer; their colors have gone politically correct and no longer have serious names."

So now colors can be politically incorrect? At least we can rely on the military for not being politically correct. In What Are Hyenas Laughing At, Anyway?, we published a letter continuing our discussion of why military forces march with the left foot first. Two readers have new contributions. In Hyenas, a reader mentioned a reference to this issue in Thoinot Arbeau's Orchesography, which addresses the Imponderable directly, but failed to see another passage in the book that was found by reader Clare Stewart of Hamilton, Ontario:

CAPRIOL: Why do you start off with the left foot?
ARBEAU: Because most men are right footed and the left foot is the weaker, so if it should come about that the left foot were to falter for any reason the right foot would immediately be ready to support it.

Walter Menzies of Satellite Beach, Florida, offers a similar theory:

"There are two causes of this habit. The first is that all animals (including man) 'test' with their nondominant foot (that is, the expendable one). For most men, it is the left foot.

"Try this. Find a rickety old footbridge, or a pond that might be frozen. Test it with your foot. Which foot did you use? Primally (not 'primarily'), you use the foot you can afford to lose, the one less developed, less strong.

"In walking, for a right-dominant person, we start out in a controlled fall by leaning forward, and then moving our 'expendable' foot (left) out to catch us, and we're off and running. Incidentally, in running, we also do the same thing, since we shove off on the most powerful leg—the right—putting the left first.

"And second, in the military, everybody has to do it the same way. And most of those in charge are right dominant—so they start on the left foot."

While we're on military subjects, Robert Griffin of Riverside, California, didn't have any disagreement with our discussion in When Did Wild Poodles Roam the Earth? *of how "hut" became the one-sentence exclamation used to count off the hike of a football; he thought we didn't talk enough about the strategy behind the cadence:*

"Allow me to share the rationale behind the use of these one-syllable commands—as they were taught to me in junior high, high school, and college.

"When offensive linemen take their stance prior to the snap of the football, they are concerned individually with beating the men opposite them to the punch as soon as the center snaps the ball, and collectively with immediately dominating the line of scrimmage. Otherwise, the called play is likely to fail. If the 'snap count' is 'on three,' they will focus on beginning their charge on the emphasized hut (or 'hip,' 'hike,' 'at,' 'go,' etc.) of 'hut-one, hut-two, hut-three.' The assumption here is that commanding their bodies into motion one half-count ('hut . . .') before the ball is snapped ('. . . one'), the line judge will see the illusion of ball and lineman moving together as one; hence, no [illegal] 'motion penalty.' Even the opposing team engages in the same practice, and the officials all know it; the actual count of one, two, or three is known only to the team on offense, which therefore still holds that advantage.

"The one-two-three count may be erratically syncopated by the quarterback, but at the risk of confusing his own linemen or being flagged by the backfield judge for unduly entrapping the opposition, especially if he further employs excessive body language (a sudden nod of his head, hunching of shoulders, or especially, shuffling his feet).

"In the modern professional game, 'hut' alone has displaced 'hut-one,' on the assumption that linemen at that accomplished level know body mechanics sufficiently to get into gear quickly, but the principle incentive of a sharp bark remains the same. In *Paper Lion,* George Plimpton relates his Walter Mitty experience as an erstwhile quarterback with the Detroit Lions. The first time he took a snap from the center, counting out 'faawwttee-one,' 'faawwttee-two . . .' his effete cadence overcame the defensive line by reducing them into hopeless giggles and belly laughs."

Several readers had transportation on their minds. One of you caught us with our feet in fresh cement, as it were. When discussing curves on highways in Do Penguins Have Knees?, *we referred to "laying cement." Whoops. Writes engineer Julian Shaw of Norcross, Georgia:*

"Cement is expensive if you were trying to cover a road, say six inches deep and twenty-four feet wide and a mile long. Cement, as its name implies, is a cementing agent, a locking together binder, if you please. To keep costs in line, we mix cement, water, sand, and typically, crushed stone to get concrete. So, it is this *concrete* that we lay."

And one enterprising reader from New Brunswick, Canada, reports that covered bridges up north are not necessarily built for the same reasons as those in New England:

"In *How Does Aspirin Find a Headache?*, you mentioned that covered bridges are covered to block the elements, particularly snow. As a lifelong resident of New Brunswick, with about seventy covered bridges still standing, that statement rang some alarm bells. Remember that many of the covered bridges have been around since the late 1800s. At that time, winter travel was often done by horse and sleigh. Because of that, not only were covered bridges not designed to keep snow off, snow actually had to be shoveled into the bridges to allow the sleighs to pass. From the New Brunswick Highway Act:

" 'Every supervisor shall, as early in the winter as possible, cause the flooring of all covered bridges in his division to be covered with snow so that the same may be easily passable during the winter by sleighs and sleds.' Source: Stephen and John Gillis, *No Faster Than a Walk: The Covered Bridges of New Brunswick* (Goose Lane Editions, 1988)."

Two Imponderables about airplanes in What *Are* Hyenas Laughing At, Anyway? *also attracted your attention. Bill Jelen, of Akron, Ohio, offers another, we must admit, excellent reason for not having shoulder harnesses for passengers on airplanes:*

"I agree that the backwards-facing seat is ideal for a crash, which probably happens once out of every ten million flights. But, it is a real pain on takeoff, which occurs on about 99.9999999 percent of flights. You know how a speeding jet pushes you back into your seat? Wow, try doing that without a seat in front of you! The seat belt (or your feet wedged on the opposite person's body) is the only thing holding you in."

And several readers sent us notes similar to New York City's Lee Middleton about why airlines dim cabin lights during takeoffs:

"You may want to check with the FAA. I seem to remember talking to a flight attendant who told me the dimming was a safety requirement. The reasoning is that if the plane crashes or has to make an emergency stop on take-off, your eyes (and the cabin crew's) will be better adjusted to the dark. When you jump out of the shoot (or swim out, in the case of the USAir incidents at LaGuardia), your pupils will already be dilated."

We did check with the FAA, and a spokesperson reiterated that there is no such regulation. Aviation experts we spoke to pooh-poohed the benefits of such a policy, but a few American companies do make the dimming a company-wide procedure for the reason Lee mentions.

Speaking of dim, have you noticed how often reader beefs are not with our explanations but with side comments we throw off breezily? Alas, in Do Penguins Have Knees?, *in a chapter about YKK zippers, we made an offhand comment about Izod's "alligator shirts." Guess what? That logo on the shirt isn't an alligator. Listen to this hard-luck story from Barbara-Anne Eden:*

"I think you should know that the figure to which you refer is not an alligator, but a crocodile. I know this because the matter was mentioned during a Final Jeopardy segment of *Jeopardy!* (a show in which, since I appeared as a contestant a few years ago, I have what you might call a proprietary interest), as part of an answer to which I couldn't furnish the question, a fact which makes it much more memorable to me.

"So, as I'm wont to do when I'm stumped, I went to the library and did some research, and I found the attached information, in Bud Collins's *Modern Encyclopedia of Tennis*. Briefly, Pierre LaCoste, a French tennis star of the 1920s, was nicknamed 'the Crocodile' for reasons I haven't yet discovered, and when he retired from tennis and started a line of clothing known as Izod LaCoste, he used the crocodile as an emblem. I remember its being quite fashionable ten or fifteen years ago, although it seems to have fallen out of favor."

Why in the world were they called "alligator shirts" then? Sorry about that Jeopardy! *problem, Barbara-Anne, but keep reading* Imponderables *books. More than one Final Jeopardy question has been based on our questions.*

One Imponderable you'd be unlikely to see featured on any program but That's Incredible *is the distasteful subject of why we don't see cockroaches in our usually crumb-filled cars. Judy Copeland and Jack Kelly of Oak Forest, Illinois, read our discussion in* How Does Aspirin Find a Headache? *and responded:*

> "The experts claim it is due to cold and lack of water. We disagree! The real reason is poverty. The cockroaches are too poor and thus are forced to take public transportation as the attached article in the *Chicago Tribune* (July 17, 1995) proves."

Thanks for sharing, Judy and Jack! The Metro front-page article, written by Gary Washburn, details in nauseating detail how the Chicago Transit Authority buses became infested with cockroaches. One unidentified rider was quoted as saying:

> " 'Suddenly, we saw them all over the place,' she said. 'I was killing them on the windows and on the walls. They were falling out of the ceiling . . . Everybody kept looking around knocking roaches off each other.' "

The solution to the infestation problem was spraying an "exciter" to attract the insects, closing the doors and windows, and then dropping bombs in the bus. The problem eased, although riders were not enamored of the overpowering stench of the insecticide. CTA authorities blamed the problem on the nasty habit of passengers—eating and drinking while aboard.

We can't have a letter section without a revisit to a few of our perennial topics. Mark E. Wild of Imperial, California, found an article, "Little Extras," in a magazine, Country Extra, that details the largest single collection of boots on fenceposts (a topic we have discussed in every Imponderables *book since* Why Do Clocks Run Clockwise? *). A reader of* *the magazine discovered that the farm of Gene Grabenstein, near Eustis, Nebraska, sported more than 300 boots hanging on fenceposts:*

> "Gene related that Walter Koch, a past neighbor, started putting the boots on fenceposts in the early part of the century. Gene and his family began to help and it soon became a hobby.
>
> "They put their own worn-out boots on the posts, along with those from friends, neighbors, and the local boot repair shop."

We're afraid that Mr. Grabenstein related a common explanation for hanging the boots—the boots shed water so that the fences don't rot during rain.

> "But for us, it's just a novelty, like some people who put wagon wheels along their driveways."

Or plastic deer on their front lawn.

Lo and behold, like clockwork, though, a reader came up with another theory to explain the boot apparitions. A longtime contributor to Imponderables, *Letty Halvorson of Sapphire, North Carolina, writes:*

> "We observed many boots on fenceposts throughout Kansas, Nebraska, the Dakotas, and Minnesota last summer. We were told that when ranchers or cowhands went out to repair the hundreds of miles of fences on their ranches, it was hard to tell where they left off, so they put the old boot on the last post. They could pick up easily next time they went out.
>
> "I took with tongue in cheek the other explanation that those old boots were salty with years of perspiration and made good, cheap salt licks for the cattle."

We took a licking from Bruce Alcan of Washington, D.C., who wanted to know how we could bring up the subject of why some women kick up their legs when kissing (Frustable 3 in How Does Aspirin Find a

Headache?) *"without bringing in [the subject of] dogs."* Gee, we didn't know women kick up their legs when kissing dogs!

Before we wrap up another volume of Imponderables, *we'd like to introduce a new feature. Evidently, we are now honor-bound to serve as a mail drop so that one reader can correspond with another. Joseph Baker of Hartford City, Indiana, noticed reader Charlene Ingulfsen's plea in the Letters section of* How Does Aspirin Find a Headache?, *to find out* "Why do I so often see loops of audiocassette tape beside the road?" *For the sake of his fellow* Imponderables *reader, Mr. Baker is about to make a startling confession:*

"When I was younger, my friends and I would round up all of our cassette tapes that we no longer wanted or that were damaged (eaten by the tape player, for example). We would then remove the plastic case to get the spool of audio tape out. We would then go out to the street with the spool of tape and hold on to the loose end and throw the rest of it down the road or at each other, kind of like streamers. Or we would get in the car and drive down the street, throw the spool of tape out the window while holding to the loose end, and let it unravel as we drove.

"Why? I don't know. I guess that question is another Imponderable. Maybe too much spare time?"

Nah. You don't want those vicious necessities like work or school to interfere with important stuff like finding single shoes on the side of the road, hunting plastic deer, and reading charming books about the little mysteries of everyday life.

Until next time, we wish you and your loved ones good health, prosperity, and altogether too much spare time.

David Feldman

Acknowledgments

If I thanked every reader by name who contributed to *Astronauts,* this book would weigh twice as much (and probably cost twice as much), so you'll have to settle for a blanket thanks for the terrific Imponderables, your fascinating Frustables theories, and your letters of praise and condemnation.

As always, I fell behind often in correspondence this year—it's the price paid for answering every letter that includes a self-addressed stamped envelope. I appreciate your patience. Many readers reached me in cyberspace this year and received much faster replies. Rest assured that I read and value *every* piece of mail I receive.

Thanks to everyone at Putnam for your support and encouragement. In particular, I'd like to thank and applaud my editor, Neil Nyren, who is as unflappable as a wingless hummingbird, and his terrific assistant, Michele Fiegoli, who flaps very little herself. Few toilers in the publishing trade are as unheralded and overworked as publicists, and I feel lucky to have found the ever-gracious Judy Burns Miller, whose high energy can only be explained by her curiously capacious capacity for Crispix consumption. And Heather D'Aurio, who helped arrange my publicity tour, who dispatches problems with ease, and who manages to maintain her equanimity on a non-Kellogg's diet.

As ever, thanks to my agent, Jim Trupin, who keeps running marathons while I try to get out of my Barcalounger without contracting a hernia.

Because my artistic technique is the equivalent of an untalented four-year-old's, I've always admired the skill with which Kassie Schwan translates Imponderables into visual images with wit and charm. Thanks for the wonderful illos, Kassie.

For his superb research assistance, I'd like to thank Phil Feldman (hey, the need to vanquish Imponderability is clearly in the genes). And my gratitude to Amie Quigley and Dara Curran for contributing to the research for several Imponderables.

And to my long-suffering friends and family, who were most subjected to my incessant moaning about my work, thanks for staying by my side:

Fred, Phil, Gilda, and Michael Feldman; Michele Gallery; Larry Prussin; Jon Blees; Brian Rose; Ken Gordon; Elizabeth Frenchman; Merrill Perlman; Harvey Kleinman; Pat O'Conner; Stewart Kellerman; Michael Barson; Jeannie Behrend; Sherry Barson; Uday Ivatury; Laura Tolkow; Terry Johnson; Christal Henner; Roy Welland; Judith Dahlman; Paul Dahlman; Bonnie Gellas; James Gleick; Cynthia Crossen; Chris McCann; Amy Glass; Judy Goulding; Mark Kohut; Rick Kot; Karen Stoddard; Eileen O'Neill; Joanna Parker; Maggie Wittenburg; Ernie Capobianco; Liz Trupin; Susie Russenberger; Nat Segaloff; Sheila Gilooly; Mark Landau; Joan Urban; Diane Burrowes; Virginia Stanley; Sean Dugan; Allison Pennels; Susan Friedland; Bill Shinker; and the Housewife Writers.

Special thanks to the terrific staff of Starbucks 839, for keeping me vertical; and to Marjan Marc and Gerard Calvo for keeping me ambulatory.

I often get asked if doing the research for my books is hard. It depends on what is meant by "hard." It's often difficult to *find* the right authorities to answer Imponderables, but once I reach them, more often than not, the consequences are illuminating at worst and great fun, at best. Nothing is more enjoyable in my work than listening to an expert excited about answering a mystery involving his or her field. *Imponderables* couldn't exist without the generosity of the hundreds of sources who are willing to share their expertise about their specialties. Below you'll find a list of the sources whose information led directly to the answers in this book.

Jeannine E. Abel, American Musical Instrument Society; Nancy Allison, Sea Straight-No Fog; Allen Allured, American Association of Candy Technologists; Ken Allweiss; Matt Anderson; Matthew Anderson, Texas A&M University; Richard Anthes, UCAR; APSCO Enterprises; Charles Ausburn, Casablanca Fan Company; Gray Autry, PGA.

John Badas, B&S Wire; Rick Baggett; Wendell Bailey, National Cable Television Assn.; Derek Bailing, GTE; Bradley Baker; Chris Ballas, Vanderbilt University; Ray Bauer, University of Louisiana Southwest; Ron Bean; Donald Beaty, College of San Mateo; Gary Becker; Pia Bergquist; Harold Blake; James Boardman; Robert D. Bonomi; Dick Botch, Print Pack; Allen Bradley, Nashville Electric Service; Marty Brenneis; Chuck Bryant, Miami Walkers; Bill Burdick.

Mary Beth Carlson, Illinois Department of Public Health; Pete Cava, The Athletics Congress of the USA; Jim Coleman, *Black Belt* magazine; Mike Courtenay, Darts & Things; John Covert; Harman Craig, Scripps Institution of Oceanography.

Bill Deane, Hall of Fame Museum; Dan DeClerck; Detroit Red Wings; Eileen Doudna, National Assn. of Watch & Clock Collectors; Lynn Downey, Levi Strauss & Co.; Jim Drath, Jimmie Jack Charters; Seymour Dupa.

Larry Eils, National Automatic Merchandising Assn.; James Eninger, TRW; Stephen C. Ertman, Florida State University.

Dale Farmer; Melissa Feinstein; Stan Ferguson, Beatrice Cheese; Mark Fletcher; Steve Forrette; Frito-Lay; Jim Frank, *Golf* magazine.

R. Bruce Gebhardt, North American Native Fishes Assn.; Peter Gesell, International Flavor & Fragrances; John Gilbert; Martin Gitten, Consolidated Edison; Dick Glass, Professional Electronics Technicians Assn.; C. E. Gostisha, G. Heileman Brewing Co.; Wilbur Gould; Judith Grabiner, Pitzer College; Richard Gralitzer; Dan Gramann, Aerial Banner Towing & Skywriting; Annette Green, Fragrance Foundation; Reitan Green, Pro Dart Shop; Kris Gudmunson, Riviera Country Club.

Bob Hale; John Hallett, Desert Research Institute; W. G. Hamlett, Fieldcrest Cannon; Pam Handley, Keyes-Davis; Scott Hansberger, Ray-Ban Sunglasses; Ruth Harmon, Miller Brewing Co.; Evan Harris; Katie Harris, American Darts Organization; Bernard Hart, National Auto Auction Assn.; James Hartsfield; Bob Heck, McNett Corp.; Bill Himmelman, Sports Nostalgia Research; Regi Hise, Wisconsin Milk Marketing Board; Jim Holmes, General Telephone of California; Scott Huffman; Wayne Huffman.

Tom Ierubino, *GOLFonline;* Janet Ivaldi, Pepsico.

Tim Jackson, Fieldcrest Cannon; Mike Jensen, Gannett Outdoor; Jan Johnson, Sky Jumpers Vertical Sports Club; Judy Johnson, USDA; Phil Johnson, USATF; Eric Jolpat; Chris Jones, Pepsi-Cola; Gary Jones, Bull's Eye News; Bob Joseph, General Mills Restaurants; David Joyce, Clark University.

Joseph Keefhaver, National Auctioneers Assn.; Glenda Kelley, International Game Fish Assn.; Randy Kendrick, ICG Access Services; Terry Kennedy, St. Peter's Computing; Douglas Kerr; Lynn Kimsey, Bohart Museum of Entomology; Dan King; H. A. Kippenhan; Lisa Kirchner; Craig Kirkland; Barbara Klein, Electric Power Institute; Dan Koch, Mt. Desert High School; Chris Kolanko, M&B Headwear Co.; Justin Kuo; Karen Kussell.

Dave Lancer, PGA; Matthew Landry; Phil Larucs, Anaheim Stadium; Wendy Lawrence; Tom LeCompte, University of Illinois; John Levine, IECC; David Lewis; Mike Lounge; David Low; Peter S. Lukasiak, National Auto Auction Assn.; Glen Lutz, NASA; Jill Lynch, Levi Strauss & Co.

Ken Mattson; Susan Mauro, Pepsi-Cola; John J. McBride, Livestock Marketing Assn.; Bob McDonald, Crane National Vendors; Anthony Meushaw, Society of Soft Drink Technologists; Matt Moran; Randy Morgan, Cincinnati Insectarium; Debbie Wales Murillo, Wales Whacker Works; David Murray, Nashville Electric Service.

Ron Natalie; Dave Nelsen, National Assn. of Oil Heating Service Managers; Marvin Nelson, Society of Cable TV Engineers; John Neves, NBA; Dave Norman, Great Explorations; Karl Newyear.

Brad Ogle, 500psi; Neil Ohlenkamp, Encino Judo Club; Doug Olander, *Sport Fishing* magazine; Rick Osgood, Cyber-Darts.

Melissa Packman, Coca-Cola; Anne Pagano, National Cable Television Assn.; C. Wayne Parker; Don Patten, Scuba Pro; Chris Patterson; Wayne Patterson, Basketball Hall of Fame; Jeff Pinsker, Great Explorations; Claudia Pope, Packaged Ice Assn.; Todd Postma, University of California, Berkeley; Lisa Prats, International Bottled Water Assn.; Pym-Dritz.

Wayne Rhodes; Jeff Robbins, Air Time Athletics; Robert R. Rofen, Aquatic Research Inst.; Jamie Rogger, PGA.

Leslie Saul-Gershenz, San Francisco Zoological Society; Robert Schmidt, North American Native Fishes Assn.; Jane Schultz, Snack Food Assn.; Alan Schwartz; Norman Scott, California Science Center; Patricia Shaeffer, Kraft; Marsha McNeil Sherman, Snack Food Association; Richard Siegel, District of Columbia Food Protection Program, Sheldon Silver, National Automatic Merchandising Assn.; Barry Sinnett, Anglo-American Dartboards; Mark Skorji; Sally Smith, Procter & Gamble; Rich Soergel, Pacific Sportswear & Emblem Co.; John Steven Soet, *Inside Karate;* Bill Sohl; Gil Stamper; Gilbert Steadman, Eller Media; Bruce Stein; Milton Stevens, American Watchmakers-Clockmakers Inst.; Jeff Stieglitz; Greg Stinis, Skytypers, Inc.; Jay Stone, Blue Cheer Scuba; Dan Strongin, American Cheese Society; Martin Swetsky, Electric Horology Society; Julie Swift, Michigan Bell.

Jim Tanenbaum, Sound Recording Services; Mike Terry, Bollé America; Sean Thomas; Milo Tichack; Don Heinrich Tolzmann, Society for German-American Studies; Pat Townson, Telecom Digest; James Turner.

Koos van den Hout; Catherine Van Evans, Cadbury Beverages; Al Barney; Matthew Vellucci, Distilled Spirits Council of U.S.; Henry Verden; John Vinson, Wysard of Information; Robert Virzi.

Marsha Walker; Shannon Walker; Raymond Lester Walters, USA-Korean Karate Assn.; George Weinstein, West Virginia University; Steve Wightman, Jack Murphy Stadium; Alfred B. Willcox, Mathematical Assn. of America; David Wilson, University of Wollongong.

Doug Yanega, University of Illinois Urbana-Champaign; Frank Young, Enertech Consultants.

Robert J. Zedik, National Confectioners Assn. of the U.S.; Zurg Ziegler, Zurg Ziegler Martial Arts Centre.

And for all the sources who preferred to remain anonymous, our thanks for toiling in obscurity.

index

A

Airplanes
  dimming of cabin lights in, 296–97
  shoulder harnesses in, 296
Alarm clocks, life before, 70–74
Algebra, X in, 131–32
"Alligator" shirts, 297–98
Area codes, middle digits of, 287
Astronauts and itching, 208–16
Auctioneers, chanting of, 201–4
Audiocassette tapes on roadsides, 300
Automobiles, cockroaches in, 298

B

Baby Ruth, origins of name, 288–89
Bands, tardiness of, in nightclubs,
  248–54
Baseball
  cap buttons, 171–72
  caps, green undersides of, 172–73
  pitcher's mounds, 195–98
Basketball, duration of periods in,
  65–69
Bathrooms, group visits by females to,
  277–78
Beds, mattresses, floral graphics on,
  1–2
Beer steins, lids of, 95–96
Belts, color of, in martial arts, 119–23

Bill posting at construction sites,
  268–70
Billboards, spinning blades on, 61–64
Birds, migration of, 91–94
Biting of fingernails, 223–28
Blue jeans and orange thread, 74
Bombs and mushroom clouds, 8–9
Boots on fenceposts, 298–99
Bracelets, migration of clasps on,
  279–81
Bridges, covered, 296
Buffet lines and clean plates, 5–6
Buzzing, bees and, 57–60

C

Cable TV and channel allocation,
  75–76
Candlestick Park, origins of, 48–51
Canada Dry, origins of name, 182–83
Candy
  origins of Baby Ruth, 288–89
  placement in vending machines,
  162–64
Caps
  buttons on baseball, 171–72
  green undersides of, 172–73
Carpenter's pencils, shape of, 290–91
Cassettes, audio, on roadsides, 300
Ceiling fans
  direction of blades, 113–14
  dust and, 111–13

Jigsaw puzzles, fitting pieces of, 3–4
Judo belts, colors of, 119–23

K

Karate belts, colors of, 119–23
Kissing, leg kicking by women during,
278, 299–300
Kodak, origins of name, 290

L

Lakes and ponds, water level of, 85–86
Left-handed string players, 108–9
Leg kicking by women while kissing,
278, 299–300
Licorice, ridges on, 188–89
Liquor distilleries during Prohibition,
54–56
Lizards and sunburn, 7
Lobsters, color of when boiled, 110

M

M&M's, blue, 286
Marching, leading of left foot during,
293–94
Math, school requirement of, 254–61
Mattresses, floral graphics on, 1–2
Meat
    children's doneness preferences in,
    273–74
    national branding of, 287
Migration of birds, 91–94
Milk
    cartons, 289–90
    national branding of, 287
Mountains, falling hot air in, 149–51
Mustaches and policemen, 278

N

Necklaces, migration of clasps of,
279–81
Nectarines, canned, 287–88
Nightclubs, lateness of bands in,
248–54
Noses, runny, kids vs. adults, 89–90

O

Octopus throwing, Detroit Red Wings
and, 183–86
Oktoberfest, September celebration
of, 156–57
Onions and crying, 169–70
Orange thread in blue jeans, 74

P

Paper cups, shape of, 289
Pebbles, spitting of by fish, 174–75
Pencils, carpenter's, shape of, 290–91
Perfumes, color of, 19
Pirates
    earrings, 43–45
    walking the plank, 37–42
Pitcher's mounds, rebuilding of,
195–98
Plastic cups, shape of, 289
Plastic deer ornaments on lawns,
262–64
Plates, repositioning of, 238–42
Pole-vaulting
    preparation for different heights,
    97–101
    women and, 102–7
Policemen and mustaches, 278
Ponds and lakes, level of, 85–86
Potato chips

R

T

S

U

V

"Use Correct Change" light on, 186–88

Videocassette boxes, configurations of, 35–36

Violins, dots on frogs of, 291

W

Walking, race, judging of, 20–23

Walking the plank, pirates and, 37–42

Water

  bottled, expiration dates on, 77–78

clouds in tap water, 126–27

Women

  and group visits to bathrooms, 277–78

  and leg kicks while kissing, 278, 299–300

X

X as symbol in algebra, 131–32

Houston, we have an Itch...

...for more Imponderables!

H e l p !

Even if finishing this book has momentarily solved our Imponderables itch, we're not naive. There are still conundrums out there to solve.

We still solicit your Imponderables, your take on outstanding Frustables, and your letters of comment.

As always, if you are the first person to send in an Imponderable we use, you'll receive an acknowledgement in the book along with an autographed copy of your contribution.

If you include a self-addressed stamped envelope, we'll send a personal reply (but please be patient—sometimes the delay can be excruciating). No need to send a SASE if you don't need a reply—all correspondence is welcomed.

We strongly recommend E-mailing us, if possible. We can reply to e-mail much more quickly, and it will save you two stamps. And while you're at it, why not check out our web page on the world wide web? Imponderability has definitely penetrated cyberspace!

Send your correspondence, along with your name, address, and (optional) phone number to:

IMPONDERABLES
P.O. BOX 24815
LOS ANGELES, CALIFORNIA 90024

or

INTERNET: feldman@imponderables.com
PRODIGY: imponderables@prodigy.com
http://www.imponderables.com

Special Call
to Imponderables Readers

As we announced in our last book, we are embarking on the project of writing an entire volume devoted to unraveling the ultimate mystery: What's the deal with the opposite sex?

Perhaps we are foolish to delve into these murky waters, which have drowned wiser folks than us. But we have a secret weapon: you. You can help us in two ways:

1. Write to us about what mystifies you, peeves you, irritates you, frustrates you, or baffles you about anything regarding the opposite sex (its beliefs, customs, anatomy, rituals, habits, psychology, and bizarre preferences are all fair game).

2. If you'd be willing to represent your gender, let us know. In the not-too-distant future, we'll send you a questionnaire that will give you the opportunity to reveal to members of the opposite sex the *ultimate truth* that they have been craving. Men and women, boys and girls of any age and background are welcome.

As always, you can reach us at *Imponderables* Central:

IMPONDERABLES
P.O. Box 24815
Los Angeles, California 90024
Internet: feldman@imponderables.com
Prodigy: imponderables@prodigy.com
http://www.imponderables.com